FORMATTING & SUBMITTING YOUR MANUSCRIPT

CHUCK SAMBUCHINO

FORMATTING & SUBMITTING YOUR MANUSCRIPT

3RD EDITION

WRITER'S DIGEST BOOKS

www.writersdigest.com
Cincinnati, Ohio

For more resources for writers, visit www.writersdigest.com/books.

To receive a free weekly e-mail newsletter delivering tips and updates about writing and about Writer's Digest products, register directly at http://newsletters.fwmedia.com.

17 16 15 14 13   8 7 6 5 4

Distributed in Canada by Fraser Direct, 100 Armstrong Avenue, Georgetown, Ontario, Canada L7G 5S4, Tel: (905) 877-4411. Distributed in the U.K. and Europe by David & Charles, Brunel House, Newton Abbot, Devon, TQ12 4PU, England, Tel: (+44) 1626-323200, Fax: (+44) 1626-323319, E-mail: postmaster@davidandcharles.co.uk. Distributed in Australia by Capricorn Link, P.O. Box 704, Windsor, NSW 2756 Australia, Tel: (02) 4577-3555.

Library of Congress Cataloging-in-Publication Data

Sambuchino, Chuck.

  Formatting & submitting your manuscript / Chuck Sambuchino. -- 3rd ed.

    p. cm.

  ISBN 978-1-58297-571-9 (pbk. : alk. paper)

  1. Manuscript preparation (Authorship) 2. Authorship--Marketing. I. Title. II. Title: Formatting and submitting your manuscript.

PN160S26 2009

808'.02--dc22

2009006662

Edited by Melissa Hill
Designed by Claudean Wheeler
Production coordinated by Mark Griffin

DEDICATION

This book is dedicated to you, the writer—whether you're a recent college graduate living in a small apartment in New York, or a retiree who's just now letting your passion for writing take flight. I wish you nothing but the best.

ACKNOWLEDGMENTS

The first person to thank is my wife, Bre, for all her love and support. It's not in my nature to do something dramatic like throw a story or manuscript in the trash, but if I ever did, she's the type of person who would pull it back out and sing its praises.

My editor, Melissa Hill, has helped me from the beginning, and I owe her much thanks. This is an immensely detailed project, and she has helped me with every line. Also deserving thanks are WD editor Kelly Nickell, who trusted me with this assignment; Nicole Klungle, who composed a wonderful introduction to the book; and Jeff Suess, who did a thorough copyedit on my text.

In no particular order, here are other people I would like to thank for their wisdom and assistance with this project: Jessica Faust, Mollie Glick, Brian A. Klems, Nick Eliopulos, Bernadette Baker, Karen McInerney, Kelly Kane, Jack Neff, Cynthia Laufenber, Don Prues, Jane Friedman, Nancy Gall-Clayton, and any agent or publishing pro who contributed an insider tip.

TABLE OF CONTENTS

INTRODUCTION:

THE BASICS BY NICOLE KLUNGLE

A crucial aspect of getting your writing sold—yes, even just as important as the writing itself—is how it is submitted. You have to engage the editor or agent, who is, after all, your first audience. You have to show professionalism and demonstrate that you know how the system works. That's where this book comes in.

Throughout this book, Chuck Sambuchino explains specific formatting guidelines for several different markets, along with samples. This introduction, then, covers the basic principles of a writer's professional correspondence, from standard letter format to professionalism to tracking submissions. Start with the guidelines presented here, then customize your queries and submissions as necessary to fit your market.

These formatting guidelines are not intended to replace publishers' guidelines. Always follow any formatting guidelines offered by the publisher, editor, or producer to whom you are submitting. Sometimes they want things done a certain way and it's important that you follow those directions to the letter. Don't give them a reason to reject your submission right from the start. In the absence of specific guidelines from your publisher or editor, though, you can safely follow the basic formatting suggestions in this section. Proper formatting will result in a clear and professional document that meets editors' expectations and secures their attention. Without proper attention to formatting, good writing often ends up in the rejection pile.

BASIC PROFESSIONALISM

Writing is a business, so it is important to appear professional. A writer's correspondence is her job application. Formatting letters and manuscripts professionally is only one aspect of professionalism. It also includes:

- Thorough research into markets before querying. Your research should help you identify the markets you are interested in, tailor your queries to those markets, and present your queries in the proper format.

- Effective business correspondence. All your business communications should be courteous, concise, and complete, as well as meet the formatting standards of the publisher.

- Professional representation of yourself in e-mail or on the Internet. The e-mail address you use for business correspondence should be professional. If you have a professional website, limit the content to material related to your writing.

- Punctual responses to requests and deadlines. Follow up on queries and requests in a timely manner, and meet your deadlines.

- Flexibility and patience when working with editors, agents, and others. It may take a long time to receive replies to your queries, to see your work in print, or even to see your check come in the mail. Your publisher or editors will likely want to make changes to your work. Showing patience and flexibility in your business relationships will likely result in more business for you in the future.

- Meeting or exceeding expectations for queries and contracted work. Make sure you give agents, editors, and publishers exactly what they want in your queries and finished work.

- Tracking submissions, following up on queries, and learning from rejections. Keeping detailed records of queries, submissions, acceptances, and rejections is essential to success in your writing career. (See the Appendix on page 301.)

BASIC RESEARCH

As a writer, you will find yourself doing a lot of research. It will be necessary throughout your career, so it is best to learn how to do it. Some research will most likely be required for anything you write—and that includes queries. Start to build this skill; it will be invaluable.

Once you have an idea for an article or a book or a play, you first need to do some basic research. Before you even write a query letter, you need to:

- Identify potential markets: Who will buy your work?
- Decide how to tailor your queries to specific markets: How can you show that your work is a good fit with an individual market?
- Learn how to query specific markets: How does each market accept queries? What materials and information do you need to provide, and in what format?

Identifying Markets

Do you have an idea for an article? Or are you writing a screenplay? Or maybe a book? If you want to sell it, you need to do some research to determine who might buy it. Send the queries for your mystery novel to editors who buy mysteries, not to editors who buy romances. If you write cozy mysteries, get even more specific and send your queries to publishers that specialize in cozies.

If you write articles, identifying your market may be more complex. A single topic idea for a magazine article can frequently be adapted for several diverse audiences—and you may want to query for all of them.

Many sources are available to help you identify publishers, agents, or editors who might be interested in your work.

Market Databases

You can start with a market database such as *Writer's Market* that provides basic information about markets for writers. They can be found in print or even online. *Writer's*

Market is updated annually in print, but is also available online at www.writersmarket.com. The online version includes a helpful search function and many other perks, including a submissions tracker.

Market databases tell you:

- what kinds of writing each market accepts (e.g., mysteries, memoirs, how-to articles, novels)
- how much each market accepts (e.g., accepts twenty to thirty articles from freelancers a year; accepts contest entries only)
- contact information of the person who accepts queries and submissions
- guidelines for how to submit queries (e.g., submit a query letter only; submit a letter and one sample chapter; no simultaneous submissions)

Pay close attention to the information in market databases, especially the guidelines for queries and submissions. Doing so can save you a lot of time, as well as drastically increase your chances of success.

Bookstores and Libraries

Bookstores and libraries can also be helpful in identifying potential markets. (For one thing, that's where you find market database books.) But there are other ways they can be useful. If you are writing a book, go to a bookstore and find the section where your book would be shelved, or go to an online bookstore and browse books in the same genre as yours. Identify the books that are the most similar to yours in content and potential readership. Find out who publishes them. That's a potential market.

If you write articles, peruse the magazine section. (Don't skip the local or regional magazines. Writing for local publications can help you break in and build a clipping file.) Think about the potential audiences for your article topic, and find the magazines that cater to those audiences. Note how magazines that appear to cater to similar markets differ from each other. Are there additional magazines that might be interested in your topic if you slant the article toward their readership?

Don't forget to read some of these books and magazines as well. Get an idea of what has already sold to the market you're aiming at your work; see what the publishers are looking for. Libraries usually have the last few back issues of magazines, so broaden your search.

Professional Organizations

Seek out professional organizations that can identify markets and help you break in to them. No matter what you write, there is some kind of organization for you. Horror writers, for instance, can join the Horror Writers Association (www.horror.org). Freelancers may be interested in the American Society of Journalists and Authors (www.asja.org). Screenwriters can find professional contacts through Writers Guild of America, East (www.wgaeast.org) or Writers Guild of America, West (www.wga.org). These organizations are rife with contacts and other networking opportunities.

Conferences and Other Opportunities

Writers' organizations frequently host conferences or retreats where you can meet and interact with publishers, editors, and agents. Many conferences offer Q&A sessions or manuscript critiques. Smaller, specialized organizations can provide a supportive online community for the sharing of ideas and contacts. One resource for learning more about conferences and writers groups is forwriters.com (www. forwriters.com).

In addition to conferences, there are other ways of professional networking to reach your potential audience—and your potential publishers. Start a website, a blog, or an e-mail newsletter. Volunteer for writing organizations or for organizations related to your field of expertise. Start your own organization or writers' group, or speak as a guest for other organizations.

The more your potential markets know you, the more opportunities will open up to you. Nonfiction publishers (and, to some extent, fiction publishers) are looking for authors who not only can reach a wide audience, but who are already reaching a wide audience. Having an existing audience or base to draw on is called platform (see more on this in part one, "Nonfiction Books").

Tailoring Your Queries

Once you have done the research to identify potential markets for your writing, you need to focus a bit more on those markets so you can demonstrate that both you and your work are a good fit with the publication or publisher.

If you are marketing an article to a specific magazine, for instance, read several issues of that magazine before you write your query letter so you can slant your article and query to the magazine. What section of the magazine is your article most likely to appear in? How long are the articles in that section? What kind of voice or style does the magazine use? Some periodicals post their editorial calendar, so you can determine lead time (how far in advance you should pitch your article) and planned content (what's coming up). When writing your query, make sure to demonstrate that you understand the magazine and its readership.

If you are querying a book publisher, demonstrate familiarity with that publisher's book line and readership so you can show how your book would fit in. If you are querying an agent, show that your book falls within that agent's area of specialization.

How to Query

Market databases provide some information about how you should query a particular agent, editor, or publisher. Some information changes with new hires or new guidelines. Make sure the information you have is up-to-date. To ensure your query reaches the right person in the right way, visit the company's website to verify:

- the name of the person who should receive your query
- the correct spelling of that person's name
- that person's gender and proper title (don't assume the gender)
- the name and address of the company

- what should be submitted (e.g., a letter only; a letter with a sample chapter)
- how the query should be submitted (e.g., hard copy, e-mail)

Request for Writers' Guidelines

Many publishers and periodicals offer a set of specific guidelines for submitting queries and other materials. Follow these to the letter. These guidelines cover what you should submit, when you should submit it, how you should format it, and how you should deliver it. Request writers' guidelines from a market before you send a query. Once you get the guidelines, follow them rigorously as you formulate your query as well as in every other document you submit.

Publishers may offer guidelines on their website, by e-mail, or by mail if you send a self-addressed, stamped envelope (SASE). Check your market listings and the publisher's website for information on requesting writers' guidelines. If you are unable to find the information that way, call the publisher and ask how to request writers' guidelines.

In addition to explaining how to submit, guidelines also provide specifics on how the market operates in terms of correspondence and money. Writers' guidelines may explain how much a market pays, what rights are purchased, if they pay on publication, how long after acceptance until the work sees print, and how long it takes them to reply to a query or manuscript submission.

THE BASIC LETTER FORMAT

No matter if you're submitting a novel, screenplay, or collection of poetry, you'll need to include a cover letter or a query letter or both. These letters precede a manuscript submission or assignment, and often pave the way to landing the writer a contract.

To be professional, don't start out with e-mails unless the market specifically requests corresponding that way. Regardless, e-mails share many of the same basic characteristics as business letters.

All business letters should follow these specifications:

- One-inch margins at the top, bottom, left, and right edges of the page
- Single-spaced text, with each section or paragraph of the letter separated by a blank line
- A single, clear, 12-point font
- Your name and contact information at the top of the page, centered or aligned flush with the middle point of the paper
- The date
- The name and address of the letter's recipient
- A salutation followed by a colon. A comma is acceptable, but a colon is preferred
- The body of the letter, with each paragraph aligned flush left (not indented), and a blank line between each paragraph

- A closing
- A space for your signature
- Your name, typed as you sign it
- Notes on enclosures, if any
- Notes on copies, if any

Your Name and Contact Information

Type your name and contact information at the top of the page, either centered or aligned with the midpoint of the page. (If you are using 1-inch margins and letter-size paper, the midpoint is 3.25 inches from the left margin, or 4.25 inches from the left edge of the page.) You contact information includes your address, telephone numbers and e-mail address, as well as your fax number, if applicable.

You may include more than one phone number—day and evening, or home and mobile—but be sure to indicate which is which. Or include your professional website if it is important that the recipient has that information. Don't include your social security number. (This may be requested on an invoice to receive payment, but never on a letter.)

John Q. Writer
123 Author Lane
Writerville, CA 95355
(323) 555-0000
johnqwriter@email.com

The Date

Leave one blank line after your name and contact information. Then type the date flush left. The traditional date format is the month spelled out, followed by the day in numerals, a comma, and then the year in numerals, as in July 4, 1976.

The Recipient's Name and Address

Insert another blank line, then type the name and address of the letter's recipient. Include the addressee's title and company name.

Dave Gregory, Editor in Chief
Cagefighter Magazine
1337 Broadway, Suite 500
New York, NY 12345

The Salutation

Another blank line precedes the salutation of the letter. Always use a formal greeting so as to appear professional: "Dear Mr. Smith" or "Dear Ms. Smith." (Substitute "Dr." or other title when appropriate.) Don't try to be clever or familiar.

If you're writing to someone for the first time, call that person's company to verify the spelling of her name, and that she's the appropriate person to receive your letter. If you can't be sure of the person's gender from the name, ask while you're on the phone.

If you are unable to verify the addressee's gender, use the person's full name, as in "Dear Chris Smith." If your letter is being sent to a committee or group, use the salutation "Dear Ladies and Gentlemen."

The Body of the Letter

After another blank line, start the body of the letter. The main text should consist of paragraphs set flush left, with no indent. Separate each paragraph with a blank line. This is called block format.

The Closure

Finally, end the letter with the closure (usually "Sincerely,"), a space for your signature, and your name, typed as you sign it.

Enclosures

If you are including additional materials with your letter, indicate this by typing "Encl:" a couple of lines down from your typed name. Then briefly list the materials you are including.

> Encl: sample chapter, SASE

Copies

If you are sending a copy of the letter to someone else, and you wish the letter's recipient to know this, insert one or two blank lines after either your typed name or the enclosures note, and then type "CC:" and the names of the people who will be receiving a copy.

> CC: June McBride

The abbreviation "CC" means "carbon copy," a term that derives from a time when carbon paper was used to make duplicates of business letters for multiple recipients. The "CC" now just means a copy, and is commonly used in e-mails as well.

Tips for Cover Letters

- Choose a simple, clear font. Serif fonts (such as Times New Roman and Garamond) are easier to read in the body of a letter than sans-serif fonts (such as Arial and Helvetica). Serifs are the tiny lines at the ends of letters. Sans serif means "without serifs."

- Strive for clarity and concision. Make sure you tell the recipient everything he needs to know, and leave out anything extraneous or unrelated to your project or query.

- Avoid informality. Unless you have an established relationship with the recipient, do not use her first name only in the salutation. Don't adopt a chatty or newsy voice, and don't use gimmicks, such as writing in the voice of a fictional character.

- Use standard white letter-size paper. If you don't want to use plain copy paper, pick a bright white paper of a slightly heavier weight. Don't bother with expensive or colored paper.

- Proofread your letter rigorously before you send it. Give it to someone else to proofread too.

Using Letterhead or Alternative Letter Formats

Remember that the purpose of your letter is to clearly and professionally communicate with the letter's recipient. Attempts to enhance your letter with colors or mixed fonts may backfire by detracting from your letter's clarity and content, or it could create a bad impression.

So, if you create your own letterhead, keep it simple. Stick with one basic, easy-to-read font for the body of the letter. Limit any customization to your contact information. Do not include color or graphics. A simple horizontal rule (a thin line) beneath your contact information communicates that it is a letterhead without sacrificing a clean, professional appearance.

Let the letter's format demonstrate your professionalism, and let the content—not the formatting—show your creativity.

FAX QUERIES

Why Not to Fax Queries

It's relatively quick and easy to slip a query on the fax—but this is the least reliable and potentially most annoying way to pitch your article. Even if the publication accepts faxed queries, try a letter or e-mail instead.

What's wrong with faxed queries?

- Faxes get lost or misrouted within organizations more frequently than letters or e-mails.

- Fax machines are extremely unreliable technology. At times faxes get jammed, shredded and stretched to the point of illegibility. They can easily fall prey to fax paper jams, get stuck in a fax machine's computer memory, or get thrown out along with scads of other unsolicited offers that clog the fax pile. Even when your fax machine or software indicates a fax has gone through, sometimes it hasn't.

- Faxes are frequently end up sent to the wrong fax machine, increasing the likelihood that your query won't even get to the editor's desk.

- Reproduction quality of faxes can be very poor, making them difficult to read. If the editor's fax uses thermal paper, your query will end up on a curly, poorly reproduced sheet that may fade before the editor has had a chance to consider it.

- You can't enclose a SASE or postcard with a fax. They don't provide the convenience of a quick e-mail response. Unless you include a toll-free number for a response, you make the editor or publisher bear the time and financial burden of a response, so they are less likely to respond.

- It's more difficult to attach clips to a fax transmission than to a mail or e-mail query. You have to push all those clips through the fax machine, consuming a lot of your time, not to mention all of the editor's fax paper. Most people don't appreciate twenty-page unsolicited faxes.

Before e-mail became widespread, faxed queries often made sense for time-sensitive topics. These days, however, editors expect you to have e-mail if you're pressed for time. Only send faxed queries if you have permission from the publisher or if submission guidelines state it is acceptable.

Formatting Tips

In those rare cases when a faxed query is called for, here are some tips for making them work as well as possible.

- Keep the format the same as a letter query, unless you're also faxing clips. If you're just faxing the letter, you don't need a cover sheet announcing the letter.

- If you do fax a clip, fax only one, preferably of no more than three pages.

- If you fax a clip, use a cover page to indicate the total page count of the transmission. Avoid Post-it-style fax notes that clutter the page.

- Try a sans-serif font, which should make it easier to read on the other end.

E-MAIL CORRESPONDENCE

Electronic communication has replaced written communication for many purposes. Use e-mails only if e-mail communication is acceptable for your query or cover letter (acceptable to the recipient, not just to you). Remember that your main goal is clear, concise, and professional communication.

E-mails are structured much like business letters (see "The Basic Letter Format" on page 5). The e-mail starts with the date, then the salutation. As usual, keep the salutation formal, ending it with a colon. Single-space the body of the letter, inserting an extra line between paragraphs. End with your typical closure including your full name. Include your contact information following your name at the bottom of the e-mail.

Also, feel free to CC (or BCC—blind carbon copy) yourself on e-mail correspondence as an easy way to track what was sent to whom and when. Make sure that the subject lines of your e-mails are clear and to the point.

Attachments

The first time you e-mail someone, do not attach anything—even a résumé or writing sample—to the e-mail. Computer viruses often come as attachments, and an e-mail with an attachment from an unknown source is likely to be deleted before it is read.

Before sending any attachment, request permission to do so. Be sure to supply the attachment in the format requested. You may be asked to send a text-only file (.txt), a Microsoft Word document (.doc), a PDF (.pdf), a JPEG (.jpg), or some other file format. If you're not sure what format to use, ask.

Special Formatting and E-Mail Stationery

Most e-mail programs allow you to specify some standard text formats, such as bold type, italics, and bulleted lists. This kind of formatting often gets lost in transmission, appearing garbled at the recipient's computer. Avoid using this kind of formatting.

Some e-mail programs give you the option to select stationery—special backgrounds, fonts, and formats—for your e-mail messages. These do not present a professional appearance. Stick to plain text e-mails.

Tips for E-Mail Letters

- Verify that the name your e-mail program sends out with your message is your full professional name, not a nickname or partial name. You can usually set the name that displays in your e-mail options.

- Make sure that the person you're writing to accepts e-mail communications.

- Do the same research before sending an e-mail as before sending a regular letter; verify that you are sending the e-mail to the correct person, that you are spelling that person's name correctly, and that you know the person's gender.

- Be just as formal in a professional e-mail as you would be in any other professional letter ("Dear Ms. Smith:"). Once you have communicated a few times with someone, you may be able to use a more informal style or format ("Dear Joan,"). Just remember to keep your e-mails professional and to the point.

BASIC MANUSCRIPT FORMATTING

How you format your manuscripts will vary depending on the type of manuscript and on the guidelines given to you by the publisher, editor, or producer. A poem manuscript, for instance, might be single-spaced, with the verse roughly centered on the page. An article manuscript would be double-spaced, with each paragraph indented. A screenplay manuscript must adhere to very specific formatting rules unique to that type of manuscript.

Ask for formatting guidelines, and then follow them, whenever you are submitting a manuscript, whether it is a sample of your writing or a finished project. Your publisher's guidelines supersede the guidelines presented in this book.

That said, most fiction and nonfiction manuscripts will feature:

- One-inch margins
- Double-spaced text
- A single, clear, 12-point typeface
- No extra space between paragraphs
- An indented first line for each paragraph

- Information identifying the author and title of the manuscript on every page
- Page numbers

The rest of this book goes into detail on formatting each type of manuscript.

Submitting Manuscripts Electronically

You may be asked to submit your manuscript electronically, either on hard media, such as a CD, or via e-mail. Ask your editor or publisher how she would like to receive the manuscript. You need answers to these questions.

- What file format should the manuscript be? The manuscript may be requested as a Microsoft Word document (.doc), a PDF (.pdf), a text-only file (.txt), or in some other format.
- How should you name the files? If your publisher has no specific naming conventions, give each file a name that indicates the title of the complete work, or use your last name as part of the file name. If submitting several files that make up one document (chapters of a book, for instance), be sure to make the proper order of the files clear.
- How should the files be divided? If the document is a long one, you may need to separate it into several individual files.
- Should you submit a paper copy of the document along with the electronic file? You may be asked to mail a hard copy of your work to accompany the electronic file.
- How should you send the files? Does the publisher want the files delivered on disk or via e-mail?
- Is there a size limit on documents that can be e-mailed? Corporations sometimes limit how much memory an individual message can consume. Messages that take up too much memory are rejected by the server. Send a large manuscript in several files over a few e-mails to ensure that your messages don't get bounced back to you.

Tracking Your Queries and Submissions

Another important part of the writing process is to keep track of your queries, proposals, and submissions. Again, this is all part of keeping a professional level to your writing career. In this way you have a record of response times, what you submitted, who you sent it to—and you can keep track of your progress or fine ways to improve your submission process. The most straightforward way to track queries and submissions is to keep a database or spreadsheet on your computer. However you track your queries and submissions, we advise that you record at least some of the following for everything you send out:

- What you sent and who you sent it to (name and complete contact information)
- The date on which you sent it
- How you sent it (mail, e-mail, or fax)

- The date when you need to follow up if there is no response. Many market database listings will state a standard response time to queries.
- The date on which you received a response
- The nature of the response (yes, no, or a request for additional material)
- What you need to do to follow-up on the response
- Notes on rejection. Record any comments you received in the rejection letter.
- Contract and payment details. What was contracted and how much was offered.
- The date the finished material is due, including intermediate deadlines
- The date you sent the finished material
- The dates you expect and receive payment and the amount received
- Date of publication (projected and actual)

Simultaneous Submissions

A simultaneous submission is material sent to multiple publishers for consideration at the same time. A poet, for example, might send the same set of poems to several magazines at once.

Simultaneous submissions have the advantage of saving time, since you don't have to wait for one publisher to respond before submitting the material to another possible market. It can take several months for a publisher to respond, and that adds up quickly. However, there are some drawbacks. Two or more publishers may offer to purchase the material, in which case you would have to disappoint at least one editor or agent—and that could mean that editor or agent won't be interested in your work in the future.

Market database listings often indicate whether a publisher accepts simultaneous submissions. It's a good idea to avoid sending simultaneous submissions to publishers unless (and perhaps even if) they explicitly state that they accept them.

Always note in your letter if you are sending the same material to others for review. Under no circumstances should you use this information to pressure publishers or agents to make a faster decision.

USING THE BASICS

The submission process is more about business than writing. Submissions are the professional face of you as a writer. Every letter, query, and manuscript needs to reflect professionalism, flexibility, courtesy and reliability. The creativity goes into your poems, stories, articles and screenplays, but not the formal correspondence. For that, use these basics of formatting and submissions and you will be received as a professional writer.

PART I:
NONFICTION

CHAPTER 1:
ARTICLES

There will always be a demand for articles in the writing market. Content that once went in newspapers is now going online. As one magazine folds, another prints its first issue. Articles can be on any topic—investigative pieces, features, interviews, travel writing, columns, sports, home & garden, lifestyle, art & music—there is a market for it all. Regardless of what type of article you want to write, you have to know how to properly submit to an editor or publisher, and how to format your work.

WHAT YOU NEED TO SUBMIT

The process of submitting articles begins with sending a query to an editor, continues through getting acceptance to write the article, and ends with submitting the article text itself. Barring some bumps along the way, the process is that simple.

Take note of the sequence: Query, acceptance, then writing. Before you write an article, you should sell it. That may sound backwards, but it is really how the publishing world works. You can submit finished articles, but this is usually a recipe for disappointment. Most editors want queries before assigning articles. Even if an editor likes the idea for an article, he usually wants to provide some guidance before it is written. That can't happen if the article is already completed. Or it means major rewrites, and major headaches. Working on spec—meaning, submitting completed articles rather than simply the ideas for different stories—is usually an unprofitable habit for freelancers.

The query letter is the time-honored traditional method for selling an article. And that method is the one that editors and publishers prefer to use. As e-mail is quickly replacing snail mail as the main form of communication, the method of delivery and the average response time from an editor may be changing, but the overall process is not.

Another thing that hasn't changed: The query is your first impression with an editor. As you start to develop relationships with editors, pitching article ideas will get measurably easier. Correspondence becomes more informal. Your story pitches become less fleshed out. You're battle-tested, so assignments come easier. But if you have no established relationship with an editor, remember to fall back on two things: professionalism and a darn good query letter.

QUERY LETTER

Submission Tips

The query should serve several primary purposes:

- Sell your idea through a brief, catchy description.
- Tell the editor how you would handle the lead and develop the article.
- Show that you are familiar with the publication and how your article would fit with it.
- Indicate why you are qualified to write this article.

When applicable—and when possible within space constraints—the query should also:

- State the availability of photography or other artwork. (If this is a key selling point, you should definitely include such information. If it's not, these details can be discussed when the editor contacts you about an assignment.) State how you'll be gathering the art, and whether you will take the pictures yourself or a third party will provide them.
- Provide a working title that succinctly and enticingly sums up your idea.
- Estimate the article's length. (It should be as long as you think is necessary to cover the topic, keeping in mind what is the typical length of pieces in the publication. Remember: The editor may think otherwise.)
- Outline possible sidebars.
- Summarize the supporting material, such as anecdotes, interviews, or statistics.
- State when the article will be available.
- Indicate if you are submitting this idea simultaneously to other publications.

A benefit for you as the writer is that preparing the query helps you define the project and develop a lead and a strategy for completing the assignment well before you actually have to do it. The downside is that a query letter can take longer to write, word for word, than the article itself.

Query letters are something of a genre unto themselves. Writing them successfully requires considerable attention to detail and tight editing to fit the one-page standard, which is a widely observed rule for article queries.

Formatting Specs

- Use a standard font or typeface, 12-point type. Avoid bold, script, or italics, except for publication titles. Arial and Times New Roman are fairly standard.
- Place your name, address, phone number, e-mail, fax, and website at the top of your letter, centered, or on your letterhead.
- Use a 1" margin on all sides.
- Keep it to one page. If necessary, separately attach a résumé or a list of credits to provide additional information.

- Use block format (no indentations, an extra space between paragraphs).
- Single-space the body of the letter and double-space between paragraphs.

Other Dos and Don'ts

- Do mention that you can send the manuscript on CD or via e-mail. Most finished articles will be sent as a Microsoft Word attachment. (Sending CDs to an editor comes in handy when dealing with high-resolution art that takes up a lot of memory.)
- Do address the query to a specific editor, preferably the editor assigned to handle freelance submissions or the section you're writing for. Call to get the appropriate name and gender.
- Do thank the editor for considering your proposal.
- Do include an SASE (self-addressed, stamped envelope) or postcard for reply. State in the letter that you have done so, either in the body or in a list of enclosures. (Postcards are cheaper and easier. Get them printed in bulk.)
- Do mention previous publishing credits that pertain to the proposed article.
- Don't take up half a page listing credits of little interest to the editor. If you have extensive credits that pertain to the query, list them on an enclosed sheet.
- Do indicate familiarity with the publication. It's okay to make a positive comment, too, if it's sincere and appropriate, but don't get obsequious.
- Don't request writers' guidelines or a sample copy in your letter. This clearly indicates you're not familiar enough to query. You should request guidelines before you send a query. (See "Request for Guidelines Letter" on p. 31.)
- Don't overpromise. If you can't deliver, it will soon become obvious to the editor.
- Don't tell the editor the idea was already rejected by another publication. Such full disclosure does you no good and isn't necessary.
- Do include clippings, especially when they're applicable to the idea you're proposing. No more than three are necessary, or even desirable.
- Do send copies, not originals, of your clippings. They can always get lost, even if you include an SASE. Photocopied clips are assumed to be disposable; if you want them back, say so in your letter, and make sure you include an SASE with sufficient postage.
- Don't discuss payment terms. It's premature.

QUERY: ARTICLE 1

This is one of many letter-head styles you can use.

John Q. Writer
123 Author Lane
Writerville, CA 95355
johnqwriter@email.com
(323) 555-0000

January 30, 2009

Date flushed right

Jane Smith, managing editor
New Mexico Magazine
4200 Magazine Blvd.
Santa Fe, NM 87501

Always address the correct editor.

Dear Ms. Smith:

According to the Bible, it took God two days to create all living creatures. The way New Mexican Regina Gordon sees it, the 48 Hour Film Project involves the same amount of time—with an only slightly less complicated task.

Use a lead designed to hook and pique interest.

"Every second counts when you only have 48 hours to make a film." That's the motto of the 48 Hour Film Project (www.48hourfilm.com), a nationwide event that challenges local filmmakers to form teams and create four-minute movies—from script to set design to finished product—in forty-eight hours or less. Albuquerque hosted more than twenty teams in 2008, and the city will again participate in the competition in 2009.

1" margin

All of these guerilla filmmakers report to one woman—the city's area producer, Regina Gordon, who must substitute passion, adrenaline, and insane amounts of coffee for sleep she certainly won't get. So what drives her and other participants to exhaust themselves like they do? I propose a 800-word short profile on Gordon along with New Mexico's involvement in the project for *New Mexico Magazine*. (I have already touched based with Gordon.) I believe that a Gordon feature would be a great fit for the "Introducing" section of your magazine. To give readers a feel for what a kinetic, exciting, shoot-from-the-hip experience this is, I would interview Gordon to hear anecdotes from last year's competition and discover what lies in store for this year as a sense of community for the project continues to build in the area.

Estimated word count

Targeting a specific section of the magazine shows you're familiar with the publication.

Highlight qualifications quickly and effectively.

In 2003, I covered Philadelphia's involvement in the project for *Artspike* magazine. Thank you for considering this piece. My résumé and clips are enclosed.

Be polite.

Respectfully,

Leave enough room here for your signature.

John Q. Writer

Encl.: Clips and résumé

Details enclosures

QUERY: ARTICLE 2

Contact information

John Q. Writer
123 Author Lane
Writerville, CA 95355
johnqwriter@email.com
(323) 555-0000

October 30, 2009

Always date letters.

Jimmy Boaz, editor
American Organic Farmer's Digest
8336 Old Dirt Road
Macon, GA 01264

Addressing the correct editor shows research.

Dear Mr. Boaz:

There are eighty-seven varieties of organic crops grown in the United States, but there's only one farm producing twelve of them. That farm is Morganic Corporation.

1" margin

Located in the heart of Arkansas, this company spent the past decade providing great organic crops at a competitive price, helping them to grow into the ninth leading organic farming operation in the country. Along the way, they developed the most unique organic offering in North America.

Single-spaced text, block format

Showing access to interview subjects is helpful.

I am a seasoned writer with access to Richard Banks, the founder and president of Morganic; I propose writing a profile piece on Banks for your Organic Shakers department. After years of reading this riveting column, I believe it is the perfect venue to cover Morganic's rise in the organic farming industry.

Explain where in the magazine this piece would fit.

Word count

The piece would run 800–1,200 words, with photographs available of Banks' and Morganic's operation.

If you will be providing or procuring art in any way, say so.

I've had pieces published in *Arkansas Farmer's Deluxe*, *Organic Farming Today*, and several newspapers. Thank you for your consideration of this article. This is a simultaneous submission. I hope to hear from you soon.

It's never a bad idea to indicate whether you're submitting the idea to multiple publications, or just to the publication in question.

When you explain your credentials, any work in similar areas of interest is most important.

Sincerely,

John Q. Writer

Signature

QUERY, MISTAKES TO AVOID: ARTICLE

John Q. Writer
123 Author Lane
Writerville, CA 95355

No e-mail or phone number is included.

March 24, 2009

Editors
Atlanta Journal-Constitution

Address is missing.

Dear Sir/Ma'am:

Not targeting a certain editor shows you didn't even do the basic research to find an editor's name.

I have an idea for newspaper article. I have a feeling that it would be a controversial and explosive story that would sell a whole bunch of copies—it's that good. What I want to do is give you some of my early thoughts, and if you're interested, we can talk some specifics over the phone (though bear with me; my cell phone gets bad reception).

There might be something here, but the idea is not fleshed out and there is no indication of how you would hook readers.

This simple grammatical error could have been caught with some proofreading.

This is what I'm thinking. I write an article on how the social networking juggernaut MySpace is affecting the dating scene in the ATL. Cool, huh? I know that I could have pitched this to *Atlanta Magazine* or even *People*, but I figured I would give you a shot. For the article, I would need some ideas for sources, and probably some upfront money to buy a laptop. At this point, I'm thinking the article will run about 5,000 words.

Always be humble. Adopting an attitude never works.

Every query recipient wants to feel like you've picked this market for a reason, and arrogant talk like this will kill a query.

My writing influences are Stephen King, James Patterson, and Joe Eszterhas. I've blogged on MySpace plenty of times before and I also regularly comment on website forums and message boards, so I think I have the necessary experience to tackle such an article.

This proposed length is way too long for virtually any publication. Suggesting such an outrageous word count will torpedo your chances.

Why does this matter?

I'm offering a seven-day window on this query because I think that's fair. After all, this is a sizzling topic. Please get back to me right quick.

Peace,

John Q. Writer

An editor doesn't need seven days. He'll just say no now.

While you want to list credentials, something worse would be to list meaningless accomplishments.

QUERY: NONFICTION COLUMN

John Q. Writer
123 Author Lane
Writerville, CA 95355
johnqwriter@email.com
(323) 555-0000

Contact information

October 30, 2009

Date flushed right

Kelly Kane, editor
Watercolor Artist
4700 Editor Road
New York, NY 00000

Dear Ms. Kane:

Address the correct editor.

It was so nice to meet you in New York at the gallery exhibit last month. Like I mentioned when we spoke, I have an idea for a recurring column for your magazine.

If the editor is already familiar with you, certainly note that.

When artists want to see excellent contemporary watercolor art and techniques, the best place to look is your magazine. Month after month, new artists are featured and their detailed work is examined to help watercolorists learn about color, style, techniques, and theme. But just as the magazine pays attention to contemporary masters, it lacks in honoring and examining classical artists.

1" margin

This paragraph tells why readers would enjoy the column, what can it do, and why it's something fresh and new.

With that in mind, I propose a column for your magazine called "Meet the Masters," which will examine famous artists through the centuries who used the medium of watercolor. The column will be an entertaining look at fabled painters—examining not only their rise to fame, but also their love for watercolor and gouache that connects with your readers. Here are three preliminary ideas for subjects:

Brief descriptions of several column ideas show you can deliver more than once.

1. **George Grosz.** Grosz, a German satirist, experimented with mixing pencil and watercolor, and used cubist techniques to exaggerate corruption he saw all around him. He was influential in Europe preceding World War II.

2. **Milton Avery.** A painter's painter, Avery was fond of painting with both watercolor and gouache. He was a master of flat shapes and simple color schemes to seize on a moment and place in nature.

3. **Arthur B. Davies.** One of "The Eight" artists who helped to progress America's art consciousness, Davies used watercolor to paint his Symbolist-influenced, ethereal compositions of female portraits and dreamlike landscapes.

Besides being a painter myself, I have written short pieces for both *American Artist* and *The Artist Magazine*. Thank you for considering my submission. I look forward to hearing from you.

Credentials listed, short and sweet

Best,

Signature

John Q. Writer

There isn't much space to list everything, but these are good choices and the writer seems familiar with both their overall accomplishments as well as their style concerning watercolor paintings.

ELECTRONIC QUERIES

Submission Tips

The digital age has brought an air of informality to communications between editors and writers, but manners have not been redefined. Communications with a new editor should still be formal and respectful whether you make contact by mail, fax, or e-mail. Once you've developed a relationship, you can afford to become less formal. Because the editor is familiar with your writing experience and ability to develop an article, you might pitch story ideas over the phone or in one- or two-sentence e-mails. But rarely will an editor make a judgment based on casual contact with a new writer.

Thus, the basic format, length, and tone of an electronic query shouldn't be much different than a query on paper, except that certain features of e-mails do dictate different strategies.

Formatting Specs

- Include the same information you would in a query on paper—your name and contact information. The biggest change is to include your contact information at the bottom left, under your signature, rather than at the top. Because an editor will have a limited view of your query in an e-mail window, it's a good idea to get right to the query text.

- Fill in the subject line of the e-mail with a description of your query. This gives you an extra selling line and can be a good place for the proposed title of your work. Don't be afraid to start the subject line with the word, "Query."

- Follow the same format you would with a query on paper, including the date, salutation, and block paragraph format. Leaving out these formalities isn't unusual, but there's no good reason to do away with them just because it's an e-mail. The information could be useful to the editor, and it never hurts to be polite.

How to Include Clips With E-Mailed Queries

When you send an e-mail query, you can provide clips five ways. Pay attention to writers' guidelines of the specific publication you are sending the query to in order to see if they would like to see clips in a particular fashion (e.g., as links inside an e-mail query). There are no generally accepted standards for which is best, but the pros and cons of each method are described. (See "Attachments" on page 79.)

1. Include a line telling the editor that clips are available on request. If the editor requests them, you can then mail, fax, or e-mail the clips according to his preference. This is a convenient solution for the writer, but not necessarily for the editor. The clips aren't available immediately, so you potentially slow the decision process by adding an additional step, and you lose any speed you've gained by e-mailing the query in the first place.

2. Include electronic versions of the clips in the body of the e-mail message. This can make for an awfully long e-mail, and it doesn't look as presentable as other alternatives, but it may be better than making the editor wait to download attachments or log on to a website. Also, since viruses are often transmitted as attachments to e-mails, editors may be leery of accepting e-mail attachments from you before they know who you are.

3. Include electronic versions of the articles as attachments. The disadvantage here is the editor has to download the clips, which can take several minutes. Also, if there's a format disparity, the editor may not be able to read the attachment.

4. Send the clips in a separate e-mail message. This cuts the download time and eliminates software-related glitches, but it clutters the editor's e-mail inbox.

5. Hypertext links in the e-mail. This may be the most convenient and reliable way for editors to access your clips electronically. If any of your stories are published online, simply include the links to those clips at the end of your e-mail. These provide a more accurate reading of what the editor can expect. If you have your own individual website dedicated to your writing career, include articles online that way.

Other Dos and Don'ts

- Don't use all caps or exclamation points in the subject line. These are among the dreaded earmarks of spam and will cause some editors to summarily delete your e-mail.

- Don't submit an e-mail query unless you know it's welcome. Listings in *Writer's Market* or *Writer's Digest* will indicate whether electronic queries are accepted. If you can't find a listing, call the publication to check.

- Don't send an e-mail query to the editor's personal e-mail address unless expressly directed to do so. Many publications maintain separate e-mail addresses for queries.

- Don't insert clip art graphics or other images.

- Do attach or provide links to photos or graphics that have digital versions stored on your computer if their availability will help sell your article. They may take a long time to download, but the editor only needs to do it if she's interested.

- Do indicate how you'll make your clips and other supporting material available.

- Do turn off your spam filter if you use EarthLink. When an editor replies, she shouldn't have to confirm her existence as a human being just so you can get her response.

ELECTRONIC QUERY: ARTICLE

It's not a bad idea to copy (CC or BCC) yourself on the e-mail to keep copies of all e-correspondence to editors.

TO: editor@fastcompany.com
CC: johnqwriter@email.com
SUBJECT: Query: Improving Attention the All Natural Way

You may capitalize key words in your subject line if you want to, but never use all caps.

August 13, 2008

Date flushed right

Starting the subject line off with "Query" will help ensure your e-mail isn't mistaken as junk mail.

Address a specific editor.

Kim Dearth, senior editor
brava
P.O. Box 45050
Madison, WI 53744-5050
kdearth@ericksonpublishing.com

Dear Ms. Dearth:

I see on your editorial calendar that you'll be covering "Adult Attention Deficit Disorder" in your December 2008 issue.

Always explain your qualifications, but never brag.

As a full-time freelance writer specializing in cognitive development, I'd like to propose an article to your upcoming issue. **"Pay Attention! Improving Attention the All Natural Way—With Brain Training"** would include the following:

The title and deck of the article are provided—making the editor's job easier.

1. Brain exercises that your readers can do at home to improve the three types of attention: selective, sustained, and divided.

2. The latest scientific research on brain training (why it works).

3. Quotes from a psychologist, a professional brain trainer in Madison, and an author.

General formatting rules—such as single-spaced paragraphs—remain the same.

I could fit the article to your desired word count.

My credentials include a B.A. in psychology and more than 1,000 published pieces including two nonfiction books for McGraw-Hill. I've written for countless parenting, health and women's magazines and currently work as a freelance editor for several publications.

If you have a working title, use quotations around it, or bold it, or both. If you can pique an editor's interest with the title alone, you're off to a good start.

Thank you in advance for your time. I look forward to hearing from you.

Best,

Instead of putting your contact information at the top of an e-mail query, place it at the bottom. Only part of an e-mail will be visible in a computer window, so you need to get down to business fast.

John Q. Writer
123 Author Lane
Writerville, CA 95355
johnqwriter@email.com
(323) 555-0000

If you aren't mailing clips, make sure you have some work online that an editor can review.

Clips available on www.johnqwriter.com

This query fits on one printed page as well. Don't abuse the formlessness of e-mail to become verbose.

ELECTRONIC QUERY, MISTAKES TO AVOID: ARTICLE

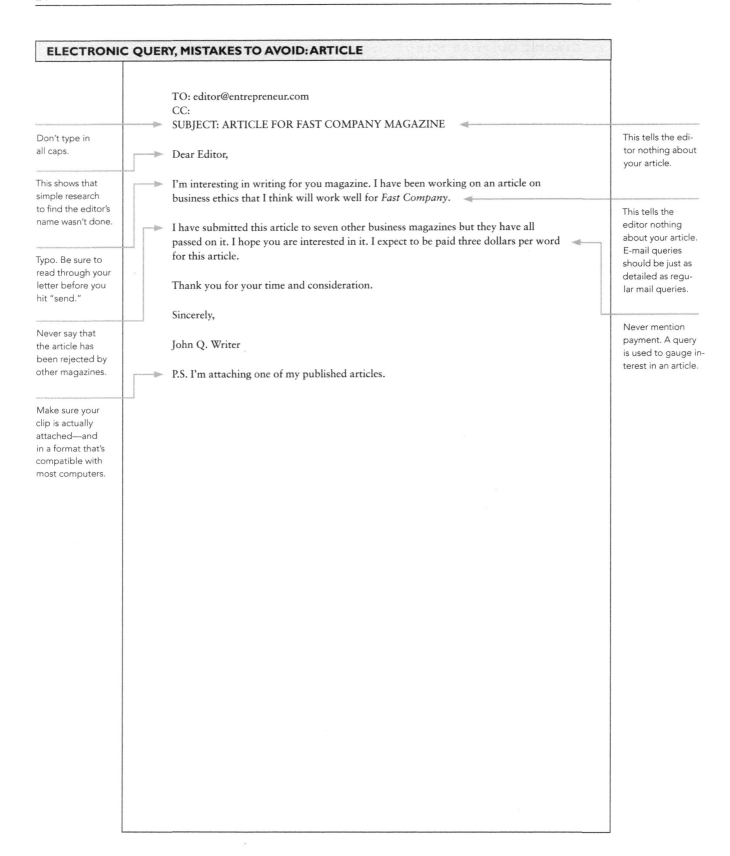

TO: editor@entrepreneur.com
CC:
SUBJECT: ARTICLE FOR FAST COMPANY MAGAZINE

Dear Editor,

I'm interesting in writing for you magazine. I have been working on an article on business ethics that I think will work well for *Fast Company*.

I have submitted this article to seven other business magazines but they have all passed on it. I hope you are interested in it. I expect to be paid three dollars per word for this article.

Thank you for your time and consideration.

Sincerely,

John Q. Writer

P.S. I'm attaching one of my published articles.

Don't type in all caps.

This shows that simple research to find the editor's name wasn't done.

Typo. Be sure to read through your letter before you hit "send."

Never say that the article has been rejected by other magazines.

Make sure your clip is actually attached—and in a format that's compatible with most computers.

This tells the editor nothing about your article.

This tells the editor nothing about your article. E-mail queries should be just as detailed as regular mail queries.

Never mention payment. A query is used to gauge interest in an article.

FOLLOW-UP LETTERS

Occasionally lines get crossed, mail gets lost, and plans change. And sometimes, editors are just plain rude. For whatever reason, your postcard or SASE is never returned, the article you submit never appears, or you don't get paid. You may need to follow up on a query, article submission, or payment. Here are some polite, gentle ways to go about it.

Submission Tips

When you haven't heard back from a publication within a reasonable time, such as sixty days or the reporting period cited in the listing in *Writer's Market*, send a brief, businesslike inquiry.

Formatting Specs

- As with queries, address it to the correct editor and use proper greeting and salutation, and letter format.
- Enclose a reply postcard or SASE (except in a follow-up on a late payment), in case your original was lost.

Other Dos and Don'ts

- Do be businesslike and polite.
- Do briefly explain the history behind your request (e.g., "I sent you a query with a prepaid reply postcard on …").
- Don't be emotional or accusatory or jump to conclusions about what happened.
- Do resubmit your query or invoice.

FOLLOW-UP TO QUERY LETTER

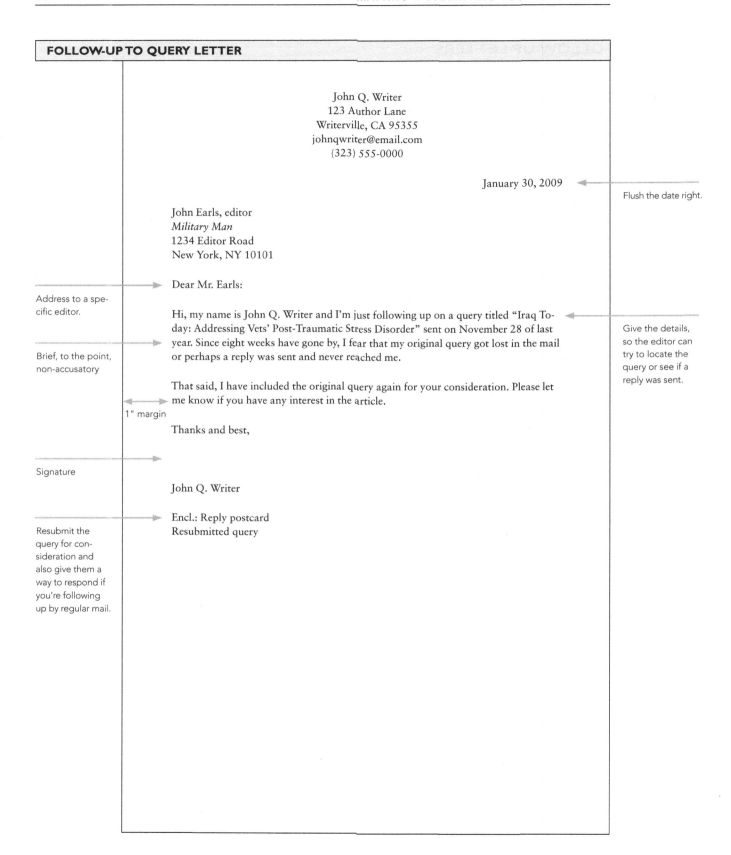

John Q. Writer
123 Author Lane
Writerville, CA 95355
johnqwriter@email.com
(323) 555-0000

January 30, 2009

Flush the date right.

John Earls, editor
Military Man
1234 Editor Road
New York, NY 10101

Dear Mr. Earls:

Address to a specific editor.

Hi, my name is John Q. Writer and I'm just following up on a query titled "Iraq Today: Addressing Vets' Post-Traumatic Stress Disorder" sent on November 28 of last year. Since eight weeks have gone by, I fear that my original query got lost in the mail or perhaps a reply was sent and never reached me.

Brief, to the point, non-accusatory

Give the details, so the editor can try to locate the query or see if a reply was sent.

That said, I have included the original query again for your consideration. Please let me know if you have any interest in the article.

1" margin

Thanks and best,

Signature

John Q. Writer

Encl.: Reply postcard
Resubmitted query

Resubmit the query for consideration and also give them a way to respond if you're following up by regular mail.

FOLLOW-UP TO ARTICLE SUBMISSION

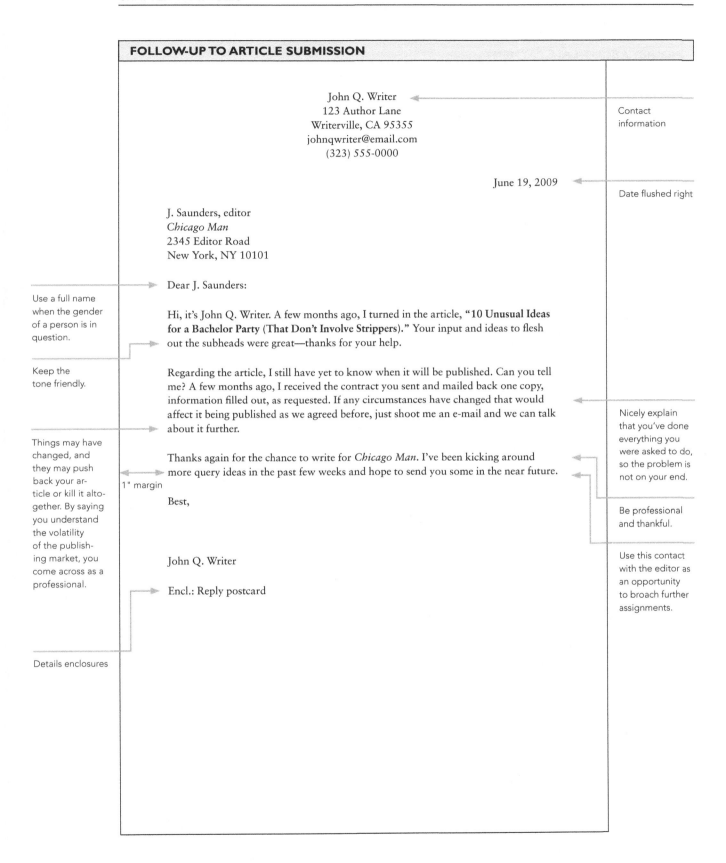

Contact information

John Q. Writer
123 Author Lane
Writerville, CA 95355
johnqwriter@email.com
(323) 555-0000

June 19, 2009

Date flushed right

J. Saunders, editor
Chicago Man
2345 Editor Road
New York, NY 10101

Use a full name when the gender of a person is in question.

Dear J. Saunders:

Hi, it's John Q. Writer. A few months ago, I turned in the article, **"10 Unusual Ideas for a Bachelor Party (That Don't Involve Strippers)."** Your input and ideas to flesh out the subheads were great—thanks for your help.

Keep the tone friendly.

Regarding the article, I still have yet to know when it will be published. Can you tell me? A few months ago, I received the contract you sent and mailed back one copy, information filled out, as requested. If any circumstances have changed that would affect it being published as we agreed before, just shoot me an e-mail and we can talk about it further.

Nicely explain that you've done everything you were asked to do, so the problem is not on your end.

Things may have changed, and they may push back your article or kill it altogether. By saying you understand the volatility of the publishing market, you come across as a professional.

Thanks again for the chance to write for *Chicago Man*. I've been kicking around more query ideas in the past few weeks and hope to send you some in the near future.

1" margin

Best,

Be professional and thankful.

John Q. Writer

Use this contact with the editor as an opportunity to broach further assignments.

Encl.: Reply postcard

Details enclosures

INQUIRY ABOUT LATE PAYMENT

John Q. Writer
123 Author Lane
Writerville, CA 95355
johnqwriter@email.com
(323) 555-0000

Contact information

June 11, 2009

Date flushed right

Mary Kay Leonetti, senior editor
Changing World
3456 Editor Road
New York, NY 10101

1" margin

Dear Ms. Leonetti:

Single-spaced text

Hi, it's John Q. Writer. I wrote the article, **"Why the World Didn't Come to an End on January 1,"** which was published in the November issue of *Changing World*. The article reached newsstands on October 27.

Be firm, but not hostile or accusatory.

I'm just writing to follow up regarding article payment. I sent an invoice on November 1 of last year. I know that your publication's policy is to pay upon publication, so I thought it would be best if I touched base to inquire about payment status. I've enclosed a second invoice, in case the first was lost.

If you ever think something was lost, always resend.

Offer to contact another department for them.

If payment matters are best discussed with another individual—such as someone in accounting—I will gladly follow up with that person instead if you can provide me with a name and e-mail.

Regarding the article: Thank you for giving me the opportunity to write for *Changing World*. It was a lot of fun and I hope to contribute more work in the future.

Be polite as usual.

Thanks very much for your help.

Sincerely,

John Q. Writer

Encl.: Invoice

No need for an SASE at this point.

LETTER OFFERING REPRINT RIGHTS

Submission Tips

When you are offering reprint rights to a publisher, send a brief letter describing the article and where it was published. Since the article is enclosed, don't give it a glowing send-off—it should sell itself. If you can provide any follow-up information on the article's impact or how it was received in its original market, however, that could help you sell reprint rights. Also offer any ideas you might have on how the article could be adapted to the publication's needs.

Formatting Specs

- Use a similar format to queries.
- Keep it short. Two or three brief paragraphs will do.
- Enclose a reply postcard.

"Today's writers will be pleased to know that a large majority of magazine editors, agents, and publishers are now accepting e-queries—that is, queries, submitted via e-mail. It's not only an incredible money-saver (stamps, paper, ink, envelopes, gas to the post office), but also a great time-saver. With some editors replying in mere seconds, you'll either be able to get right to work, or right back to the drawing board."

—WENDY BURT-THOMAS

author, *The Writer's Digest Guide to Query Letters*

LETTER OFFERING REPRINT RIGHTS

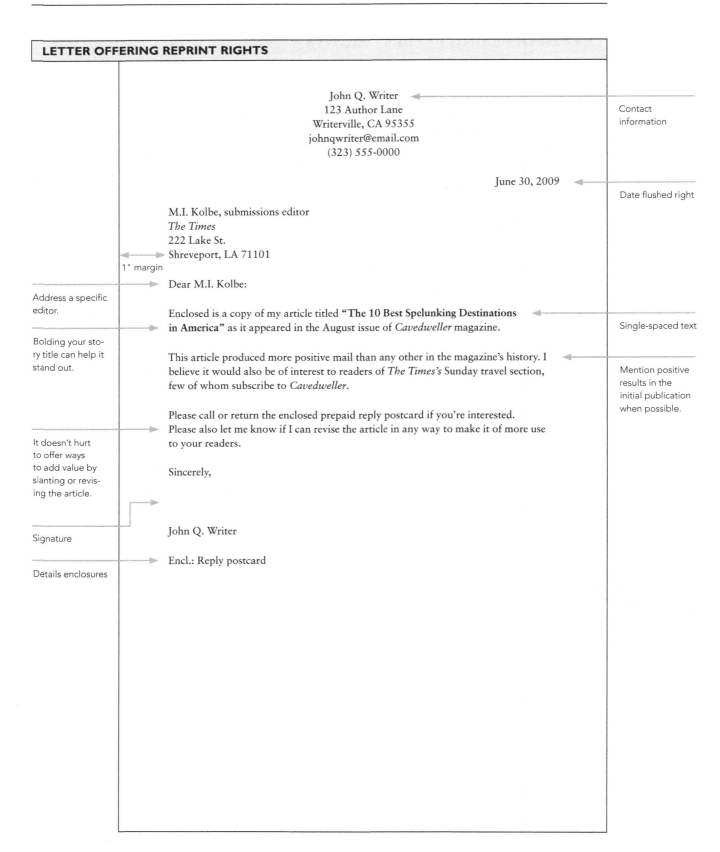

John Q. Writer
123 Author Lane
Writerville, CA 95355
johnqwriter@email.com
(323) 555-0000

June 30, 2009

M.I. Kolbe, submissions editor
The Times
222 Lake St.
Shreveport, LA 71101

Dear M.I. Kolbe:

Enclosed is a copy of my article titled **"The 10 Best Spelunking Destinations in America"** as it appeared in the August issue of *Cavedweller* magazine.

This article produced more positive mail than any other in the magazine's history. I believe it would also be of interest to readers of *The Times's* Sunday travel section, few of whom subscribe to *Cavedweller*.

Please call or return the enclosed prepaid reply postcard if you're interested. Please also let me know if I can revise the article in any way to make it of more use to your readers.

Sincerely,

John Q. Writer

Encl.: Reply postcard

Contact information

Date flushed right

Address a specific editor.

Bolding your story title can help it stand out.

It doesn't hurt to offer ways to add value by slanting or revising the article.

Signature

Details enclosures

1" margin

Single-spaced text

Mention positive results in the initial publication when possible.

REQUEST FOR GUIDELINES LETTER

Submission Tips

Send a brief letter stating that you want to receive the publication's writers' guidelines. Before you send the letter, use an Internet search engine such as Google (www.google.com) to find the publication's website and see if the writers' guidelines are included on the site.

Formatting Specs

- Address the letter to the correct editor. Check *Writer's Market* listings when available, or use the phone (you needn't ask for the editor—just get the name and address).
- Use block format.
- Keep it simple. One paragraph will do.
- Include your name, address, phone number, and e-mail.
- Enclose an SASE.

Other Dos and Don'ts

- Don't try to pitch yourself or a story at this point. It may not even be an editor who reads this letter, and all you need are the guidelines, anyway.
- Don't use "Dear Sir," "To whom it may concern," or other indications that you don't know who the editor is.

Before a columnist can get published, he has to find a subject niche—something specific about which to write, but not so specific as to narrow the potential audience and topics of the column. He has to find out whether other columnists are writing on the same subject and study their work to see how his differs from theirs. Then he has to outline topic ideas and flesh out at least several finished columns to show editors. To sell the idea to an editor, he has to position himself as the right person for the job. Once the column is published, he must continually think about the next topic, striving to make every one better.

—MONICA MCCABE CARDOZA

author, *You Can Write a Column*

ELECTRONIC REQUEST FOR GUIDELINES LETTER: ARTICLE

TO: afortin@motherjonesmag.com
CC: johnqwriter@email.com
SUBJECT: Request for Writers' Guidelines

Copy yourself on an e-mail to keep all e-correspondence.

June 30, 2009

Flush the date right.

April Fortin, executive editor
Mother Jones
4567 Editor Ave.
New York, NY 10001

Even here, it can pay to know the editor's name.

Dear Ms. Fortin:

Stay formal, even in e-mail.

I'm interested in writing for *Mother Jones* magazine, and would like to request a copy of your writers' submission guidelines. I can't find the guidelines on your website and wondered if you could point me to a web page that can help.

Short and sweet

If they are only available in print form, just say so and I will mail an SASE to your attention.

Thanks for your help.

Sincerely,

John Q. Writer
123 Author Lane
Writerville, CA 95355
(323) 555-0000
johnqwriter@email.com

Since it's an e-mail letter, put your information at the bottom of the letter.

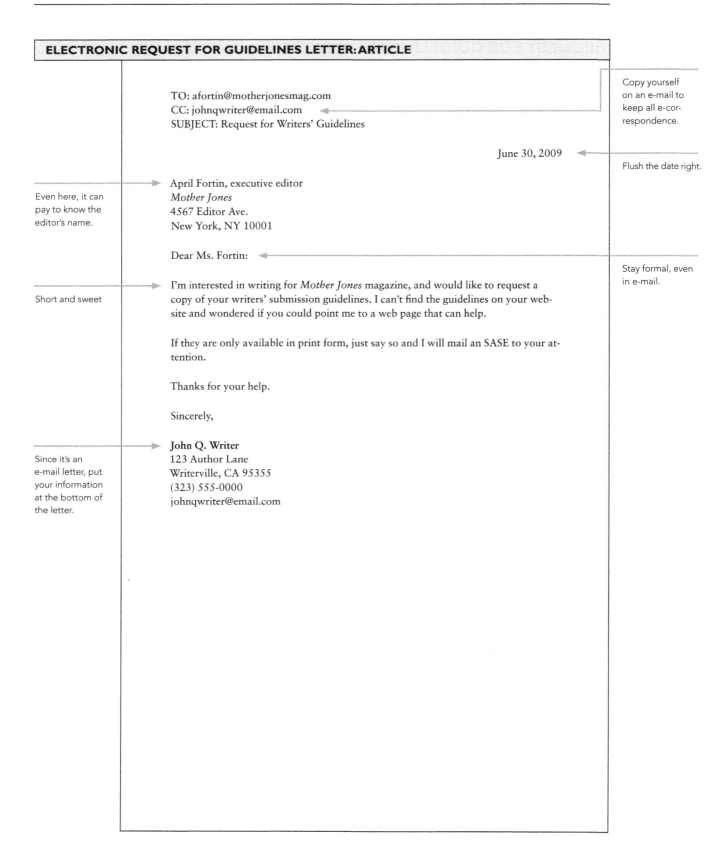

A good query letter outlines the specific proposal, with definitive subject matter, sources, and applicable expertise. Are you well versed enough on your subject matter to write knowledgeably about it? It's your job in the query letter to convince the editor that you are the writer for the job. What captures my attention is clear, concise writing that showcases the writer's attention to detail. Standouts include well-documented research, interviews with well-known writers, and relevant essays.

—NAN LESLIE

fiction editor, *The Green Hills Literary Lantern*

REPLY POSTCARD

If you're a bit worried about whether your submission package actually makes it to the publication, enclose a reply postcard to be signed by the editor (or someone on the staff) and sent back to you. Two caveats: (1) Not all editors are gracious enough to send your reply postcards back, but most do. (2) Just because you receive a postcard reply from a publication, you cannot assume your story has been read or will be read in the next few days or weeks. The only function of your reply postcard is to let you know your submission was received.

Your best bet to ensure an editor will return your reply postcard is to make it neat and simple to use. That means typing your postcard and not asking the editor to do anything other than note your submission has been received. Although it's okay to leave a small space for "Comments," keep the space small and don't expect it to be filled in—most editors simply don't have the time or a reason to write anything in it. You'll turn off an editor if you ask him to do too much.

Follow the examples here to create a suitable and functional reply postcard. Remember to keep things short and sweet—and, of course, always supply the postage.

REPLY POSTCARDS: ARTICLE

Front of card:

John Q. Writer
123 Author Lane
Writerville, CA 95355

Back of card (query):

Your query was received on_____

___ We need more time to consider your query and will be in touch.
___ Yes, we are interested in your idea. An editor will be in touch soon.
___ No, we are not interested in your article at this time.
___ Please send the following additional information (see below).

Comments: _____
_____
_____

Back of card (follow-up):

Yes, your article was received on _____

___ We need more time to consider your query and will be in touch.
___ No, we are not interested in your article at this time.
___ Please send the following additional information (see below).

Comments: _____
_____
_____

Back of card (reprint):

___ I would like to reprint your article. Please call me.
___ No, we are not interested in your article.
___ Please send the following additional information (see below).

Comments: _____
_____
_____

ARTICLE

What You Need to Submit

Compared to the query letter that leads up to the article, formatting the article itself is relatively easy. The style and approach of each article is different, of course, and beyond the scope of this book. However, the layout of the printed page and the information is relatively clear-cut. All you need is:

- A cover letter
- Your article

This section will guide you through the cover letter and the article itself.

COVER LETTER

Submission Tips

By the time you send the article, the editor should already know who you are and about the article. Use the cover letter to accomplish a few additional functions:

- Provide details that may be important in the editing and fact-checking process, including names, addresses, and phone numbers of sources.
- Inform the editor of the status of photographs and graphics that will accompany the article (whether they're enclosed or coming from another party).
- Provide information about how you can be reached for questions.
- Mention any details the editor should know in editing the manuscript, such as difficulty in reaching a particular source or conflicting data you received and how you resolved the conflict.
- Thank the editor for the assignment and express your interest in writing for the publication again.

Formatting Specs

- Use a standard font, 12-point type. Avoid bold or italics, except for titles.
- Put your name and contact information at the top of your letter, centered, or on your letterhead.
- Use 1" margins on all sides.
- Address the cover letter to a specific editor. (Call and get the appropriate editor's name and gender.)
- If you need more than a page, use it. The editor will need this information in handling your manuscript.
- Provide a word count.
- Provide contact names of sources if needed.

ELECTRONIC COVER LETTER

Submission Tips

Once an editor is interested in seeing your article, he may ask you to send the article via e-mail. Don't send the article by itself; just because you're using e-mail doesn't mean you should forego a cover letter. The cover letter will provide the editor with valuable information regarding your article and should include the same information as one sent via mail.

The text of the cover letter should be submitted in the e-mail body. The article should be attached, preferably as a Microsoft Word document (.doc).

Formatting Specs

- Include the same information in your cover letter as you would in a paper cover letter—name, address, phone, fax, and website.
- Use the subject line to introduce the title of your article.
- Follow the same format you would with a paper cover letter, including date, salutation, and block paragraph format.

Other Dos and Don'ts

- Don't use all caps or exclamation points in the subject line.
- Don't insert clip art graphics or other images in your cover letter. Keep it simple.

Pitching an article to a newspaper can be an intimidating prospect, especially if you're new to the market. But you might be surprised to find out that editors aren't always looking for highly experienced wordsmiths with extensive résumés. Of course, writers must have a grasp of basic journalistic writing style and grammar. Still, many editors say enthusiasm or proficiency in a particular subject is more prized in a freelance writer than a thick packet of published clips.

—FEOSHIA HENDERSON

freelancer, *The Lane Report, Kentucky Monthly*

COVER LETTER: ARTICLE

John Q. Writer
123 Author Lane
Writerville, CA 95355
johnqwriter@email.com
(323) 555-0000

Contact
information

January 5, 2009

Elizabeth Cook
Food Processing
6789 Editor Ave.
Chicago, IL 60612

Some informality
is acceptable at
this point.

Dear Libby:

Enclosed is "Foods for (Shelf) Life" (1,500 words) for the March issue.

Photos should have arrived from the National Sunflower Association and USDA. If
you don't receive them by the end of the week, please let me know and I'll call to
check on their status.

1" margin

Provide informa-
tion about pho-
tography, if you
have it.

Tell how you can
be reached for
questions when
necessary.

I'll be away on business from January 7–10, but I will be checking voice mail daily.
Feel free to leave any questions on my voice mail, and I'll answer them on yours if I
can't return the call when you're in the office.

Here are the contact numbers for sources:

- Jeff Miller, agronomist with the U.S. Department of Agriculture,
  (716) 555-4322

- Pamela J. White, professor of food science at Iowa State University,
  (515) 555-1224

- Larry Kleingartner, executive director of the National Sunflower
  Association, Bismarck, ND, (716) 555-3400

- Shin Hasegawa, a biochemist at the USDA's Agricultural Research
  Service in Albany, CA, (510) 555-6070

Many publica-
tions require
contact names
and numbers.
The cover letter
is a good place
for this.

It's always a good
idea to mention
that you are
available to do re-
quested changes.

Thanks again for the assignment. I look forward to working with you again soon. As
I mentioned before, let me know if this piece needs any revisions or tweaks.

Best wishes,

Signature

John Q. Writer

Encl.: Manuscript, "Foods for (Shelf) Life"

If you're sending
an article through
the mail, consider
including a CD
data disk that con-
tains the article in
electronic format.

ARTICLE MANUSCRIPT

Submission Tips

Show you're a professional by submitting a clean, grammatically correct and properly spelled manuscript that hews as closely as possible to the style of the publication (see "Winning Style Points" on page 39).

Formatting Specs

- Use a 1" margin on all sides.

- Don't number the first page.

- Include rights offered or negotiated and a word count in the top right corner of the first page.

- If you have one or more sidebars, indicate this in the top right corner of the first page, along with the word count for each sidebar.

- Put the working title in all caps or boldface and the subtitle underlined or in italic, centered, about one-third of the way down the page from the top margin.

- Skip one line and write "by" in lowercase, then skip another line and put your name. (If you're using a pseudonym, put that name in all caps, and then on the next line put your real name in parentheses.)

- Drop four lines and begin the article. Indent all paragraphs except the first one.

- Double-space the entire text of the story.

- Put a slug, a one- to two-word name, at the top left corner of the header in the second and preceding pages.

- Put page numbers (from page 2 to the end of the article) in the top right corner of the header.

- Use 12-point type.

- Optional: At the article's end, put a "–30–" or "–###–" notation. This is more of a relic in publishing than a necessity, but some writers feel insecure without it. It won't hurt to do it or leave it out.

- When sending an accepted article, be sure to include a copy of the article on disk or CD along with the hard copy.

Other Dos and Don'ts

- Do use paper clips in the top left corner of your manuscript (butterfly clips or paper clamps for articles of more than ten pages).

- Don't use staples.

- Don't clip, and especially don't staple, your cover letter to the manuscript.

- Don't use a separate cover page. It's pretentious for an article-length manuscript and wholly unnecessary.

Before you spend weeks writing sample columns or drawing cartoon strips, it is wise to invest at least a few hours researching your idea. Is something like it already out there? How is your idea unique? Does it fit with current trends? Be sure you know the competition, how your pitch can fill an empty niche in the market or why it is better than what is currently out there. Being aware of this information can make all the difference with a national syndicate.

—LISA ABEYTA

columnist, *Albuquerque Tribune*

- Don't justify text or align the right margin. Ragged right is fine.
- Don't insult the editor's intelligence or intentions by putting a copyright notice on the manuscript. It's copyrighted as soon as you write it.
- Don't use unusual fonts. A simple Times Roman will do fine.
- Do include suggested subheads in the body of your manuscript if the magazine's style is to use subheads; however, don't rely on subheads as a substitute for transitions. Subheads may need to be removed for layout or page composition purposes. Besides, they're an editor's prerogative. Don't count on them staying where you put them.

Winning Style Points

Virtually all newspapers and many magazines use some variation of Associated Press style. Other magazines and most books use *The Chicago Manual of Style* from the University of Chicago Press. Every freelancer should have the books *The Associated Press Stylebook and Libel Manual* and *The Chicago Manual of Style* on her shelf. *CMS* also provides useful general guidance on grammar and usage issues in addition to style points. Both books also offer online versions to which you can subscribe.

The most common style questions concern such areas as numbers, localities, abbreviations, and capitalization. Style manuals also cover such fine points as the difference in usage between *lawyer* and *attorney*. It's a good idea to at least skim through the style manuals to become familiar with the usage issues they cover, in addition to using them as references when unsure about a style issue.

Most publications have style rules of their own that deviate from whichever standard they use. Freelancers can't realistically be expected to know all the rules before first being published in a magazine, but try to be familiar with the publication's basic style standards.

MANUSCRIPT: ARTICLE

Include contact information here.

John Q. Writer
123 Author Lane
Writerville, CA 95355
(323) 555-0000
johnqwriter@email.com

First North American Rights
Approximately 1,500 words

Provide a word count.

Title one-third of the way down the page

FOODS FOR (SHELF) LIFE
For advances in shelf life, researchers increasingly change foods themselves

by
John Q. Writer

Underline or italicize the subhead or deck head.

1" margin

Enhancing shelf life used to mean finding better preservatives. But food scientists increasingly are changing the food itself as they search for cleaner-reading labels, better taste, and stronger nutritional profiles to go along with improved shelf life.

Indent paragraphs except for the first one.

Researchers are modifying such basic foods as oils, beef, and fruit on the molecular or genetic level for the sake of preserving flavor or preventing spoilage.

One of the bigger changes in the next few years could be in oils for frying snacks and other foods. Research into high-oleic versions of sunflower, soybean,

Double-spaced text

and corn oils is bringing to market oils that offer extended shelf life for fried and other foods without requiring hydrogenation. Higher oleic oils may offer relatively modest or no gains in shelf life compared to hydrogenated oils, but they offer substantial gains over unmodified oils and provide an alternative to the costs and health risks of hydrogenation.

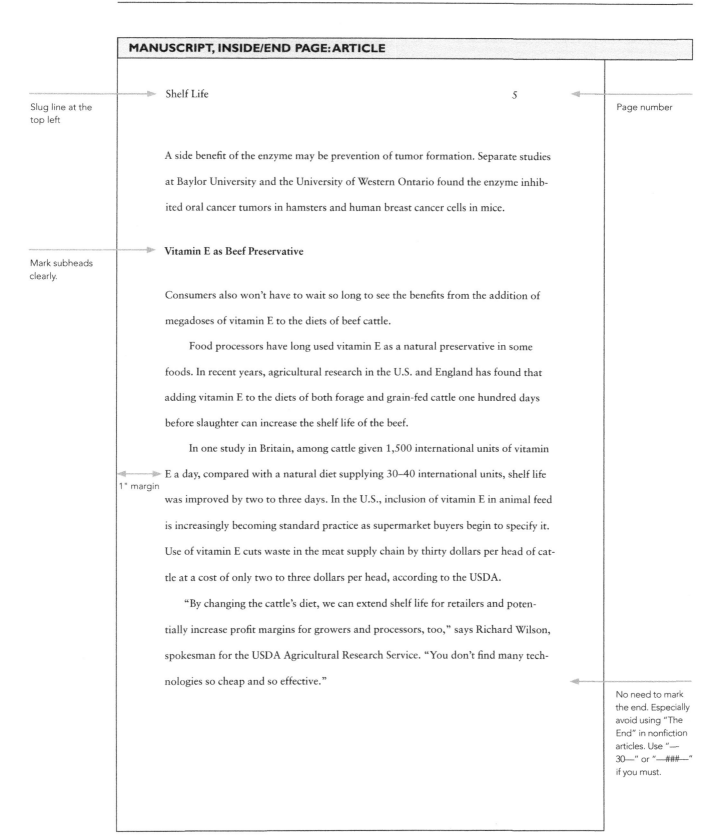

MANUSCRIPT, INSIDE/END PAGE: ARTICLE

Slug line at the top left

Shelf Life   5

Page number

A side benefit of the enzyme may be prevention of tumor formation. Separate studies at Baylor University and the University of Western Ontario found the enzyme inhibited oral cancer tumors in hamsters and human breast cancer cells in mice.

Mark subheads clearly.

Vitamin E as Beef Preservative

Consumers also won't have to wait so long to see the benefits from the addition of megadoses of vitamin E to the diets of beef cattle.

Food processors have long used vitamin E as a natural preservative in some foods. In recent years, agricultural research in the U.S. and England has found that adding vitamin E to the diets of both forage and grain-fed cattle one hundred days before slaughter can increase the shelf life of the beef.

In one study in Britain, among cattle given 1,500 international units of vitamin E a day, compared with a natural diet supplying 30–40 international units, shelf life

1" margin

was improved by two to three days. In the U.S., inclusion of vitamin E in animal feed is increasingly becoming standard practice as supermarket buyers begin to specify it. Use of vitamin E cuts waste in the meat supply chain by thirty dollars per head of cattle at a cost of only two to three dollars per head, according to the USDA.

"By changing the cattle's diet, we can extend shelf life for retailers and potentially increase profit margins for growers and processors, too," says Richard Wilson, spokesman for the USDA Agricultural Research Service. "You don't find many technologies so cheap and so effective."

No need to mark the end. Especially avoid using "The End" in nonfiction articles. Use "—30—" or "—###—" if you must.

"When you're just starting out, clips and experience are more important than money. So if that means writing for free for a while, then do it. Once you become a truly good writer, it won't be an issue, because you'll get paid for your work. The biggest consideration when deciding on whether to take a writing assignment should always be: What's in it for me? Will what I get out of this experience make it worth what I put into it? That might be money, experience, a great clip, or a great contact."

—LARRY GETLEN

freelancer, *Esquire, Variety, New York Post*

SIDEBARS

Submission Tips

For sidebars included with articles, start the sidebar on a new page immediately following the last page of the main text. Don't include all the front-page information you put at the beginning of the main text. Simply use a header that says "Sidebar: (Same slug you used for the article)" in the top left corner and a word count in the top right corner.

Formatting Specs

- With the exception just noted, follow the same formatting specs used with the article manuscript.
- Don't number the first page of the sidebar, but do number subsequent pages, if there are any.
- Use the sidebar slug in the header of the second and following pages, along with a page number, in the same format as a regular article.

Other Dos and Don'ts

- Don't use staples to attach your sidebar page.
- Don't justify text or align the right margin.
- Do include suggested heads and subheads for your sidebar.

MANUSCRIPT WITH SIDEBARS: ARTICLE

Contact information

John Q. Writer
123 Author Lane
Approximately 1,500 words
Writerville, CA 95355
johnqwriter@email.com
(323) 555-0000

First North American Rights

Sidebars of 225 and 150 words

Indicate the sidebars separately here as part of the package.

Timid Steps Toward Brave 'Nute' World
*Major food players get feet wet
but produce few patents so far*

by
John Q. Writer

Bold title

Italicized subhead

Title one-third of the way down the page

Nutraceuticals may have captured the interest and imagination of major food companies. But at least based on patent activity, they don't appear to have captured many research and development dollars yet.

A Food Processing review of patents granted in the 1990s shows that major food companies have received fewer than sixty patents for nutraceutical products. One company alone, Procter & Gamble Co., accounts for more than half of those. Even P&G, however, denies it has a "nutraceutical" business.

That doesn't necessarily mean the food industry's R&D or patent activity in nutraceuticals is slack. But it does show that functional foods research has yet to produce the types of breakthroughs that can be easily patented. That could change quickly as interest in the area grows.

Double-spaced text

Indent paragraphs except for the first one.

1" margin

SIDEBAR: ARTICLE

Sidebar slug line
on the first page.

Sidebar: Nutraceuticals   Approximately 225 words

Patents From Major Food Companies

Here's how the major food companies rank by number of nutraceutical-related pat-

ents, and a roundup of products for which they hold patents.

1. Procter & Gamble Co., 37

    Psyllium and other cholesterol-lowering drinks and compounds, tea extracts,

fortified drink mixes, enhanced bioavailability of nutrients and system for physiologi-

cal feedback in administration of nutrients.

2. Kellogg Co., 7

1" margin

    Psyllium and other cholesterol-lowering foods, improved iron fortification.

3. Unilever NV, 4

    Probiotic for treating irritable bowel syndrome, antioxidant tea extracts.

Source: U.S. Patent and Trademark Office, Food Processing Research

Repeat the
word count for
the sidebar. If
the sidebar goes
more than one
page, there's no
need to repeat
the word count
on the subse-
quent pages.
Instead, write
"Sidebar Page 2"
and so on.

Double-spaced,
just like manu-
script text

ELECTRONIC ARTICLE MANUSCRIPTS

Submission Tips

Submitting articles electronically isn't so much about what you do as what you don't do.

A certain amount of attention to detail is necessary to get the article's format across, but you don't have to try to design an article. That's a graphic designer's job.

More than likely, you'll submit your articles electronically as an attachment—preferably as a Microsoft Word document (.doc).

Formatting Specs

- Find out from the editor how she prefers to receive electronic files.

- Formatting is mainly a matter of removing potential glitches from your copy. For instance, don't put two spaces after a sentence. Typesetters automatically handle the space, and your extra spaces may need to be removed by an editor.

- Use the formatting function in your word processing software to double-space electronic files. Don't double-space by using hard returns, as the spacing could foul up production.

- If you mail a disk or CD, use the same kind of cover letter you would with a paper manuscript. Include a hard copy of the manuscript in the envelope as a point of reference if glitches appear in the electronic copy.

Other Dos and Don'ts

- Do ask for a confirmation receipt after you've sent a file to make sure it can be received. Electronic transfers can be unreliable, and deadlines for news publications are tight.

- Do note at the top of the file where you can be reached if you're not going to be close to the phone, especially if your editor is working on a daily deadline.

- Don't use "–30–" or "–###–" to mark the end of your article. In an electronic format, it's just another thing that will have to be removed.

- Do try to learn the style, especially with news publications. On tight deadlines, copyeditors can get very testy about having to make style changes.

- Do include a suggested headline. It isn't necessary, and it probably won't fit, but it could be a starting point for the editor.

- Don't put any copyright information on the manuscript. It's copyrighted when you write it, and the editor knows this.

SUBMITTING PHOTOS AND GRAPHICS

Submission Tips

When submitting photos, graphics, and information graphic material for your article, give editors as much information as possible. Few things are as frustrating for an editor as scrambling to find artwork or a bit of information about it at the last minute.

Formatting Specs

- Provide suggested captions for photos on a separate page after your article.

- Captions should be brief, descriptive, action-oriented, and in the present tense. Ultimately, caption writing is an editor's job, but she probably won't mind your help.

- Attach a form to the back of prints with key information (see the "Photo and Graphic Identification Form" on page 48).

- Use tape to attach the form to prints. Never use staples.

- Use a code on the margin of slides to identify them, corresponding to an information form. Put the slides in an envelope and then attach the envelope to the necessary form with tape or staples.

- Put each transparency in its own coded envelope with the code corresponding to the information form.

- If the photo needs to be returned, provide a preaddressed, stamped mailer with sufficient strength and postage to get it through the mail intact. Preferably, allow the publication to keep prints when possible.

- If you have more than one photo or slide, use a coding system to keep captions and identifications straight.

- The most common and universal forms of electronic photos are JPEG and TIFF.

Other Dos and Don'ts

- Do make sure digital images are high-resolution. The minimum requirement for most high-resolution images is 300 dpi (dots per inch), and the image should be at least 3" × 3" (8cm × 8cm) in size. The publisher's guidelines will indicate the resolution and size of the image required, as well as the preferred file format. Follow these guidelines! Do not refer editors to a website and ask them to copy the images; the resolution of these photos will not be high enough to reproduce a high-quality image.

- Don't send extremely large files via e-mail. If you have many high-resolution images, put the files on a disk or CD (ask the editor which format is preferred) and mail it to the editor along with a copy of your article.

CAPTION LIST: ARTICLE

Slug line for
the article

Captions: Nutraceuticals

Photo A:

Researchers at Procter & Gamble Co.'s Sharon Woods laboratory display tea

beverage.

Credit: Procter & Gamble Co.

Photo B:

Bill Mayer, president and general manager of Kellogg Co.'s Functional Foods

Division, discusses strategies for capitalizing on the company's recent Food and Drug

Double-
spaced text

Administration approval for health claims on psyllium-based cereals.

1" margin

Credit: Andy Goodshot, The Associated Press

Graphic

Kellogg Co. wasted no time getting its health claims into advertising copy, plac-

ing this ad in women's and health magazines within two weeks of FDA approval.

Use codes
with more than
one photo.

Always include a
credit, even when
it's simply the
company that pro-
vided the photo.

Reproduction
of an ad also
needs a caption
for context.

PHOTO AND GRAPHIC IDENTIFICATION FORM

Date: _____   Code: _____

Slug: _____

Subject (in artwork): _____

_____

Editor: _____

Date article submitted: _____

Credit: _____

Direct questions to: Please return after use
John Q. Writer   Keep this for your files
123 Author Lane
Writerville, CA 95355
(323) 555-0000
johnqwriter@email.com

SUBMITTING INFORMATION GRAPHIC MATERIAL

Submission Tips

Providing information graphics isn't part of your job as a writer, but providing the information that goes into those graphics is. Since *USA Today* debuted in 1982, information graphics—with or without articles attached—have become a staple of journalism.

If you and your publication have the know-how, one of the best ways to submit information graphic material is in the form of a spreadsheet. A variety of word processing and graphics programs can create simple graphics using spreadsheet information.

You can also submit your information in tabular form on a separate page appended to the end of your article.

Because of the hundreds of ways such information can be presented, you'll have to tackle each situation on a case-by-case basis. Here are a few simple formatting specs.

Formatting Specs

- Use a slug atop the printed page that links the graphic information to the article, i.e., "Graphic Information: Storyslug."

- Always include a line citing the source, even if it's only your own research (usually cited in the name of the publication, i.e., "Source: Your publication research").

- Take special care to double-check the numbers and make sure the column material is properly matched. A relatively simple miscue can render an informational graphic useless, ludicrous, or embarrassing.

Other Dos and Don'ts

- Do ask the editor if the publication has a preferred format for receiving information graphic material.

- Don't forget to cite the source of your information.

- Do put the story slug at the top of each page.

INFORMATION GRAPHIC TEXT: ARTICLE

Story slug line

Graphic information: DTC-Direct

Table 1

This could be used in a bar chart or a graph.

New database and direct-response pharmaceutical drug marketing programs by year:

1999 108
2000 201
2001 258
2002 38 (through mid-February)

Source: John Cummings and Partners

Table 2

Top drug companies in database marketing:

1. GlaxoSmithKline
2. Merck
3. Pharmacia & Upjohn
4. Schering-Plough

Cite the source of the information.

Source: John Cummings and Partners

CHAPTER 2:

NONFICTION BOOKS

Nonfiction books can be on any number of subjects—from a gigantic hardcover book about architecture to your run-of-the-mill diet book to a small pocket prayer guide. If it's true and it's a book, you can learn how to submit it to agents and editors by reading on. Note that unlike fiction, writers do not have to finish their nonfiction project prior to submitting work for consideration. Instead of writing the book's text and chapters, the all-important, complicated first step is composing a nonfiction book proposal, which will serve as a business plan for your book and its release.

CONCERNING MEMOIR

Memoirs are true-life stories, but they read like novels. They are nonfiction tales that employ common fiction devices, such as cliffhangers, character arcs, and a three-act structure. For this reason, memoir is treated like fiction. If you're writing a memoir, follow the instructions in Chapter Five: Novels.

WHAT YOU NEED TO SUBMIT

The first step in selling a nonfiction book is creating a book proposal. Typically, the proposal will include a query letter, a detailed proposal, and at least one sample chapter. This all must be completed and reviewed—usually over the course of several months, by agents, editors, and business managers of the publisher—before the book writing begins in earnest. If you're writing out the entire book now, you should stop and start on a proposal instead.

For the writer, the proposal process begins with solid market research, which can prevent a considerable waste of time and energy. This means spending time in a bookstore and searching on Amazon.com for similar works to prove there is a market for your book. From the agent or editor's point of view, however, the process starts with the query. That's where this chapter will begin.

QUERY LETTER TO AN AGENT

Submission Tips

Most authors published by major commercial publishers are represented by agents. Establishing a relationship with an agent is often the first step toward selling your first book. Though you can present a proposal to an agent without a query, it makes more sense to query first. Inability to interest agents in your proposal is a strong sign that you need to rework or scrap your idea. When you send a query, be sure to check the agent's specific submission guidelines.

A query letter to an agent should:

- Make a convincing case for a compelling book concept

- Show why you are the person to write the book

- Outline the market potential for the book, including who the readers will be and what the competition is like

Sum up your concept in a single paragraph. It may seem impossible, but if you can't do it now, your agent won't be able to do it later when he pitches the book to a publisher. This may even be the same hook an editor uses to convince the committee that ultimately decides on your book. Later, it may be used by the publisher's sales rep to get your book into stores. Ultimately, a paragraph description will be used on the jacket to convince readers to buy it, generating the royalties that make this all a paying venture. So spend considerable time refining this concept.

A brief description of the market for this book is equally vital to your query. Why is it better than the competition? Why will it fly off the shelves?

The last paragraph of the query is an explanation why you are the perfect person to write this book. What qualifies you to write it? Are you a working professional in the field? This is also an important selling point of the book.

Formatting Specs

- The basic setup for a query to agents is similar to an article query (on page 17).

- Use a standard font or typeface, 12-point type.

- Use 1" margins on all sides.

- Use block format—single-space the body; double-space between paragraphs.

- Use letterhead or type your personal information in the top right corner.

- Keep the query to one page.

Other Dos and Don'ts

- Do address an agent by name.

- Don't use "To whom it may concern" or other nondescript salutations.

- Do the basic research to find out what kinds of books the agent handles.

- Do summarize any relevant experience you have, especially in publishing books. (This query model assumes a first-time book author.)

- Do keep your query brief. As noted earlier, your pitch rides on three basic paragraphs.

- Do ask if the agent would like you to submit a full proposal. Indicate whether the proposal is ready now.

Limit your query to one page, single-spaced, and address the editor by name (Mr. or Ms. and the surname). Do not assume that a person is a Mr. or Ms. unless it is obvious from the name listed. For example, if you are contacting a D.J. Smith, do not assume that D.J. should be preceded by Mr. or Ms. Instead, address the letter to D.J. Smith.

—ROBERT BREWER

editor, *Writer's Market*

- Don't ask for proposal guidelines. Some agents offer these, but express the confidence that you can handle a proposal on your own. After all, you bought this book.
- Don't fax your query unless you have permission from the agent.

QUERY TO AN AGENT: NONFICTION BOOK

John Q. Writer
123 Author Lane
Writerville, CA 95355
(323) 555-0000
johnqwriter@email.com

July 5, 2009

Sabrina Smith
Smith & Smith Literary Agency
222 Forty-ninth St.
New York, NY 10111

Dear Ms. Smith:

When was the last time you tried selling an idea? Probably it was the last time you had a conversation.

In today's economy, regardless of your career, selling ideas is what you really do. And you do it in more directions than ever. Companies sell to customers, but they also sell ideas to suppliers. Employees pitch ideas to their bosses, and vice versa. In the modern team-filled corporation, you may be selling your ideas simultaneously to a wide array of peers, bosses, and subordinates. Until now, however, there was no definitive book on how to sell ideas.

That's about to change. I am preparing a book, *Selling Your Ideas: The Career Survival Strategy of the 21st Century*, to fill the void. Hundreds of highly successful books have addressed sales tactics for salespeople, and dozens of highly successful books address persuasion skills for everyone else. But, up to now, no one has addressed a book to cover the one sales job in which everyone in corporate America engages—selling ideas. Unlike other sales and persuasion books, *Selling Your Ideas* addresses everyone in business on a department-by-department, function-by-function basis. Because virtually anyone at any walk of corporate life will be reflected in this book, the appeal is considerably wider than any previous work of its kind.

Included will be dozens of real-life case studies drawn from my twenty years as a corporate executive, trainer, marketing consultant, and columnist for management publications. I am also an adjunct professor in the business department of the University of Denver and a past president of and consultant for the Business Executives Council. I would be interested in sharing my detailed proposal with you at your convenience.

Sincerely,

John Q. Writer

Encl.: SASE

Margin annotations:

- Contact information
- Always address a specific agent.
- The hook
- Single-spaced text
- 1" margin
- Differentiate this book from the competition.
- Explain why you should write this book.
- A polite offer
- Signature
- Always include an SASE.

QUERY TO AN EDITOR

Do You Need an Agent?

When trying to sell a novel, you almost always need a literary agent. In nonfiction, however, it's more common to skip the agent and deal directly with a publisher. Books and ideas considered "small scope, small sales" are more likely to not need the shepherding of an agent. For example, a book about the role of Rhode Island in the Civil War is a project that has a small scope (a simple, regional appeal) that will likely have a small sales number (because of its limited audience). A book like this won't sell for much money, so an agent wouldn't be quick to take it on in the first place because her 15% commission would not be worth the effort.

Submission Tips

The goals and strategies for a query to a book editor are essentially the same as with an agent query. Both the agent and editor are looking for a marketable book. The book editor may play a role in shepherding the book through production—or at least hear about it when there are problems—so she may place a somewhat higher priority on the author's writing ability and track record in completing projects. Agents certainly care whether their authors have writing ability, but they're willing to work with or help find ghostwriters for books that are clear winners.

It pays to be familiar with the publishing house, its imprints, recent titles published, and how successful they've been. When possible, link your idea to a past success without portraying your book as a knockoff. This not only helps the book editor understand why your book will succeed, but also helps the editor sell the idea internally. Publishers love nothing more than a proven formula for success, and frequently shape new acquisitions along the lines of successful past ones. If you take this approach, do your homework. Misfiring by making an unsupported comparison or claiming a book was a success that really wasn't can hurt you badly. If you're not sure of your facts, you're better to forego this tactic.

The easiest and most effective way to do the kind of research you need is by using the search engine of an online bookseller, such as Amazon.com. Not only do the search engines allow you to search by topic and publisher, but some of them also tell you where the title ranks against all others in sales for that particular bookseller.

Of course, agents are the ones most likely to have the current information on publishing trends and to know the hot buttons of individual book editors, publishing houses and imprints, but if you think you can handle it on your own, or if your book's concept doesn't require an editor, go for it.

Formatting Specs

- Format your letter for an editor similar to that for an agent (see page 54).
- Address your letter to a specific editor. Do the research in *Writer's Market* or call to find the appropriate editor for your query.

You may have heard the word "platform" floating around and wondered what it means. Put simply, there are two kinds of platforms, and ideally you want to demonstrate that you've got both. First: What makes you an expert and the clear choice to write the book you're proposing? Second: What media connections do you have that will help you reach your intended audience with your message?

—MOLLIE GLICK

literary agent, Foundry Literary + Media

Other Dos and Don'ts

- Do keep your letter to one page.
- Do avoid rambling and wordiness, regardless of length.
- Don't overreach. Build a case for your qualifications based on reality.
- Don't come off as pompous, even if you do know everything about your topic.
- Don't fax or e-mail your query unless you have permission from the publisher or if submission guidelines state it is acceptable.
- Do show you're familiar with the publisher, possibly by comparing your book with other successful titles from the imprint.
- Do build your query on a strong, succinct concept, market insight, and a convincing reason why you're the right person to write the book. Ultimately, the hook could be any of those three, or a combination, but you need all three to build your case.

QUERY TO A BOOK EDITOR, MISTAKES TO AVOID: NONFICTION BOOK

To: AMACOM BOOKS

New York City

Dear Editor,

I have written a great book on how to get a job in today's tight employment market. I think you'll want to add this book to your list and will be very happy when it sells like gangbusters.

Options today abound for those looking for work, but many folks don't know where to start—the newspaper, the Internet, friends, family, cold calling, there are many ways to get a job that may seem confusing to most job seekers, they are not sure where to start and sometimes just give up before they really start and end up standing on the umemployment line and feel unfulfilled and unhappy and eventually those checks will run out, and where will they end up?

My book will tell readers where to start to find a job and how to best find a job that will make them happy. My book has been read by my many friends and family and they all said, wow, I wish I had this book when I was looking for a job, it really would have helped and I'd be much happier than I am now.

A book like this will hit the best-seller lists right away because it's the only one that tells it like it really is and doesn't kiss up to big corporations.

If you will send me your e-mail address I can e-mail you an electronic copy of the manuscript so you can see for yourself what a great book it is, and how we will be raking in the money on this one.

Thanks for your time, and I look forward to working with you!

Sincerely,

John Q. Writer
(323) 555-0000

This is set up like a memo, not a formal letter, and doesn't include any information on whom the letter is from, whom it is going to, or even the date.

Always address your queries to a specific editor that works with the type of book you're submitting.

Typo! Proofread your work

How will your book do this? Be specific.

More bragging, with no information to back up such an outrageous claim.

Don't offer to send your book via e-mail. If the editor is interested, she will ask for more.

Be sure to include your address, phone number, and e-mail.

Boring! You need to capture the editor's interest. This is the time to sell your idea, not your book.

This is a rambling, run-on sentence that doesn't tell the editor needed information.

Editors don't care what friends and family think. State why you are the most qualified person to write this book and how you plan to differentiate it from the competition.

Being confident in your work is one thing—being arrogant and obnoxious is quite another.

ELECTRONIC QUERY LETTER TO AN EDITOR OR AGENT

Submission Tips

Many publishers and agents now accept queries via e-mail. Before you send a query off to a publisher or agent electronically, though, you must either have permission to send it via e-mail or make sure that her guidelines indicate that it is acceptable. Communicating with an editor or agent via e-mail should be just as formal and respectful as if you were sending it through the mail. The basic tone and format of the electronic query shouldn't be much different from a query sent on paper.

Formatting Specs

- Include the same information you would in a paper query, including your name, address, phone number, fax, and website. For e-queries, put your contact information at the bottom left of the e-mail. It isn't necessary to include your e-mail address in the body of the e-mail, though, since the editor can reply easily with the click of a button.
- Put a description of your book or its title in the subject line.
- Follow the same format you would with a paper query, including the date, salutation to a specific editor, and block paragraph format.

Other Dos and Don'ts

- Don't use all caps or exclamation points in the subject line unless the exclamation point is part of your book's title.
- Don't submit an e-mail query unless specifically requested by the publisher or agent, or if it is stated clearly in his guidelines that it is acceptable.
- Don't insert clip art graphics or other images into your query letter. Keep it simple.

There are two areas in which I find most nonfiction proposals to be delinquent. The most apparent is the concept itself. Typically, it's been done before in some fashion or another and doesn't stand out enough from the crowd. The second and more common shortfall I find in proposals is that the author has little or no platform.

—JEFFERY MCGRAW
literary agent, The August Agency

ELECTRONIC QUERY LETTER TO AN AGENT, MISTAKES TO AVOID: NONFICTION BOOK

TO: submissions@smithsmith.com
CC:
SUBJECT: Got a Book 4 U

Put a brief description or the title in the subject line.

John Q. Writer
Writerville, CA 95355
johnqwriter@email.com

First of all, this contact information is incomplete. Secondly, it should be at the bottom of a query if you're contacting by e-mail.

March 3, 2009

Smith and Smith Literary Agency
222 Forty-ninth St.
New York, NY 10111

Address your query to a specific agent.

To Whom It May Concern:

I hope you are interested in nonfiction books about birds, because that is the type of book I have written. I would like to sell it to a publisher, which of course means that I need an agent.

Do your homework. Know what kinds of books an agent works with before sending a query.

Don't be obvious—an agent knows why writers need agents.

The subject of birds is a big one, but I know that my book stands out from all the others. People all over the country love to read interesting stories about these fascinating creatures, so the book will appeal to just about anyone who loves birds—they don't even have to be birdwatchers or nature enthusiasts. I've attached the first four chapters of my book and will send the rest at your request.

This tells the agent absolutely nothing about the book. Explain how your book differs from others currently on the market.

I had such a good time writing about this, my favorite subject, over the past ten years. I am a bird enthusiast and even met my wife while on a birding expedition in the mountains of New England in 1999.

Don't send book chapters unless asked by the agent. This is just a query.

This is my first attempt at writing a book. I have written many articles that were never published on the subject so I thought it would be a good idea to put them all together in one book. I think that with the right editor's expertise and input this book has the potential to be a huge bestseller.

Keep all your information focused on the book itself. Don't waste time with anecdotes that have nothing to do with the book.

Thanks,

John Q. Writer

Don't point out your (or the book's) shortcomings. If it needs editorial help, get some before you send it to an agent.

Don't exaggerate. Be confident in your work, but don't overstate it.

BOOK PROPOSAL

What You Need to Submit

Like the article query, the book proposal is something of a genre in its own right. The differences are that it takes much more time and can vary considerably in length. A fully thought-out book proposal should include the following:

- Cover letter
- Cover page
- Overview
- Marketing information or business case
- Competitive analysis
- Author information
- Chapter outline
- Sample chapters
- Attachments that support your case

You really should send in a query letter before submitting a complete book proposal, but if your proposal is unsolicited, include an SASE or postcard for a reply.

Submission Tips

The thing agents and editors cite as most frequently lacking in book proposals is the marketing information. Authors often don't have a firm vision of whom the readers of the book will be and how to reach them, or they don't know what the competition is and how to differentiate their books from existing titles. It's strange that the marketing information is so often missing, because it's really where any author should start. Before you ever begin the painstaking process to create a book proposal, you have to know there's a market for your book. If you can't build a convincing business case for your book, go back to the drawing board. That's why, even if the marketing and competition information doesn't come first in the proposal lineup, you should prepare these sections first. In fact, you should do your homework on these sections before you query an agent or book editor to submit a proposal.

The other element that a proposal often lacks is the author's platform. This term, which has come to prominence in recent years, is defined as the author's avenues to sell his book to audiences that will buy it. In other words, what ability to do you have to market the book, sell the book, gain press for the book, and tap into its potential audience?

Read sample book proposals and seek out other books that help break down what makes up a winning proposal. Start with *Bulletproof Book Proposals* by Pam Brodowsky and Eric Neuhaus, and *How to Write a Book Proposal* by Michael Larsen.

Here is a piece-by-piece look at the elements of the proposal, along with some special instructions for book proposals sent electronically.

ELECTRONIC BOOK PROPOSAL

Submission Tips

Once you send a query and an editor is interested in seeing your proposal, he may ask you to send it via e-mail. The editor will indicate what format he prefers to receive files. Be sure to follow his guidelines.

- Don't forget the cover letter. Just because you're using e-mail doesn't mean you don't need to introduce your proposal.
- An electronic proposal should include the same components as a proposal sent via regular mail. Pages 60-80 detail what each part of the proposal should contain.
- Your cover letter may be included in the body of the e-mail. The additional elements of the proposal, including the cover page and overview, marketing/competitive analysis, author information, chapter outline, and sample chapters, should be sent as a file attachment unless otherwise requested from the editor.

Formatting Specs

- Use the subject line of the e-mail to introduce the title of your book.
- Make it simple by keeping all the components together. It's not necessary to create a separate file each for the cover page, overview, marketing analysis, competitive analysis, author information, chapter outlines, and chapter samples unless the editor specifically requests them as separate files.
- A book proposal should follow the same format as a paper proposal, including a header and page numbers on every page. This will make it easy for the editor to keep everything in order when it's printed.

Other Dos and Don'ts

- Don't use all caps in your subject line.
- Don't submit a book proposal electronically unless the editor or publisher's guidelines specifically request it.
- Do send your proposal as an attachment of a Microsoft Word document (.doc) unless specified otherwise.
- Don't insert clip art graphics or images in your e-mail.
- Do proofread your work.

COVER LETTER

Submission Tips

Because so much information is included in the rest of the proposal, and because you should have already queried the agent or editor, the cover letter can be fairly brief. Don't use more than one page. Follow the same guidelines for submission to agents or book editors (see page 58).

If you are submitting an unsolicited proposal, the cover letter should incorporate elements of the query letters provided earlier in this chapter on pages 51 and 55, as well as introduce the proposal. The cover letter for a solicited manuscript, which is modeled on pages 63, simply serves to introduce a proposal and covers the following points:

- An introductory paragraph introducing the proposal
- An outline of the information included in the proposal
- A concluding paragraph politely seeking a response

Formatting Specs

- Use a standard font or typeface for the body of the letter, 12-point type.
- Letterhead is fine, but not required. If you don't use letterhead, put your name, address, phone number, e-mail, etc., in the top right corner.
- Use 1" margins on all sides.
- Keep it to one page.
- Use block format—single-space the body; double-space between paragraphs.

Other Dos and Don'ts

- Do address a specific editor.
- Don't start your pitch all over again in the cover letter. If your query made enough of an impression to spark interest, assume that the agent or editor remembers the book idea and who you are.
- Don't ask for advice or criticism regarding your proposal. Asking can appear unprofessional. Many agents will offer advice or guidelines for proposals when they ask you to submit one.
- Don't mention copyright information. What you've put down here is copyrighted, and you shouldn't imply the agent or editor is out to steal your idea.
- Don't discuss payment or terms. It's still premature.
- Don't staple your cover letter to anything. Use a butterfly or clamp-style paper clip to hold the proposal elements together, while the cover letter stands alone in front.

COVER LETTER: NONFICTION BOOK

John Q. Writer
123 Author Lane
Writerville, CA 95355
(323) 555-0000
johnqwriter@email.com

August 30, 2009

Sabrina Smith
Smith & Smith Literary Agency
222 Forty-ninth St.
New York, NY 10111

Dear Ms. Smith:

Enclosed is the proposal you requested for *Selling Your Ideas: The Career Survival Strategy of the 21st Century.*

Included in the proposal are detailed market and competitive analyses, my biographical information, a complete chapter outline, and three sample chapters.

I hope after you've had a chance to review the proposal that you'll understand why I believe this book has so much promise. Please let me know if I can make any revisions or add any information to make the proposal more salable.

Thanks for your time. I look forward to hearing from you.

Sincerely,

John Q. Writer

Encl.: Proposal

Contact information

Date flushed right

1" margin

Brief preview

Offer help.

Continue to address a specific agent.

Don't waste time. Get right to the point.

Single-spaced text, block format

Signature

Details enclosures

A great lead (the first paragraph or two of the query) captures my attention. This could be a question, an anecdote, a statistic showing how many people make up the book's potential market, even a joke—if appropriate. The lead should be creative and intriguing. It should make me want to read on. A great lead does double duty—it not only captures my attention, it suggests to me that the author knows how to write.

—STEPHEN BLAKE METTEE

founder and publisher, Quill Driver/Word Dancer Press

COVER PAGE

Submission Tips

This is the same as the cover page you'll use with the ultimate manuscript. It includes the title, estimated word count, and either your contact information (if submitting directly to an editor) or your agent's contact information (if submitting through an agent).

Formatting Specs

- Contact information goes in the bottom right corner.
- Put an estimated word count (for the entire book, not for the proposal) in the top right corner. This is optional at this point, but it could be helpful
- Center the title, subtitle, and author's name in the middle of the page.
- Conventionally, the title is in all capital letters and the subtitle is uppercase and lowercase. If you want, use boldface for the title and italics for the subtitle.

Other Dos and Don'ts

- Don't include both your address and the agent's. Use one or the other.
- Don't use a header or number the title page.

COVER PAGE: NONFICTION BOOK PROPOSAL

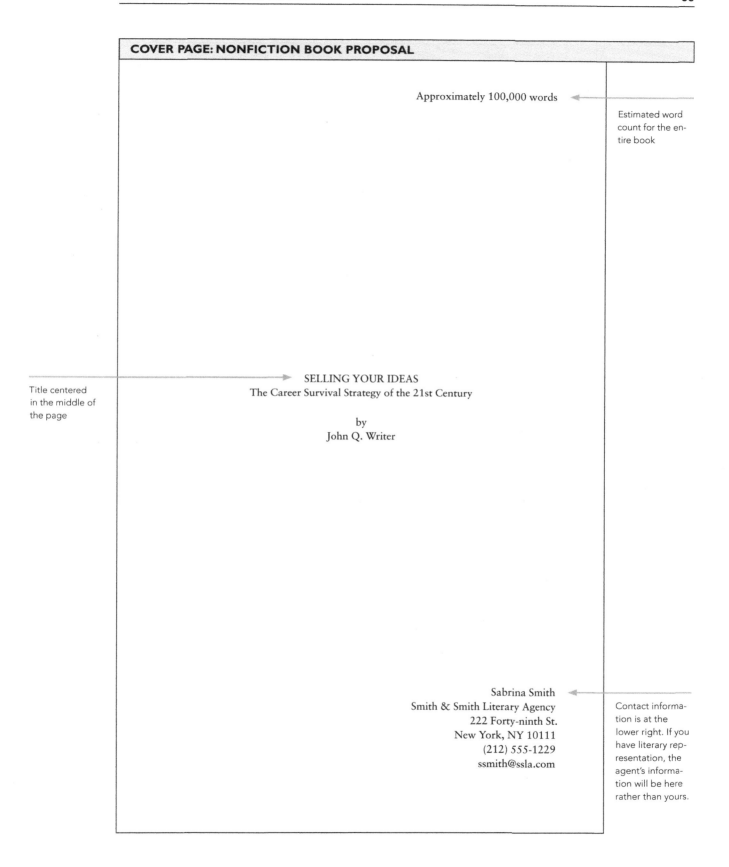

Approximately 100,000 words

Estimated word count for the entire book

Title centered in the middle of the page

SELLING YOUR IDEAS
The Career Survival Strategy of the 21st Century

by
John Q. Writer

Sabrina Smith
Smith & Smith Literary Agency
222 Forty-ninth St.
New York, NY 10111
(212) 555-1229
ssmith@ssla.com

Contact information is at the lower right. If you have literary representation, the agent's information will be here rather than yours.

There's a lot of information available to writers on how to write "the greatest," "the most compelling," "the no-fail" nonfiction book proposal, so I'm often surprised when authors fail to mention their reasons and credentials for writing the work. Like publishers, I often jump to the credentials section of the proposal before getting to the meat of the proposal. I need to know why an author is qualified to write what they're writing.

—JANET BENREY

literary agent, Benrey Literary

OVERVIEW

Submission Tips

The overview is the place for your thirty-second sound-bite pitch. It incorporates elements of the concept, marketing and competitive analyses, and author information that is to be presented in the proposal and ties them together convincingly, forcefully, and coherently. Even though it's a small element of the proposal, it's a powerful one.

The overview of the concept should be only one page. Use the same approach you used in the query to concisely explain the concept, but the overview should be even more focused. Boil the pitch down to a single sentence, then use a paragraph or two to describe the contents of your book.

Resist the urge to give a blow-by-blow description of the rest of the proposal. No one needs a preview of a proposal. The overview is simply, to borrow from the corporate buzzword lexicon, "the top-line analysis," "the big picture," "the view from ten thousand feet."

Formatting Specs

- Begin numbering your proposal with this page. Place the page numbers in the top right corner.
- Use a slug in the top left corner of the header in this and succeeding pages.
- The slug should read "Proposal: Your Book Title Here."
- Center your heading, "Overview," and underline it.
- Double-space the text and use a 1" margin on all sides for the whole proposal.

Other Dos and Don'ts

- Do make sure the overview conveys a convincing hook, even though it's a free-style exercise. Think of the overview as the speech the agent will make to the editor, the editor to the people on the editorial committee, the sales rep to the buyer, and the book jacket to the reader.
- Do write your entire proposal in the third person.

OVERVIEW: NONFICTION BOOK PROPOSAL

Selling Your Ideas / Writer   1

Header includes the title, your last name, and the page number.

<u>Overview</u>

Heading centered, one-third of the way down the page, and underlined

Selling Your Ideas is the sales how-to manual for the rest of us.

And it's long overdue.

No matter what you do, selling ideas is your job. And you do it in more directions than ever before. Companies sell to customers, but they also sell ideas to suppliers. Employees pitch ideas to their bosses, and vice versa. In the modern team-filled corporation, you may be selling your ideas simultaneously to a wide array of peers, bosses, and subordinates.

1" margin

Double-spaced text

Yet, among the thousands of sales how-to books, none has really been geared to help non-salespeople develop the fundamental skill of selling ideas—until now. *Selling Your Ideas* offers practical, time-tested strategies for all kinds of employees to sell all kinds of ideas to all kinds of audiences. Included will be dozens of real-life case studies drawn from corporate executive and marketing consultant John Q. Writer's twenty years as a corporate executive, trainer, marketing consultant, and writer.

The hook

Write in the third person.

Rather than relying on one-nostrum-fits-all approaches typical of sales and persuasion books, *Selling Your Ideas* takes a detailed approach to selling ideas within and outside the organization.

More information will follow.

MARKETING ANALYSIS

Submission Tips

The marketing information section of your proposal answers that all-important question: Will this book sell? And it should answer the question in as much detail as possible. There are no limits on length here, beyond your ability to research and write. As with any part of your proposal, make this as tight and compelling as you can, and offer any facts or figures you can find to prove your book will be a hit.

The marketing analysis section covers the product (your book) and the consumers (its readers). The areas to cover in the analysis include:

- Who is the audience? Describe them. How big is the potential readership base? Is it growing? What are some important facts about the readership base that a marketer would want to know? What kind of media do they like? What organizations do they belong to? Where do they shop? Can you provide concrete numbers to prove that the audience is sizeable?

- What trends could affect the book? Why would the audience be growing, buying more books, or suddenly taking more interest in your book?

- Where, besides bookstores, could this book be sold? Are there special events, seasonal approaches, or other special channels through which this book can be sold?

- What information will the book provide? How will that appeal to readers?

- How will you approach the book? Will it have sidebars, callouts, interviews, pictures, charts, or other special features?

- What are the sources of information? What will the research be based on?

Closely linked to the marketing analysis is the competitive information that follows it. You may choose to combine these into a single section.

Other Dos and Don'ts

- Do write concisely and in the third person.
- Don't be too worried about the length. Take as long as you need to present all relevant marketing information.
- Do use charts, tables, and graphs if you have them.

MARKETING ANALYSIS: NONFICTION BOOK PROPOSAL

Selling Your Ideas / Writer   4

<u>Marketing Analysis</u>

> *Heading centered, one-third of the way down the page, and underlined*

Potential readers of this book include anyone who works, but it will especially appeal to upwardly mobile middle and upper managers who have the difficult job of selling in many directions at once. Because of the growing acceptance of such management philosophies and tactics as "empowerment," cross-functional teams, consensus building, and vendor-management quality efforts, these corporate soldiers have seen their roles change dramatically in ways that force them to sell their ideas more.

> *1" margin*

This is a market of more than 2.5 million people who are heavy book buyers. According to a recent report by the American Association of Middle Managers and the Business Executive Council (see attached report), middle managers buy an average of six management and career-related titles annually—a higher average than any other job classification in the survey.

> *Full report is attached.*

Special Distribution Opportunities

> *Subheads help clarify.*

This book's special appeal opens additional distribution channels beyond bookstores. As a general-interest business book with wide application to a variety of consumers, including the small-office/home-office (SOHO) market, *Selling Your Ideas* should have the power to win shelf space in end-aisle displays at office superstores.

> *Double-spaced text*

COMPETITIVE ANALYSIS

Submission Tips

The competitive analysis details what books are similar to yours, how they have done in the marketplace, and how your book is different and better than they are. There's no set format for handling this information, but it helps to begin with an overview of the genre or category into which your book fits, how that category is doing generally, and what the leading competitive titles are.

Then go into an analysis of the leading competitors, looking at how those books have done and why yours is still needed. Even if the subject already has been covered, it may not have been covered for your audience, or the information may be hopelessly out of date because of changes in social mores or technology.

The traditional method for gathering this information is to visit a good-size bookstore, look for competing titles, and then research through Amazon.com and possibly BookScan (though this is a pay service) to see how the books are selling. Pay attention to how a competing book is similar to yours and how it is different. What is the print size of the book? Does it have illustrations or art of any kind? Is it told in a folksy, joke-filled manner?

Amazon.com provides a varied amount of information on books. You can compare sales rank, get commentaries from readers, and see what other books and authors are also popular with buyers of the title. You can't get information on total number of books sold, but if you combine some inside sales information from other authors with their Amazon.com ranking, you might be able to determine a ballpark estimate of how many copies a book has sold.

Other Dos and Don'ts

- Do use as much space as needed, but write concisely.

- Don't critique the competing titles. Point out what shortcomings they have that make room or create demand for your book, though.

- Don't contend that your book is so unique that it has no competition. Agents and editors will conclude that you didn't do enough research or that you are offering an idea so bizarre or unappealing that no book should be published. You can always find a comparable book if you try hard enough.

COMPETITIVE ANALYSIS: NONFICTION BOOK PROPOSAL

Selling Your Ideas / Writer   7

Header includes the title, your last name, and the page number.

Competitive Analysis

Heading centered, one-third of the way down the page, and underlined

1" margin

Thousands of titles have tackled various aspects of selling or persuasion over the years, but none have directly tackled the subject of selling ideas to a wide range of constituencies inside and outside the corporation.

Double-spaced text

Sales and persuasion titles are consistently strong performers. An analysis of titles listed by Amazon.com shows that more than fifty such titles have been published in the past year. They rank between 5 and 64,000 in sales for Amazon.com. In addition, analysis of older titles shows that the top twenty sales and persuasion books have a median ranking of 5,000, compared to 10,000 for the top twenty management theory books and 12,000 for the top twenty time-management books. Backlist sales potential in this category is substantial.

The four recent titles that come closest in subject to *Selling Your Ideas* have an average sales rank of 11,000. Two of those focus narrowly on presentations; the broader books rank 2,000 and 5,000, respectively.

Below is a detailed analysis of each title.

1) ***The Anatomy of Persuasion: How to Persuade Others to Act on Your Ideas, Accept Your Proposals, Buy Your Products or Services, Hire You, Promote You and More*** by Norbert Aubuchon. This book covers ground similar to *Selling Your Ideas*, but without the department-by-department, case study-based approach. This is primarily a Dale Carnegie-style book that doesn't entirely reflect the forces at play in the modern organization.

The closest competing books are listed, with all the book's publisher information.

There is a lot of information you could include here, depending on how detailed you want to get. You can include the book's ISBN, publisher, and year of release, for instance.

Always pitch. Accept that rejection is a part of life, and, whatever you do, don't get cocky and don't let your business slip. If you find that you have finally gotten to the point where you don't have to worry about paying the rent and/or you're finally financially comfortable, that is not the time to relax and rest on your laurels. Work can dry up as fast as it comes in and you have to constantly work to keep things flowing.

—LARRY GETLEN

freelancer, *Esquire, Variety, New York Post*

AUTHOR INFORMATION

Submission Tips
The author information section is about you, but only in the context of what makes you the perfect person to write this book. Highlight any other information that makes you a salable author as well. This is not your life story; this is the story of how you will help the publisher sell books. It is the author platform.

Good points to include in the author information are:

- Teaching credentials (professors can often sell their books to their students and other professors).

- Organizational affiliations, groups you head, or any special audiences with whom you are connected and which could become channels for marketing the book.

- Previous publishing credits (including books, which show you can write one; articles, which show your expertise; and columns, which show a possible avenue of promotion). If you are still getting published—through a column or articles, for instance—your name will continue to get out there.

- Any experience you have in other media (radio shows, TV shows, radio commentaries, websites, blogs—anything that shows you could promote your book effectively in a variety of media).

- Compelling personal history that could help generate publicity and get you booked on talk shows.

- Any blogs, websites, or newsletters you run where you are receiving plenty of hits each day.

- Any public speaking engagements where you get in front of large crowds.

This is not a résumé. It's a narrative description similar to what might appear on a book jacket. Don't be crass or belabor the obvious. Editors know that if you're a professor or the founder and president of a group, you can use these positions to sell books. The author section is more subtle than the rest of the proposal. Try to come off as qualified and marketable without sounding like a jerk.

Formatting Specs

- Double-space the text.

- Keep this to one page, regardless of how fascinating you are.

- Write this in the third person.

Other Dos and Don'ts

- Do write concisely.

- Don't overreach. State your history and qualifications accurately.

- Don't provide information that's irrelevant to the book's marketing, such as the story of your life ("He was born in a small log cabin just outside ..."). Family and other details that may be appropriate in a jacket blurb aren't necessarily helpful here.

AUTHOR INFORMATION: NONFICTION BOOK PROPOSAL

Selling Your Ideas / Writer   12

Header includes the title, your last name, and the page number.

<u>Author Information</u>

Heading centered, one-third of the way down the page, and underlined

1" margin

John Q. Writer has been selling ideas successfully both inside and outside the cor-

Double-spaced text

poration for more than twenty years. He is a former senior vice president of sales

and marketing for Henderson Steel Plating Corporation who now serves as a con-

sultant on customer service and marketing issues for more than two dozen Fortune

500 corporations.

Qualifications are extensive without bragging.

He is also adjunct professor of business administration at Colorado State Uni-

versity and former president of the Business Executive Council, a 300,000-member-

strong educational and advocacy group for middle managers. He continues to serve

as a consultant on sales and marketing issues for the BEC, and he is active in Mentors

International, a nationwide network of mentors and protégés.

Shows he has a following— several really.

Writer also writes a regular column on career planning for *Middle Manager*

Shows media-savvy and promotion skills.

magazine and hosts a call-in radio show on Denver public radio station WBZN-FM.

He is also a frequent speaker at business and trade organizations, having spoken at

fifteen events with a combined attendance of 25,000 over the past year.

CHAPTER OUTLINE

Submission Tips

The chapter outline provides an extended table of contents for your book and includes a brief description of each chapter. This should not be in the classic outline format you learned in your high school composition class. Such an outline may help you write the book, but it's a little dry for the purposes of a proposal, which is meant to sell an editor on the merits of each chapter and show how it fits into the book.

Formatting Specs

- Describe one chapter per page.
- If the book is divided into parts as well as chapters, first list the part and part heading, then the chapter and chapter heading.
- Indent paragraphs and otherwise follow the same format as the rest of the proposal.

Other Dos and Don'ts

- Don't insert a new title page and start numbering all over again with the outline. The proposal is a single entity.
- Do describe how the chapter will unfold, including any sidebars, tables, charts, photos, or other illustrations that will be included.
- Don't approximate how many pages or photos you'll have in each chapter. Assuming you haven't actually written the book yet, it's impossible to know, and the information isn't likely to sway an editor.

CHAPTER OUTLINE: NONFICTION BOOK PROPOSAL

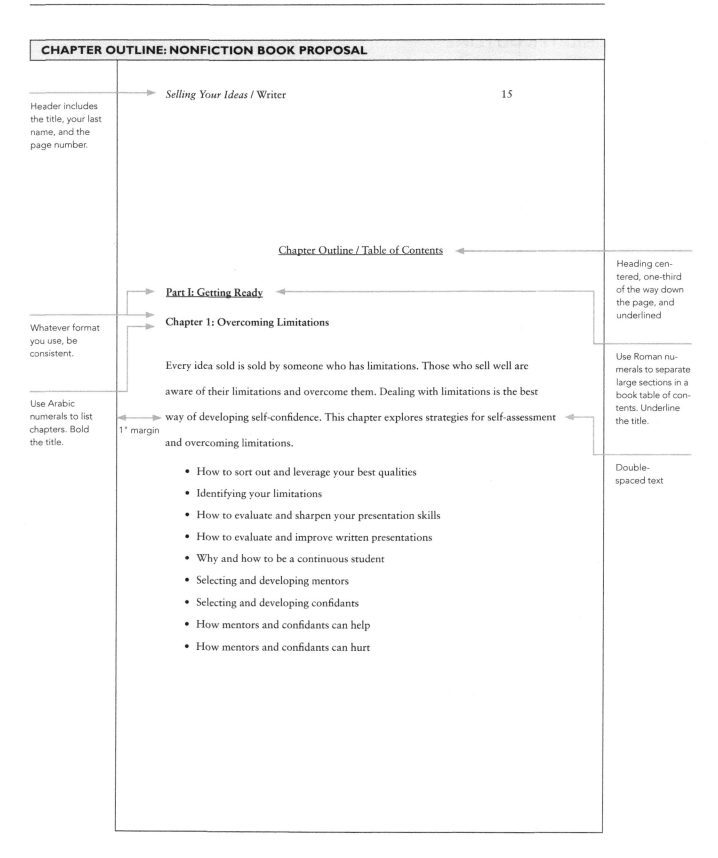

Selling Your Ideas / Writer   15

Header includes the title, your last name, and the page number.

Chapter Outline / Table of Contents

Heading centered, one-third of the way down the page, and underlined

Part I: Getting Ready

Chapter 1: Overcoming Limitations

Whatever format you use, be consistent.

Every idea sold is sold by someone who has limitations. Those who sell well are

aware of their limitations and overcome them. Dealing with limitations is the best

way of developing self-confidence. This chapter explores strategies for self-assessment

and overcoming limitations.

Use Arabic numerals to list chapters. Bold the title.

1" margin

Use Roman numerals to separate large sections in a book table of contents. Underline the title.

Double-spaced text

- How to sort out and leverage your best qualities
- Identifying your limitations
- How to evaluate and sharpen your presentation skills
- How to evaluate and improve written presentations
- Why and how to be a continuous student
- Selecting and developing mentors
- Selecting and developing confidants
- How mentors and confidants can help
- How mentors and confidants can hurt

SAMPLE CHAPTERS

Submission Tips

Agents and editors almost always want to see at least one sample chapter, even from established authors. If you've already written a book in the same subject area, you might get by without a sample chapter. Even then, however, some editors insist.

Most authors' natural inclination is to send chapter one, but some agents recommend against this. If chapter one seems too complete, they argue, it might be hard to make a case for the rest of the book.

Ultimately, the number of sample chapters and which ones to send is your judgment call. Look at the chapter outline. Which chapters are the most intriguing, or the most needed to make a case for the book? These are the chapters you should include. Submit up to three.

Formatting Specs

- Use the same formatting as in the rest of the proposal. This is not exactly like manuscript format—it is a section of the proposal and should appear the same.

- After the first page of the sample chapter, continue using the header and page number as in the rest of the proposal. You need not indicate the chapter number or title in subsequent pages.

Other Dos and Don'ts

- Do center the chapter number and chapter title about one-third of the way down the page.

- Don't assume you must submit chapter one. Submit the most compelling chapter or chapters.

- Do submit a sample chapter that's already been published, if you can. For example, if your article in *Texas Parent* magazine can be a chapter in the book, submit the published article. It shows your writing style, and proves that the idea has a market because it is published.

SAMPLE CHAPTER: NONFICTION BOOK PROPOSAL

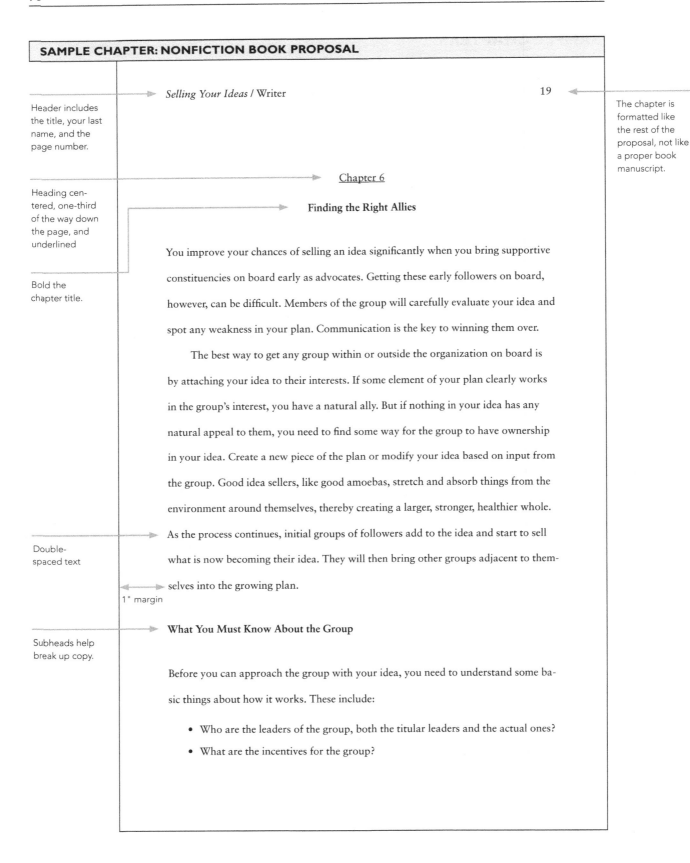

Header includes the title, your last name, and the page number.

The chapter is formatted like the rest of the proposal, not like a proper book manuscript.

Heading centered, one-third of the way down the page, and underlined

Bold the chapter title.

Double-spaced text

1" margin

Subheads help break up copy.

Selling Your Ideas / Writer   19

<u>Chapter 6</u>

Finding the Right Allies

You improve your chances of selling an idea significantly when you bring supportive constituencies on board early as advocates. Getting these early followers on board, however, can be difficult. Members of the group will carefully evaluate your idea and spot any weakness in your plan. Communication is the key to winning them over.

The best way to get any group within or outside the organization on board is by attaching your idea to their interests. If some element of your plan clearly works in the group's interest, you have a natural ally. But if nothing in your idea has any natural appeal to them, you need to find some way for the group to have ownership in your idea. Create a new piece of the plan or modify your idea based on input from the group. Good idea sellers, like good amoebas, stretch and absorb things from the environment around themselves, thereby creating a larger, stronger, healthier whole. As the process continues, initial groups of followers add to the idea and start to sell what is now becoming their idea. They will then bring other groups adjacent to themselves into the growing plan.

What You Must Know About the Group

Before you can approach the group with your idea, you need to understand some basic things about how it works. These include:

- Who are the leaders of the group, both the titular leaders and the actual ones?
- What are the incentives for the group?

ATTACHMENTS

Submission Tips

If you have supporting materials for your proposal, attach them at the end, preceded by a page that serves as a brief table of contents for them.

Articles from magazines or newspapers that support comments made in your proposal, and articles and columns you have published on the subject are good examples of the types of material that should be attached.

Formatting Specs

- Use a single page with the heading "Attachments" or "Supporting Documents," followed by lines describing the documents.

- Number the introduction, but not the pages of the documents attached.

Other Dos and Don'ts

- Don't attach material just to make your proposal look more impressive. Size does not matter.

> Three tips concerning book proposals. 1) Spill the beans. Don't try to tantalize and hold back the juice. 2) No BS! We learn to see through BS, or we fail rapidly. 3) Get published small. Local papers, literary journals, websites, anything. The more credits you have, the better.
>
> **—GARY HEIDT**
>
> literary agent, Signature Literary Agency

ATTACHMENTS: NONFICTION BOOK PROPOSAL

Selling Your Ideas / Writer   21

Header includes the title, your last name, and the page number.

Attachments

Header centered, one-third of the way down the page, and underlined

Keep it brief.

Report from the American Association of Middle Managers and the Business Executive Council, April 2006, "The Middle Manager in America: Growing Pressures on the Sandwich Generation."

Double-spaced text

Flush left, no indent

Column by John Q. Writer, "Primacy of the Idea in Modern Business Culture," *Middle Manager*, October 2006.

BOOK MANUSCRIPT

Submission Tips

The book manuscript is similar in most respects to the proposal format. This section begins with an explanation of the basics of the body of the manuscript, then looks at the specific requirements for various elements of the front matter and back matter.

You may end up submitting the manuscript in several stages to the publisher rather than in one installment, and you may not necessarily do this in sequential order.

Books, like newspapers and magazines, have become increasingly varied in design in recent years. Sidebars, callout quotes, subheads, and short pieces within chapters abound. No universal guidelines exist for handling these formats within books, so confer with your editor early on for guidelines.

Formatting Specs

- Use a 1" margin on all sides.

- Use a cover page (see "Cover Page" for book proposals on page 65).

- Don't number the title page. Begin numbering with the first page of the text of the book, which usually will be the introduction or chapter one.

- Use a header, with your last name or the title of the book.

- Double-space the entire text of the book.

- Use a 10- or 12-point plain font such as Times New Roman, Arial, or Courier.

- Put sidebars, captions, and other elements that fall outside the flow of the main chapter at the end of the chapter rather than where you think they should fall. Design and space constraints will dictate their placement, and it's easier for editors and designers to have the elements in a single location.

- When sending an accepted manuscript, send a disk or CD containing the manuscript along with the hard copy. See the section "Electronic Book Manuscripts" on page 82 for tips on formatting your manuscript for disk or CD.

- Feel free to use plenty of subheads and page breaks to add white space and break up what will be a very long document.

Other Dos and Don'ts

- Don't staple anything.

- Don't punch holes in the pages or submit it in a three-ring binder.

- Do keep an original copy for yourself both on your computer hard drive and on a separate storage medium kept in a secure place, such as a fireproof safe.

- Don't justify text or align the right margin.

- Don't put any copyright information on the manuscript. It's copyrighted when you write it, and the editor knows this.

ELECTRONIC BOOK MANUSCRIPT

Submission Tips

Some editors might ask you to submit your manuscript via e-mail or on a disk or CD. The editor can provide you with specific formatting guidelines indicating how she wants the manuscript sent and the type of files she prefers. Microsoft Word is the oft-used default.

Formatting Specs

- Use a 1" margin on all sides.
- Use a cover page.
- Remove any formatting that might cause potential glitches when the manuscript is typeset. Don't put two spaces after a sentence, and don't double-space electronic files by using hard returns.
- Put sidebars, captions, and other elements at the end of each chapter.
- Send the manuscript as an attachment unless the editor requests otherwise.

Other Dos and Don'ts

- Don't use all caps in your subject line.
- Don't submit a manuscript electronically unless the editor specifically requests it.
- Do ask for specific file format guidelines to make sure the editor can open your files.
- Don't justify text or align the right margin.
- Don't put any copyright information on the manuscript. It's copyrighted when you write it, and the editor is aware of this.
- Do write after you've sent a file to make sure the editor has received it.

Mentioning your awards in a query, even out of the genre of the proposal, is going to be helpful. Withholding any information about your qualifications as a writer isn't a good idea.

—DR. ROBERT D. WOLGEMUTH

literary agent, Wolgemuth & Associates

COVER PAGE: NONFICTION BOOK

Approximately 50,000 words

Rough word count in the upper-right corner

Title in all caps

THE 10 DIRTY LITTLE SECRETS TO DIETING

by
John Q. Writer

Title centered, halfway down the page

John Q. Writer
123 Author Lane
Writerville, CA 95355
(323) 555-0000
johnqwriter@email.com

If you don't submit the manuscript through an agent, the contact information in the lower right corner will be your own, including address, phone number, and e-mail.

MANUSCRIPT: NONFICTION BOOK

Header includes the title, your last name, and the page number.

Writer—*Make Your Woodworking Pay For Itself*   1

Chapter 1
Shop Smarts—Saving Money and Space

Chapter and title centered, one-third of the way down the page

Before you find ways to make money by selling woodworking projects, it makes

sense to study your workshop. Consider what tools you really need, and create a plan

for acquiring them. Find ways to squeeze every penny you can out of the dollars you

spend on wood, tools, and other supplies. The money you save by shopping smart

and cutting waste adds substantially to the money you make. You don't have to pay

tax on it, and it will make everything you sell more profitable. And, waste hurts the

environment as much as your pocketbook.

Double-spaced text

1" margin

Equipment Basics—What You Really Need

Just which tools you need in your shop will depend on your projects. Few tools are

absolutely essential if you are ingenious in finding a way around them, but there are

some items most woodworkers would rather not do without.

Use a line space to separate subheads in your text. Any white space is pleasing to the eye.

Your Shop

Develop a consistent hierarchy for the heads.

How much room do you really need to set up shop? The answer always depends on

what you do. A woodcarver may be able to work in the corner of a bedroom or base-

ment. Some furniture makers may feel the need for a 1,000-square-foot workshop,

plus additional room for milling and storing wood.

FRONT MATTER

Submission Tips

The term "front matter" refers to a wide variety of items that fall between the cover and the body of the finished product. These include:

- Table of contents
- Dedication
- Epigraph or inscription
- Foreword
- Preface
- Prologue
- Acknowledgments

As books have become increasingly graphic, publishers largely have done away with such genteel niceties as lists of illustrations or photos, which could become a book unto themselves and take up space without conveying much useful information.

Tables of contents, on the other hand, have grown to become more detailed and complex, as publishers push for more page breaks, sidebars, and other nontraditional points of entry to appease readers with increasingly short attention spans.

One thing all front matter has in common is that it is not numbered as part of your manuscript. In some cases, publishers number these elements separately with Roman numerals in the actual book. Generally, you don't need to worry about this unless you have a lot of front matter, or individual elements begin to span more than two pages. If your front matter is lengthy, number it using Roman numerals, or Arabic numerals and an altered slug that indicates the pages belong to the front matter.

Formatting Specs

- Generally, front-matter pages are not numbered.
- Front-matter pages get slugs in the header.
- Heads for each element are centered.

Other Dos and Don'ts

- Don't get carried away with most of these elements. Readers routinely skip over them, and they take up space that should be devoted to the text of the book.
- Do have a good reason for including any of these elements.

Being known as someone easy to work with can distinguish you from other writers who also deliver solid work. Acting like a professional means a number of things. Dressing a certain way. Acting a certain way. Hitting deadlines. Returning calls and e-mails promptly. In this business just like any other, people, and circumstances will irk you—but in almost every case it behooves you to take the high road. Reacting emotionally can only harm you; staying cool can only benefit you.

—I.J. SCHETER

freelancer, *Golf Monthly*, *Pregnancy*

TABLE OF CONTENTS

Submission Tips

The table of contents is one of the first places a potential consumer goes to evaluate a nonfiction book. Publishers got wise to this fact, so now editors look for the table of contents to be more complete, descriptive, and compelling than ever.

Tables of contents in nonfiction books are as varied as the books they describe, so prescribing a slapdash formula for them is pointless. Many remain bare bones, merely listing the chapter titles and page numbers. Increasingly, however, the table of contents for many books looks like the chapter outline in the book proposal—no-holds-barred hucksterism aimed at doing the same sales job on the reader as the author and agent did on the editor. So, keep that book proposal handy as you prepare the table of contents.

Formatting Specs

- Center the heading "Table of Contents" or "Contents" one-third of the way down the page.
- Provide extra-wide margins, at least 1.5".
- Don't number pages as part of the manuscript.
- Use a slug in the same place as the header in the rest of the manuscript.
- At the very least, include the chapter titles.
- Include such front-matter elements as prefaces, forewords, and prologues.
- Include back matter, such as the appendix or glossary.
- Don't include acknowledgments, dedications, and other short bits of front matter.
- Page numbers are the numbers as they occur in your manuscript. The numbers in the book will be different, of course, and impossible for you to predict.

TABLE OF CONTENTS: NONFICTION BOOK

Writer—*Make Your Woodworking Pay For Itself*

Header includes your last name and the title, but no page number.

Table of Contents

Head centered, one-third of the way down the page, and underlined

1.5" margin

Indent second and subsequent lines in the same chapter.

Double-spaced text

DEDICATIONS, EPIGRAPHS, AND INSCRIPTIONS

Submission Tips

These short pieces are all handled similarly from a format standpoint. A dedication is a short statement dedicating the book to a person or persons, often in combination with some expression of affection. An epigraph or inscription is a quote that sums up, signifies, or sets the tone for the book.

Formatting Specs

- Dedications and epigraphs are centered about one-third of the way down the page.
- Keep them to two or three lines.
- Don't put a heading above these to label them (e.g., "Dedication").
- Don't number the page.

DEDICATION: NONFICTION BOOK

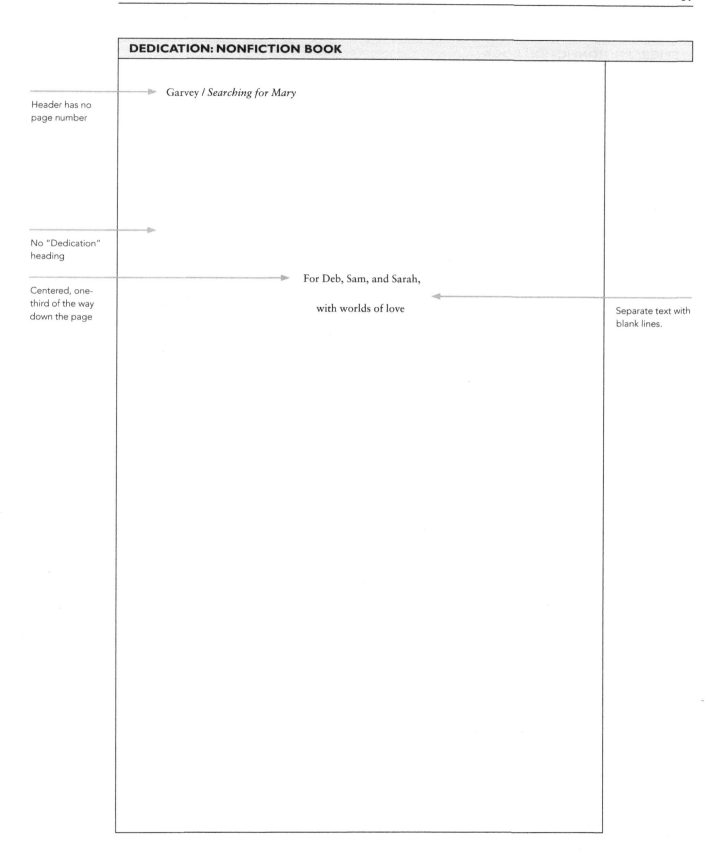

Garvey / *Searching for Mary*

For Deb, Sam, and Sarah,

with worlds of love

Header has no page number

No "Dedication" heading

Centered, one-third of the way down the page

Separate text with blank lines.

EPIGRAPH: NONFICTION BOOK

Garvey / *Searching for Mary*

Header has no
page number.

Oh! Blessed rage for order ...

—WALLACE STEVENS

Separate text
with blank lines.

Centered, one-
third of the way
down the page

FOREWORD

Submission Tips

A foreword is a commentary or review of the book written by an expert in the field or someone familiar with the story of the book's creation. If the name and the review do not add something to the appeal of the book, they serve no function.

Formatting Specs

- Like the rest of the front matter, the foreword has a header but no page numbers.
- Use a heading, starting about one-third of the way down the first page.
- The name of the foreword's author goes flush right at the end of the text, followed by his title and affiliation.
- Optional: The city and year where and when the foreword was written may go after the text, flush left.

FOREWORD: NONFICTION BOOK

Foreword: *Selling Your Ideas*

Foreword

I was there when John Q. Writer had his first big idea in business. He was a twenty-two-year-old sales representative for Cyclops Steel just out of college when he returned from a sales call very excited, clutching a handful of napkins covered with notes, scribbles, and diagrams. After he calmed down a bit, I soon discovered that he had landed on a concept that would radically change the steel industry forever.

I never did quite understand how a sales rep fresh out of college came up with what would be known as the continuous casting process, but I quickly realized the power of his proposal. Unfortunately, the guys in engineering weren't used to taking cues from downy-faced salesmen just out of college. Good thing John already had an instinct for how to work the system. He had enlisted the help of his boss—me—and given me ownership of the idea at an early stage. Soon, I was using my contacts with junior-level executives in the engineering department to find out if this idea truly had legs. By the time we made a formal presentation to the engineering department, we already had the support of key people in that organization. I watched John's career skyrocket after that day, and was witness to plenty more good ideas where the first came from. But more than just having good ideas, John learned quickly how to get other people to embrace them as their own. When he came into my office twenty-three years later with the idea for this book, I knew he had a winner. If there was one person I would want selling my idea up and down the organization chart, John is the man. I know readers will come away armed with insights into how the system works and how ideas go from napkins to blueprints.

Pittsburgh, 2006

John Masterson
CEO, TronicCorp.

PREFACE, PROLOGUE, AND ACKNOWLEDGMENTS

Submission Tips

Formatting for each of these front-matter elements is very similar, though each serves a different purpose. The example here is a sample acknowledgments page, but the same formatting applies to the preface and prologue as well.

A preface explains the story behind the book—the reason why it was written, the background, the unusual stories that were part of its creation. In other cases, a preface may serve as another pitch for the book, explaining why it's needed and how to use it. At least that's the theory. A preface sometimes gets muddled in with the purposes of an introduction or a prologue.

A prologue explains events or history that provide a context for the book. If you're writing a book that chronicles an event, for instance, the prologue might describe the events or forces that led up to that event.

The acknowledgments page is where you thank the folks who helped you put the book together. The preface and prologue may be optional, but the acknowledgments are not. It's virtually impossible to write a nonfiction book without someone's help, and it's impolite not to thank those people. Though this is front matter, it's among the last things you'll write.

Publishers and editors generally consider the introduction part of the body of the book. But in some cases, the book's introduction is treated as front matter, too, and handled the same way as these other elements.

Formatting Specs

- As with other front-matter elements, these are not numbered as part of the rest of the manuscript. They do, however, use headers.
- The introduction can be part of the main book, or it may be in the front matter.
- For each element, drop about one-third of the way down the page and use a centered heading.
- After the heading, drop an extra line, indent, and get started.

Other Dos and Don'ts

- Do include these elements if they add something to the book.
- Don't include prefaces or prologues just to appear impressive. This is the mark of an amateur.
- Don't forget anyone who helped in preparation of the book when you write the acknowledgments, unless they don't want to be mentioned. Keep a running file of names and ways that people helped so you don't have to scramble for this information at the end.

ACKNOWLEDGMENTS: NONFICTION BOOK

Writer—*Insiders' Guide to Greater Cincinnati*

Header includes the book title and your last name.

No page number

<u>Acknowledgments</u>

Heading centered, one-third of the way down the page, and underlined

Thanks to the many folks who provided tips and other assistance in the preparation of this book, particularly Gordon Baer for the back cover photo, Mary Anna Dusablon and Rita Heikenfeld for their insights on Cincinnati cuisine, and tipsters Julie Harrison, Michelle Howard, Bob Humble, Gail Paul, Irene Schaeffer, Joan Schaffield, Karen Tennant, Julie Whaley, and Joel Williams.

Among the librarians and public relations people who went out of their way to help include Alliea Phipps, who must operate the fastest fax/modem this side of the Alleghenies, and Bea Rose for her assistance in procuring photos of Albert Sabin.

Double-spaced text

Thanks to coauthor Skip Tate for his help, not least of which was writing half the book. Also thanks to editor Molly Brewster and to Beth Storie and the rest of the crew at The Insiders' Guides for making this possible.

Special thanks go to my wife, Glenda, for general forbearance and for again taking everyone but the dogs away for the occasional cramming to meet deadlines.

1" margin

BACK MATTER

Submission Tips

It's a dirty job, but somebody has to do it—that would be you. Back matter is that mostly unglamorous but necessary part of any nonfiction book that includes the endnotes, appendix, glossary, bibliography, epilogue, and index. You won't always have all of these, but you should know how to handle each section.

The epilogue provides a final thought from the author, perhaps summing up the work's impact on the author or, in a revised edition, detailing changes that have occurred since or because of the book.

Endnotes are used mainly for scholarly manuscripts and business proposals, but they are sometimes included in other nonfiction books based on significant documentary research. They can be handy in eliminating the need to pepper the manuscript with attributions, allowing instead a quick reference to the endnote for anyone seeking the source of information. Endnotes may also be included in more scholarly articles. *The Chicago Manual of Style* is the definitive source on handling these and other back-matter issues.

The appendix is used for material that supports information or arguments in the book but which is too lengthy to include or would hamper the natural flow of the book. It's similar to the attachments found on a book proposal.

A glossary lists and defines special terminology used in the book, such as technical phrases, foreign words and phrases, and any other specialized lexicon or jargon.

The bibliography is a list of books cited in the manuscript, used in researching the manuscript, or otherwise useful as further reading. A bibliography with a brief commentary or review of significant titles and why they're helpful adds some value to an otherwise fairly dry formality. The bibliography may also be called "Recommended Reading" or incorporated into a section on "Resources" that includes information on websites of interest, events, or where to buy products related to the book's subject.

The index is a detailed listing of all the people, places, things, and concepts cited in the book, along with the page numbers. Generally, publishers hire professional indexers to prepare these.

Formatting Specs

- Unlike front matter, back matter is numbered as part of your manuscript.
- Back-matter pages take the same slug as the rest of the manuscript.
- All elements of the back matter start with a centered heading about one-third of the way down the page and are double-spaced.
- The format for the appendix and epilogue are the same as for front-matter elements, except that they are numbered as part of the manuscript. See the front matter section on page 85 for details.
- The details of these elements are easier to grasp by seeing them, so look to the models that follow for additional details.

Other Dos and Don'ts

- Do include these elements only if you have a good reason. As with front matter, you don't get any extra credit for having a well-rounded assortment of back matter. Except for the index, and at times the bibliography, none of these elements are indispensable.

The compulsion to blanket-submit is understandable. As writers, we are informed constantly about the odds against succeeding, the astronomical rations of submissions to acceptances and the necessity of long response times. So we decide to send our work to as many places as possible, hoping the odds will deliver a match. In truth, the best response to the inherent challenges of the publishing trade is to be as tactical as possible. In the long run, this will prove a much greater boon to your career than blitzing the market with every piece you write.

—I.J. SCHETER

freelancer, *Golf Monthly, Pregnancy*

ENDNOTES: NONFICTION BOOK

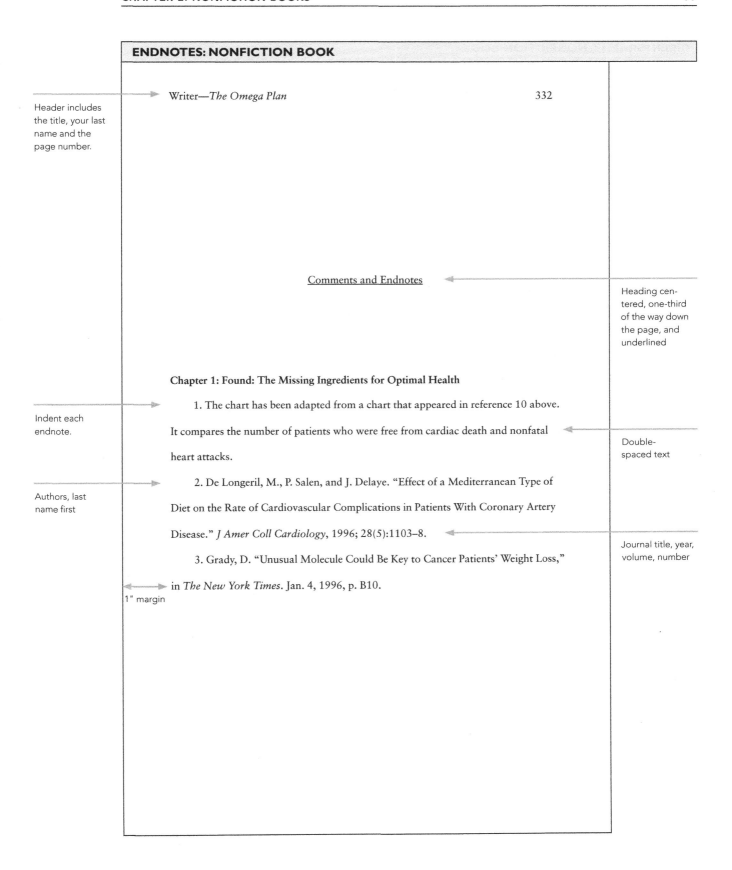

Writer—*The Omega Plan*   332

Header includes the title, your last name and the page number.

Comments and Endnotes

Heading centered, one-third of the way down the page, and underlined

Chapter 1: Found: The Missing Ingredients for Optimal Health

1. The chart has been adapted from a chart that appeared in reference 10 above. It compares the number of patients who were free from cardiac death and nonfatal heart attacks.

Indent each endnote.

Double-spaced text

2. De Longeril, M., P. Salen, and J. Delaye. "Effect of a Mediterranean Type of Diet on the Rate of Cardiovascular Complications in Patients With Coronary Artery Disease." *J Amer Coll Cardiology*, 1996; 28(5):1103–8.

Authors, last name first

Journal title, year, volume, number

3. Grady, D. "Unusual Molecule Could Be Key to Cancer Patients' Weight Loss," in *The New York Times*. Jan. 4, 1996, p. B10.

1" margin

BIBLIOGRAPHY: NONFICTION BOOK

Header includes the title, your last name and the page number.

Writer—*Searching for Mary*   235

Heading centered, one-third of the way down the page, and underlined

<u>Bibliography</u>

Literature available on the subject of Marian apparitions is copious and of wildly varying quality and credibility. Of works consulted in the course of my research, most of which are listed below, a few stand out as superior tools for readers interested in plumbing the subject to greater depths.

Commentary adds value to the listings.

Sandra Zimdars-Swartz's *Encountering Mary* has set the standard for balanced, scholarly treatment of the phenomena of popularity among communities of believers. If you read only one more book on the subject, this should be the one.

No more succinct and helpful presentation of the Catholic Church's position in regard to claims of private revelation is to be found than in Benedict Groeschel's *A Still, Small Voice.*

Though only tangentially related to the subject of Marian apparitions, *The Physical Phenomena of Mysticism* by Herbert Thurston is a sublimely creepy compendium from the outer fringes of Roman Catholic lore—everything from stigmata to miraculous corpses. This book is out of print, but well worth searching for in the stacks of your local library—makes Stephen King read like A.A. Milne.

Ashton, Joan. *Mother of All Nations.* San Francisco: Harper and Row, 1989.

1" margin

Book citations flush left

Christian, William A., Jr. *Apparitions in Late Medieval and Renaissance Spain.*
    Princeton, N.J.: Princeton University Press, 1981.

Double-spaced text

Indent second line of two-line listing.

GLOSSARY: NONFICTION BOOK

Header includes the title, your last name, and the page number.

Writer—*Insider's Guide to Greater Cincinnati* 405

<u>Glossary</u>

Heading centered, one-third of the way down the page, and underlined

Goetta: *A mixture of oats and pork sausage developed by German immigrants and peculiar to Cincinnati.*

1" margin

Please?: What many Cincinnatians say for "Pardon me?" or "Come again?"

Three-Way: Cincinnati chili in its fundamental form, including, from the bottom up, spaghetti, a runny meat-filled chili seasoned with cocoa and cinnamon, and grated cheddar cheese. Note: There is no one- or two-way. This, or the higher-order ways, are the only ways. A four-way also includes onions or beans and a five-way also includes both.

Double-spaced text

Indent the second line of a two-line definition.

CHAPTER 3:

SHORT AND SPECIALIZED PIECES

When you think of short nonfiction pieces for magazines and newspaper, you probably think of articles. But don't forget about other short-form work, such as fillers and anecdotes, which many publications still seek and purchase. Submission guidelines for short pieces generally follow the same guidelines as for articles, with a few exceptions. Specialized pieces, such as radio and television commentaries, require specific submission formats, so read on to learn more.

FILLERS AND ANECDOTES

Submission Tips

Short pieces such as fillers or anecdotes follow the same submission guidelines as articles (see pages 14–15); however, since these are short pieces, it would be pointless to query editors on them. Simply submit these items with a brief cover letter noting what's enclosed, along with a brief paragraph on your background and a polite request for a response. These items together usually take up a page or less. When they take more, follow the same guidelines for pagination and headers as you would with articles. It's okay to leave less white space above the item to make it fit on one page.

Formatting Specs

- Use a 1" margin on all sides.
- Don't number the first page.
- Put your name and contact information in the top left corner of the first page.
- Put the rights offered and a word count in the top right corner.
- If you need a second page, put a one- to two-word slug at the top left corner of the header. Put a page number at the top right corner.
- When appropriate, put the working title in all caps or boldface and the subtitle underlined or in italic centered, about one-third of the way down the page from the top margin.
- Don't include a byline. Such short items rarely get them. Occasionally, an editor will give the writer credit in a tag line, but you don't need to include your name with the manuscript.
- Drop four lines, indent, and begin the item.

- Double-space the entire text of the item.
- Use 12-point type.

Other Dos and Don'ts

- Don't use a notation at the end of the item, such as "–30–" or "–###–".
- Don't staple the manuscript to the cover letter.
- Don't use a separate cover page.
- Do put one item per page when making multiple submissions.
- Don't insult the editor by putting a copyright notice on the manuscript. It's copyrighted as soon as you write it.
- Don't use unusual fonts. A simple Times Roman will do fine.
- Don't fax or e-mail your items unless you have permission from the publisher or if the submission guidelines state it is acceptable.

ELECTRONIC SUBMISSIONS

These short items are ideally suited for electronic submissions, but don't go clicking away until you've ascertained the electronic submission policies of the publication to which you're sending material. Writers' guidelines (see "Request for Guidelines Letter" on page 110) should spell out the electronic guidelines. Send unformatted text files as attachments or in the body of the e-mail, unless the guidelines specify different directions.

> If you don't have a bio and clips to die for, major magazine editors aren't likely to trust you with a long feature assignment right away. Instead, aim for the short articles in the front of the magazine, and stay on the lookout for appropriate ideas you can flesh out in a few hundred words or less. For truly short articles, you can skip the query and just write the whole thing if you prefer—it usually requires about the same amount of effort.
>
> **—JENNA GLATZER**
> author, *Make a Real Living as a Freelance Writer*

MANUSCRIPT: FILLER OR ANECDOTE

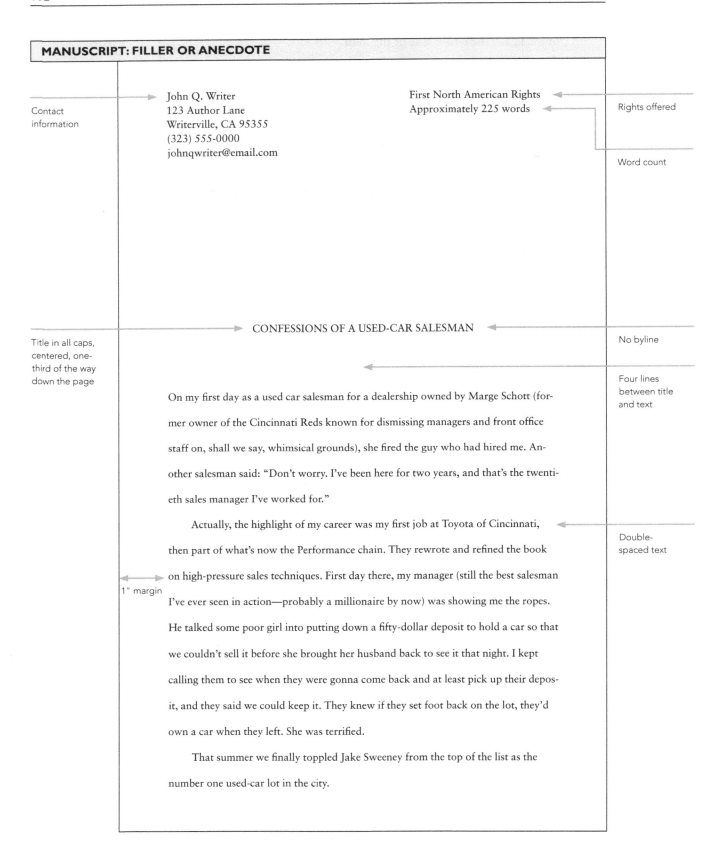

Contact information

John Q. Writer
123 Author Lane
Writerville, CA 95355
(323) 555-0000
johnqwriter@email.com

First North American Rights
Approximately 225 words

Rights offered

Word count

Title in all caps, centered, one-third of the way down the page

CONFESSIONS OF A USED-CAR SALESMAN

No byline

Four lines between title and text

On my first day as a used car salesman for a dealership owned by Marge Schott (former owner of the Cincinnati Reds known for dismissing managers and front office staff on, shall we say, whimsical grounds), she fired the guy who had hired me. Another salesman said: "Don't worry. I've been here for two years, and that's the twentieth sales manager I've worked for."

Actually, the highlight of my career was my first job at Toyota of Cincinnati, then part of what's now the Performance chain. They rewrote and refined the book on high-pressure sales techniques. First day there, my manager (still the best salesman I've ever seen in action—probably a millionaire by now) was showing me the ropes. He talked some poor girl into putting down a fifty-dollar deposit to hold a car so that we couldn't sell it before she brought her husband back to see it that night. I kept calling them to see when they were gonna come back and at least pick up their deposit, and they said we could keep it. They knew if they set foot back on the lot, they'd own a car when they left. She was terrified.

That summer we finally toppled Jake Sweeney from the top of the list as the number one used-car lot in the city.

1" margin

Double-spaced text

COLUMNS AND OP-EDS

Submission Tips

Columns and commentaries, including humor, business, how-to or op-ed pieces, are really articles and so follow the article format described on pages 38–39. The only difference with columns and opinion pieces is a brief (usually one sentence) biographical paragraph appended to the end of the column.

It isn't necessary to send a query for an op-ed submission, as it is a one-time short piece, though it can certainly help to write ahead for writers' guidelines (especially with magazines) before submitting. When trying to land a regular column assignment, however, a query is required, along with three or more ideas for column entries.

Craft a brief cover letter introducing the submissions, along with a note on the enclosures and any other information that may help in editing the piece. Include your e-mail address and the best times to reach you at the phone numbers you provide. Editors' hours can vary widely, especially at newspapers, so give both a daytime and evening phone number. Also provide any information or contact phone numbers that could help in fact checking.

Formatting Specs

- Use a 1" margin on all sides.
- Put your name and contact information in the top left corner.
- Put the rights offered and a word count in the top right corner.
- Put the suggested title or headline in all caps or boldface centered, starting about one-third of the way down the page.
- Drop a line and put "by" in lowercase, centered.
- Drop a line and type your name, centered.
- Double-space the rest of the column or op-ed piece.
- Indent paragraphs, except for your bio at the end of the piece.
- On the second and subsequent pages, use a slug (your last name) in the top left corner, and number pages in the top right corner.
- At the end of the column, skip a line, then, with no indentation, write your bio. Keep it to one sentence, mentioning your name, what you do, where you live, and any other fact that may be of relevance to readers of the column or op-ed. This can be in italics, but it doesn't need to be.

Other Dos and Don'ts

- Do research your column or op-ed as thoroughly as you would anything else you write. Just because it's an opinion doesn't mean you don't need facts. Indeed, verifying facts is even more important in an opinion piece.
- Do use your real name in an op-ed submission. No worthwhile publication accepts opinion pieces from anonymous contributors.

- Do be brief. About 700 words is the top end for opinion pieces. Generally, the shorter the piece, the better its chance of being published, though anything under 250 words is probably letter-to-the-editor material rather than an op-ed piece.

- Don't e-mail or fax your submission unless you have permission from the publication or if the submission guidelines state it is acceptable.

Electronic Submissions

Many newspapers have electronic submission guidelines that can be found on their editorial or op-ed pages. Magazines with regular opinion features may mail their writers' guidelines to you if you request them (see "Request for Guidelines Letter" on page 31), and many magazines have their guidelines posted on their websites.

PERSONAL ESSAYS

Submission Tips

Personal essays, also known as personal narratives, provide a glimpse into a writer's life and can run the gamut from opinionated rants to whimsical observations. Those found in newspapers and magazines typically run under 2,000 words. A query usually isn't necessary, but check a publication's guidelines before you send an unsolicited essay to make sure. Include a brief cover letter describing the essay you are sending and provide any other information that indicates why you are qualified to write on the subject you are covering. Be sure to include your e-mail address and day and evening phone numbers.

Formatting Specs

- Use a 1" margin on all sides.
- Put your name and contact information in the top left corner.
- Put the rights offered and a word count in the top right corner.
- Put your suggested title in all caps or boldface, centered, about a third of the way down the page.
- Drop a line and put "by" in lowercase, centered.
- Drop a line and put your name, centered.
- The rest of the essay should be double-spaced.
- Indent paragraphs.
- On the second page, use a header and number the pages.
- At the end of the column, drop a line, then, with no indentation, write your one-sentence bio. It should include your name, what you do, and where you live.

Other Dos and Don'ts

- Do use your real name in a personal essay submission.
- Don't forget to verify names, places, and facts that you mention in your essay. Just because it's personal doesn't mean it shouldn't be accurate.
- Don't fax or e-mail your essay unless you have permission from the publication or if submission guidelines state it is acceptable.

ELECTRONIC SUBMISSIONS

Check a magazine or newspaper's submission guidelines to see if they accept personal essay submissions via e-mail. If they do, send an unformatted text file of your essay as an attachment or in the body of your e-mail, unless otherwise instructed in the guidelines.

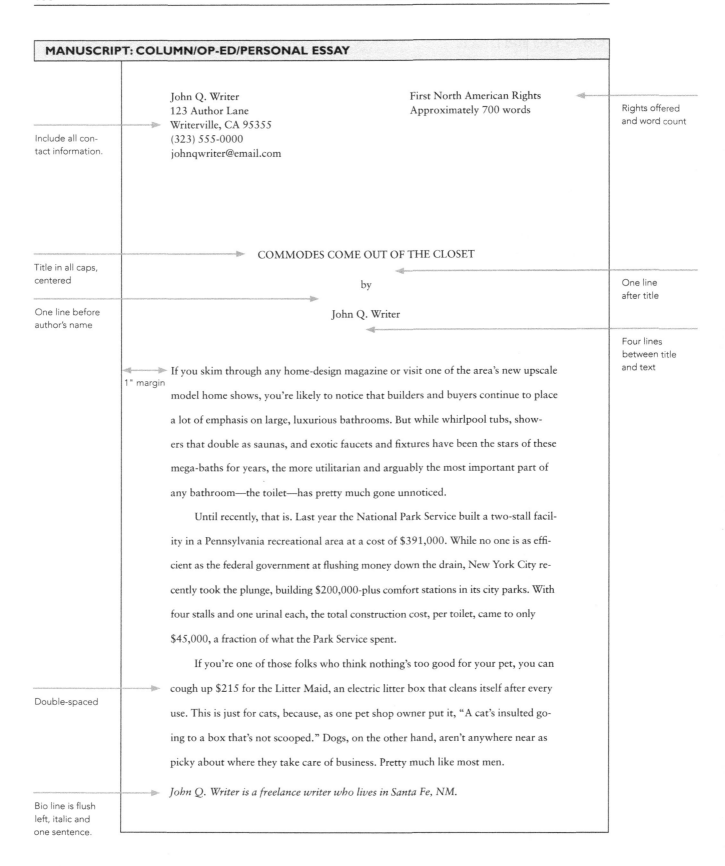

MANUSCRIPT: COLUMN/OP-ED/PERSONAL ESSAY

John Q. Writer
123 Author Lane
Writerville, CA 95355
(323) 555-0000
johnqwriter@email.com

First North American Rights
Approximately 700 words

Include all contact information.

Rights offered and word count

COMMODES COME OUT OF THE CLOSET

by

John Q. Writer

Title in all caps, centered

One line after title

One line before author's name

Four lines between title and text

1" margin

If you skim through any home-design magazine or visit one of the area's new upscale model home shows, you're likely to notice that builders and buyers continue to place a lot of emphasis on large, luxurious bathrooms. But while whirlpool tubs, showers that double as saunas, and exotic faucets and fixtures have been the stars of these mega-baths for years, the more utilitarian and arguably the most important part of any bathroom—the toilet—has pretty much gone unnoticed.

Until recently, that is. Last year the National Park Service built a two-stall facility in a Pennsylvania recreational area at a cost of $391,000. While no one is as efficient as the federal government at flushing money down the drain, New York City recently took the plunge, building $200,000-plus comfort stations in its city parks. With four stalls and one urinal each, the total construction cost, per toilet, came to only $45,000, a fraction of what the Park Service spent.

If you're one of those folks who think nothing's too good for your pet, you can cough up $215 for the Litter Maid, an electric litter box that cleans itself after every use. This is just for cats, because, as one pet shop owner put it, "A cat's insulted going to a box that's not scooped." Dogs, on the other hand, aren't anywhere near as picky about where they take care of business. Pretty much like most men.

Double-spaced

John Q. Writer is a freelance writer who lives in Santa Fe, NM.

Bio line is flush left, italic and one sentence.

RADIO AND TELEVISION COMMENTARIES

Submission Tips

Many radio and TV commentaries come from people who don't write for a living, and some are submitted in the form of demo tapes rather than manuscripts. Therefore, the style of submissions is fairly informal. It's best to contact the station directly, find out who deals with commentary submissions and discuss with them what form they prefer. The manuscript should indicate how long it will take to deliver the piece and also include a brief bio and a suggested lead-in for the announcer. Otherwise, commentaries follow the same formats as other articles and short forms.

Formatting Specs

- Use a 1" margin on all sides.
- Put the title for your piece along with your name and contact information in the top left corner.
- Put a word count and an estimated air time length in the top right corner.
- Put suggested title in all caps or boldface centered, starting about one-third of the way down the page.
- Drop a line and put "by" in lowercase, centered.
- Drop a line and type your name, centered.
- Include a brief, one- or two-sentence lead-in that can be used by an announcer to introduce your piece.
- Double-space the text of the commentary.
- Indent paragraphs, except for your bio at the end of the piece.
- Use a header on the second and subsequent pages.
- At the end of the column, with no indentation, include your bio. Generally, keep your bio to one sentence, mentioning your name, what you do, where you live, and any other relevant fact. This can be in italics, but it doesn't need to be.

Other Dos and Don'ts

- Do research your commentary as thoroughly as you would anything else you write. Just because it's an opinion doesn't mean you don't need facts. Indeed, the need to verify facts is even more pronounced in an opinion piece.
- Do use your real name.

ELECTRONIC SUBMISSIONS

Some stations may accept electronic submissions. Check with the contact person at the station for guidelines.

MANUSCRIPT: RADIO AND TELEVISION COMMENTARY

Out of the Water Closet   513 words, Time: 2:25
John Q. Writer
123 Author Lane
Writerville, CA 95355
(323) 555-0000
johnqwriter@email.com

COMMODES COME OUT OF THE CLOSET

by

John Q. Writer

INTRO: Skim through any home-design magazine or tour any new upscale model homes and you'll discover builders and buyers place a lot of emphasis on large, luxurious bathrooms. But, as commentator John Q. Writer noticed, until recently, the spotlight has been focused on all but the most important part of any bathroom.

If you visited one of the area's recent home shows, you have noticed that lavish bathrooms are still a hot-selling feature. While whirlpool tubs and exotic faucets and fixtures have been the stars of these mega-baths for years, the more utilitarian and arguably the most important part of any bathroom—the toilet—has gone unnoticed.

Until recently. It looks as if the toilet has finally come into its own. Last year the National Park Service built a two-stall facility in Pennsylvania at a cost of $391,000. And while no one is as efficient as the federal government at flushing money down the drain, New York City recently took the plunge, building $200,000-plus comfort stations in its city parks. But with four stalls and one urinal each, the total per-toilet cost came to only $45,000, a fraction of what the Park Service spent.

If you can't swing the money for one of these pricey privies, do the next best thing and upgrade your current commode. Toto offers a seat with antibacterial glazing, a water spray, heat, and a fan, for just $800—though you may feel a bit nervous settling down onto a seat that's plugged into an electric outlet. For the true music lover, Jammin Johns offers toilet lids shaped like guitars and pianos for $150 to $250.

John Q. Writer is a freelance writer who lives in Santa Fe, NM.

Word count
and estimated air
time length

One line
after title

Four lines
between title
and text

Contact
information

One line before
author's name

Lead-in introduc-
ing the piece

Two lines
between intro
and text

1" margin

Double-spaced

Bio line is flush
left, italic and
one sentence.

PART 2:
FICTION

CHAPTER 4:
SHORT STORIES

Fiction short story markets are mostly in magazines, literary journals, anthologies, and some online websites. And, like novels, they can run the gamut of literature to genre tales to children's stories. The main difference between short stories and novels is length—short stories run anywhere from 1,000 to 20,000 words, whereas novels are much longer. Short stories are a medium all their own, and require a specific format and submission policy. Read on to learn how to submit your short stories to print and electronic publications.

WHAT YOU NEED TO SUBMIT

Submitting short stories is relatively simple. Unlike with novels where you typically need to submit a query letter as well as a few sample chapters and a synopsis, with a short story you only need to send a cover letter and the story in its entirety.

REQUEST FOR GUIDELINES LETTER

Submission Tips
Before you actually submit your story, obtain a copy of the publication's writers' guidelines. To save time, try the publication's website to see if the guidelines are available online. If you can't find the website, or if the guidelines are not there, then write to the publication.

Send a brief letter stating that you'd like to receive the writers' guidelines. Receiving guidelines will allow you to do the following:

- See what rights the publisher acquires.
- Find out what kind of material they're looking for.
- Learn if and what they pay.
- Learn how to submit material.

Formatting Specs
- Address the letter to the correct editor.
- Use a 1" margin on all sides.
- Use block format.

- Keep it to one paragraph.
- Include your name, address, phone number, and e-mail.
- Enclose an SASE.

Other Dos and Dont's

- Don't mention anything about your story at this point.
- Don't mention anything about yourself.
- Do address the request to a specific editor. Call to get the appropriate name.
- Do keep the letter brief and to the point.
- Don't fax or e-mail a request for guidelines unless the publication indicates it is acceptable to do so.

Always mail your manuscript flat. It doesn't matter if it's two pages and will fit nicely into a #10 envelope. Mail it flat. The editor will appreciate it.

—JOHN JOSEPH ADAMS

anthology editor

REQUEST FOR GUIDELINES: SHORT STORY

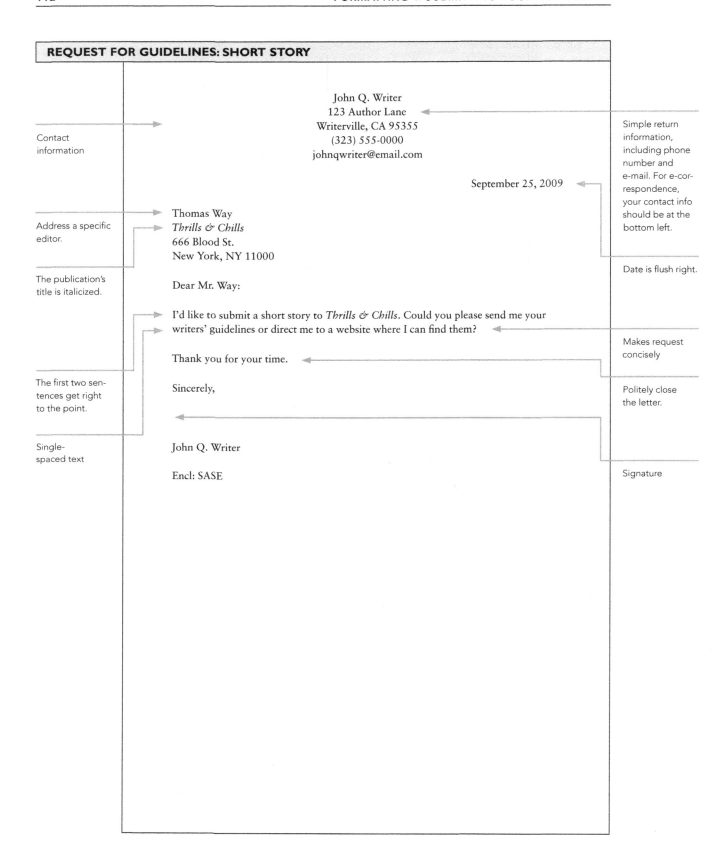

Contact information

Address a specific editor.

The publication's title is italicized.

The first two sentences get right to the point.

Single-spaced text

John Q. Writer
123 Author Lane
Writerville, CA 95355
(323) 555-0000
johnqwriter@email.com

September 25, 2009

Thomas Way
Thrills & Chills
666 Blood St.
New York, NY 11000

Dear Mr. Way:

I'd like to submit a short story to *Thrills & Chills*. Could you please send me your writers' guidelines or direct me to a website where I can find them?

Thank you for your time.

Sincerely,

John Q. Writer

Encl: SASE

Simple return information, including phone number and e-mail. For e-correspondence, your contact info should be at the bottom left.

Date is flush right.

Makes request concisely

Politely close the letter.

Signature

COVER LETTER

Submission Tips

Your cover letter is important for two reasons: It lets the editor know who you are and how you write. This is different than a query because you are submitting the story along with the letter. The best cover letters contain three short paragraphs, in the following order:

- The **introductory paragraph** states the story's title, then hooks the editor with a brief description of the story.

- The **biographical paragraph** explains, in one or two sentences, a bit about yourself that is pertinent to the story, such as previous publishing credits, why you're sending it to this particular publication or how a personal experience influenced your story.

- The **concluding paragraph** politely closes the letter.

While publication will hinge on the story itself, a strong cover letter will ensure your story will at least get a close read. Remember to keep it brief and to the point.

Formatting Specs

- Use a standard font, 12-point type. Avoid bold or italics, except for titles.
- Place your name and contact information at the top of your letter, centered.
- Use a 1" margin on all sides.
- Address the cover letter to a specific editor. Call to get the appropriate editor's name and gender.
- Keep it to one page.
- Use block format (no indentations, an extra space between paragraphs).
- Single-space the body of the letter and double-space between paragraphs.
- Give the story's exact word count.

Other Dos and Don'ts

- Do mention if your story has been—or will be—published in another publication.
- Do indicate familiarity with the publication. Make a brief positive comment about the publication. Be sincere, but don't go overboard.
- Do address the letter to a specific editor, preferably the editor assigned to handle freelance submissions. (Call to get the appropriate name and gender.)
- Don't state that another publication has rejected your story.
- Don't ask for advice or criticism—that's not the editor's job at this stage.
- Don't mention anything about yourself that's not pertinent to the story, for instance that you're a first-time writer, that you've never been published, or how much time you've spent on the story. Your story must stand on its own merit.

- Don't bring up payment for the story. It's premature.

- Don't mention copyright information.

- Don't staple your cover letter to your story (a paper clip is okay).

- Don't fax or e-mail your cover letter and story unless you have permission from the editor or if submission guidelines state it is acceptable.

- Do thank the editor for considering your story.

- Do include an SASE (self-addressed, stamped envelope) or postcard for reply, and state in the letter that you have done so. (Postcards are cheaper and easier. Get them printed in bulk.)

- Do state that you're able to send your story on disk, CD or via e-mail, but this won't be necessary until the editor actually wants to publish your story.

ELECTRONIC COVER LETTER

Submission Tips

Before you send a cover letter and story to a publication via e-mail, make sure they accept electronic submissions by contacting the publication directly or checking out their writers' guidelines in a trusted guide or online. Never send a story via e-mail unless you have permission from the editor or if their submission guidelines state it is acceptable.

Formatting Specs

- Include the same contact information in your cover letter as you would in a paper cover, but it is not necessary to include your e-mail address in the body of the e-mail, since the editor can easily click "Reply" to respond.

- Use the subject line to introduce the title of your story.

- Follow the same format you would with a paper cover letter, including the date, salutation, and block paragraph format.

Other Dos and Don'ts

- Don't use all caps or exclamation points in the subject line.

- Don't insert clip art graphics or other images in your cover letter. Keep it simple.

COVER LETTER: SHORT STORY

John Q. Writer
123 Author Lane
Writerville, CA 95355
(323) 555-0000
johnqwriter@email.com

December 29, 2009

Thomas Way
Thrills & Chills
666 Blood St.
New York, NY 11000

Dear Mr. Way:

Enclosed is my short story, "Spitfire Sunday" (2,500 words). It's about Pastor Donald White, who spends every Sunday preaching hellfire and brimstone. But his little routine changes when atheist Katherine Condon comes to town. She doesn't just preach about perpetual suffering—she delivers it. The target of her latest sadistic crusade is none other than the preacher himself, as she kidnaps, tortures and prepares to set him ablaze just before the clock strikes midnight on Easter Sunday.

I am a full-time pastor by day and part-time writer by night. My published stories have appeared in three mystery magazines (*Murderously Yours* 12/02, *Crime Pays* 1/03, and *Mystery Times*, 7/03). You are the first editor I'm soliciting with this story, and I will wait six weeks for your response before I approach another magazine. If you are not interested in the story, feel free to dispose of the manuscript, but please notify me with the enclosed SASE. If, however, you do want to publish it, I can send you an electronic version in a Microsoft Word attachment.

Thank you for considering "Spitfire Sunday." I look forward to hearing from you.

Sincerely,

John Q. Writer

Encl.: Short story, "Spitfire Sunday"
SASE

Address a specific editor.

Story title and word count

Single-spaced text

1" margin

Allows disposal of manuscript

Offer to send electronic version of story.

Polite closing; positive without being overbearing

Details enclosures

Simple contact information, including phone, fax, and e-mail.

Date flushed right

Good introductory paragraph. It succinctly states the story's title, the word count, the central characters and sets the hook by revealing what the story's about.

Pertinent personal information—he's a pastor so he knows the business of preaching—and publishing credits, including titles and dates of publication.

Lets the editor know this magazine gets first dibs on publishing this story, and how long he'll wait for a response.

Signature

ELECTRONIC COVER LETTER: SHORT STORY

Make sure you have the correct e-mail address.

TO: tgraham@cimarron.com
CC: johnqwriter@email.com
SUBJECT: Short Story Submission
March 2, 2009

It's not a bad idea to copy (CC or BCC) yourself to keep a record of all e-correspondence.

Toni Graham
Cimarron Review
Oklahoma State University
205 Morrill Hall
Stillwater, OK 74078

Since Toni could be male or female, take no chances and write out the full name.

Dear Toni Graham:

I am submitting my short story, "Things From Which You Can Never Recover" (6,465 words) for your consideration in *Cimarron Review*. The story is attached in a Microsoft Word document.

Word count

State how the story is attached. Make sure the publication accepts e-mailed stories.

I am currently a freelancer for several newspapers and magazines, including the *Indianapolis Star*. Your website says you are seeking work with "unusual perspective, language, imagery, and character," and I think my story fits this description.

Informs the editor that other publications are considering the piece.

This is a simultaneous submission. As per your online guidelines, if I do not hear back within three months, I will assume the story was not a fit for *Cimarron Review*. Thank you in advance for your time and consideration.

Give a reason for contacting this publication.

Sincerely,

Polite and short

John Q. Writer
123 Author Lane
Writerville, CA 95355
(323) 555-0000
johnqwriter@email.com

Contact information goes at the bottom of e-mails.

Let the editor know this magazine gets first dibs on publishing this story, and how long he'll wait for a response.

COVER LETTER, MISTAKES TO AVOID: SHORT STORY

John Q. Writer
123 Author Lane
Writerville, CA 95355

No telephone number or e-mail.

December 29, 2005

The strange date is either a mistake, or a clue that this letter has been copied and pasted many times—neither being a good sign.

Thomas Way
Thrills & Chills
666 Blood St.
New York, NY 11000

Hey Tommy,

Salutation is far too informal.

I have been a man of the pulpit for the last twenty-two years and I know about faith and evil and sin and redemption. I am also a published poet and fiction writer. I've had numerous poems published in our local paper and I write weekly stories for the church bulletin. I get lots of praise from my congregation for my stories, and other people in the community have made glowing remarks about my poetry.

Every sentence in this paragraph begins with "I." Should begin with information about the story, not himself.

Who cares? What qualifies them to give a valued opinion?

Anyhow, I've been working on this one short story for about five months now that I'd like your magazine to publish. It's about a minister who gets caught on fire and burned to death by a new woman in town that doesn't agree with his preaching practices.

Too colloquial

Doesn't tell enough about the story, but does reveal the ending!

Always a bad idea to tell the editor how much time you spent on the story. It's irrelevant.

I'm sure you'll appreciate this story as it is based on some real people I have known and therefore it is based in reality but I made a lot of it up too. It'll scare the heck out of your readers.

If for some reason you do not wish to publish this story, I would appreciate your wise and professional opinion about how to make it better.

Never ask for advice or criticism—that's not the editor's job at this stage.

Nowhere on this page does the writer mention the word count, the story's title, or the main characters.

Thank you for your time.

Sincerely,

John Q. Writer

Encl.: Manuscript
SASE

Even if the enclosed story is spectacular, the editor will be skeptical when reading it (if he bothers reading it after wading through this poor cover letter).

REPLY POSTCARD

If you're a bit worried about whether your story actually makes it to the publisher, you may enclose a reply postcard to be signed by the editor (or someone on the staff) and sent back to you. Two caveats: (1) Not all editors are gracious enough to send your reply postcards back, but most do. (2) Just because you receive a postcard reply from a publication, you cannot assume your story has been read or will be read in the next few days or weeks. The only function of your reply postcard is to let you know your submission has been received.

Your best bet to ensure an editor will return your reply postcard is to make it neat and simple to use. That means typing your postcard and not asking the editor to do anything other than note your submission has been received and stick the postcard in their outgoing mail pile. Although it's okay to leave a space for "Comments," keep the space small and don't expect it to be filled in—most editors simply don't have the time or a reason to write anything in it. You'll turn off an editor if you ask him to do too much.

Follow the examples here to create a suitable and functional reply postcard. Remember to keep things short and sweet—and, of course, always supply the postage.

I would say 10,000 words is definitely a long story. A writer who feels the need to apologize for the lengthy of her submission in the cover letter is quite possibly sending us too long a story.

—SARAH BLACKMAN

fiction editor, *The Black Warrior Review*

REPLY POSTCARD: SHORT STORY

Front of card:

John Q. Writer
123 Author Lane
Writerville, CA 95355

Back of card:

Your query/story was received on _____

___ We need more time to consider your query and will be in touch.

___ Yes, we are interested in your idea. An editor will be in touch soon.

___ No, we are not interested in your article at this time.

Comments: _____

_____

_____

SHORT STORY MANUSCRIPT

Submission Tips

Establish yourself as a professional by following the correct short story format. A separate cover or title page is not necessary. Don't submit any materials that have handwritten notes on them. And as with all parts of your submission, make sure your work is revised and proofread.

Formatting Specs

- Use a 1" margin on all sides.
- Do not number the first page.
- Put your name and contact information at the top, centered, on the first page.
- Put the word count and rights offered in the top right corner.
- Put the story's title, centered in all caps, approximately one-third of the way down the page from the top margin.
- Skip a line and write "by" in lowercase, then skip another line and put your name in all caps. (If using a pseudonym, put that name in all caps, and then on the next line put your real name in parentheses.)
- Drop four lines, indent, and begin your story.
- Double-space the entire text of the story.
- Put a header at the top of every page (except the first) including the title, your last name, and the page number).
- Optional: Type "THE END" in all caps when the story is finished. (Some editors like this because it closes the story; others do not. It's your call.)

Other Dos and Don'ts

- Do use a paper clip in the top left corner to attach pages together (butterfly clamps work well for stories longer than ten pages).
- Do keep an original copy of the story for yourself.
- Don't put your social security number on the manuscript.
- Don't use a separate cover or title page.
- Don't justify the text or align the right margin. Ragged right is fine.
- Don't put a copyright notice on the manuscript. It's copyrighted as soon as you write it.
- Don't include your story on a disk or CD unless the editor asks for it.
- Don't use unusual fonts. A simple Times Roman, Arial, or Courier is fine.
- Don't e-mail or fax your story to a publication unless you have permission from the editor or if their submission guidelines state it is acceptable.

If you wish to make some positive comment about the publisher or publication (e.g., "I've been reading and enjoying *Yankee* for more than a decade"), you may do so in a sentence or two toward the end of your letter. Be sincere; avoid overt flattery.

—SCOTT EDELSTEIN

author *1,818 Ways to Write Better & Get Published*

ELECTRONIC SHORT STORY MANUSCRIPT

Submission Tips

Make sure that the publication accepts e-mail submissions before you send your story in that way. Either get permission from the editor, or check to see if their submission guidelines allow it. Don't forget to include your cover letter in the body of your e-mail.

Send the story file as an attachment. You can also cut and paste the entire story below your electronic cover letter in the e-mail itself. This will allow the editor to see the story whichever way she wants.

Formatting Specs

- Before you send the manuscript, find out how the editor prefers to receive files.
- Follow the same formatting specs as above for a paper manuscript submission.
- If you are sending the manuscript via e-mail, send it as an attachment to your e-mail unless the editor requests otherwise.

Other Dos and Don'ts

- Don't use all caps in your subject line.
- Do ask for specific file format guidelines to make sure the editor can open your files.
- Don't use a separate cover or title page.
- Don't justify text or align the right margin.
- Don't put any copyright information on the manuscript. It's copyrighted when you write it.
- Don't put two spaces after sentences within the manuscript.
- Don't use hard returns to double-space the manuscript.

MANUSCRIPT, PAGE 1: SHORT STORY

Contact
information

John Q. Writer
123 Author Lane
Writerville, CA 95355
(323) 555-0000
johnqwriter@email.com

First North American Rights Only
2,500 words

The author has
already discussed
the rights with
the editor. If you
haven't, leave
this blank.

Word count

Title is centered,
all caps, one-third
of the way down
the page.

SPITFIRE SUNDAY

by

JOHN Q. WRITER

Name is centered,
all caps.

Four lines
between title
and text

I was in a small white church south of Somerset, Kentucky, when I first heard the fol-

lowing words: "You will not love yourself until you love Jesus."

Indented
paragraphs

Pastor Donald White was no ordinary preacher. He was intense, and modera-

tion was not his game. He preached love but was full of hate. He hated women. He

1" margin

hated divorce. He hated gays. He hated mixed couples. He hated abortion-rights ad-

vocates. He hated unbaptized children. He hated sex. He certainly hated the Presi-

Double-
spaced text

dent of the United States. Yes, I'd say he pretty much hated everyone and everything.

I'd honestly like to at least say he hated everything except Jesus, but that wouldn't be

true. He didn't love Jesus; he only loved talking about Jesus.

Anyway, a more self-righteous man I've never seen. He even ran for city council

last year—and won—on the motto "You Can Only Go Right With White."

As she poked and prodded him with that scalding hot branding iron, he danced

amidst the flames, cursing and wailing at her.

MANUSCRIPT, LAST PAGE: SHORT STORY

Writer/Spitfire Sunday   15

"You shall not be torn between loving yourself and loving Jesus," he said. "For Jesus is life, and if you do not love Jesus, you cannot love your own life. You can hate me and torture me all you want. I know you're only doing it because you don't love Jesus. You don't love yourself!"

Katherine couldn't bear to hear one more word. She took the branding iron and pressed it to his mouth. He could not speak; he could barely scream. A look of horror fell over his face as he collapsed in the ring of fire. Then she pointed the gun at him. I thought she was finally going to shoot him, to put an end to this poor man's suffering. But she didn't. She dropped the gun, watched him burn, and smiled. Once his screaming stopped, Katherine picked up the pistol as if to finish the act, to make sure he'd be dead.

To my surprise, she put the pistol in her mouth and fired.

THE END

Header includes your name, the title, and the page number. Number all pages except the first.

Optional, but perfectly placed if used

CHAPTER 5:

NOVELS

Novels are lengthy works of literary fiction—usually totaling 60,000 words or more. They come in all sorts genres and types, from a paperback Harlequin romance to heavy literature to an installment in a mystery series. No matter what type it is, this chapter will provide guidelines for formatting a professional manuscript submission.

CONCERNING MEMOIR

Memoirs are true-life stories, but they read like novels. They are nonfiction tales that employ common fiction devices, such as cliffhangers, character arcs, and a three-act structure. For this reason, memoir is treated like fiction. If you're writing a memoir, follow the instructions in this chapter.

THE NOVEL PACKAGE

Before You Submit

Before you submit your novel to an agent or publisher, there are things you need to do. First and foremost, you must finish the work. If you contact an agent and she likes your idea, she will ask to see some or all of the manuscript. You don't want to tell her it won't be finished for another six months. After it's complete, set it aside for a short time, then return with fresh eyes for revisions. Following your own rewrites and revisions, it's not a bad idea to have a trusted peer read over the story. Look for someone who is both skilled and honest. Some writers choose to hire an independent editor to critique their work. This route can be very effective—but know that freelance editors are not cheap. Always get a referral from a friend and ask for a free editing sample before signing any contract.

If your novel is complete and polished, it's time to write your query and synopsis. After that, you're ready to test the agent and editor waters.

What You Need to Submit

There are a few ways to submit your novel package to an agent or publisher, depending on the individual's submission guidelines. Some want only a query letter; others request a query letter and the complete manuscript; some demand a query letter plus three sample chapters and a synopsis; and still others request that you submit a query letter, a few sample chapters, an outline, and a synopsis. All want an SASE (self-addressed stamped envelope) with adequate postage, unless they request an electronic submission.

To determine what you need to submit, consult the current edition of market databases such as *Novel & Short Story Writer's Market*, *Writer's Market*, or *Guide to Literary Agents*. Or try the market's individual website. These sources have submission specifications that come straight from the editors and agents telling you just what to send, how to send it, when to expect a response, and other information unique to the agent or editor you will be soliciting.

Expect to send at least a query letter, a synopsis, and three consecutive sample chapters. These are the most important—and most requested—parts of your novel package. However, if you don't know whom you'll be soliciting and what they demand, try to have the following prepared before you start sending out submissions:

- A query or cover letter
- A synopsis
- At least three consecutive sample chapters
- A chapter-by-chapter outline
- An author biography

Rarely will you need to send them all in the same submission package, since each agent and editor has his own preferences. But you probably will need to use each of them at one time or another, so prepare everything before you actually start submitting your novel. Always include an SASE if you're sending your submission through the mail.

QUERY LETTER

Submission Tips

A query letter two functions: to tell the agent or editor what you have to offer, and to ask if she is interested in seeing it.

Though you can send the query letter attached to a novel package, many agents and editors prefer you send the query letter either by itself or with a synopsis and a few sample pages from your novel. This is called a "blind query" or a "prepackage query," because you're sending it without having been asked to send it. No matter what you call it, it's your quick chance to hook the agent or editor on your novel.

If she likes your query, she'll call and ask for either specific parts of your novel package or the entire manuscript. Then she'll make her decision.

Some agents and editors prefer that you accompany your initial query letter with other parts of your novel package. If that's the case, include the required materials specified by the particular agent or publisher in the market database listing. When you accompany your query with your novel package, the query becomes your cover letter.

The query is the vital component to the submission, no matter whether you submit the query by itself or accompanying other material. Make it compelling, interesting, even funny—anything to make it outstanding to the agent or editor. And do it all in just one page. The query shows that you have a good grasp of your novel and can boil down the concept into a concise and compelling pitch. Although every winning query works its own magic, all good queries should contain the following:

- A "grabber" or hook sentence that makes the reader want to get his hands on the actual novel
- One to three paragraphs about your novel
- A short paragraph about you and your publishing credentials (if you have any)
- A good reason why you're soliciting the person you're soliciting (why this agent or publisher instead of another?)
- The length and genre of the novel
- A sentence or two about the intended audience
- An indication that an SASE is enclosed if you are sending it through the mail

Arguably the most important aspect of any query is the grabber, the hook that lures the reader into wanting to read—your novel. Your grabber should be part of the paragraphs—the pitch—you devote to telling about the novel. Another good idea is to point out why your novel is different from all the others.

Then spend a few sentences telling about yourself; list your publishing credentials (if you have any), or toss in a personal anecdote that's pertinent to the novel (explain that you spent two years in the Peace Corps in Somalia if that's where your story takes place). Ideally, what information you include in your bio paragraph shouldn't matter much because your pitch will have already hooked the agent in. That said, if you don't really have anything to say about yourself, skip talking about yourself and instead simply thank the agent or editor for her time.

Then, in another paragraph, mention why you're sending your query to this particular agent or editor. Feel free to allude to an author the publisher publishes (or the agent represents) whose work is similar to yours. Doing this is not just name-dropping, but also that proof you've done your research.

Finally, always include an SASE if you're sending your query through the mail.

Formatting Specs

- The basic setup for a query to an agent or publisher is similar to an article query or short story cover letter (see pages 15 and 113).
- Use a standard font, 12-point type. Avoid bold or italic except for titles.
- Use a 1" margin on all sides.
- Use block format (no indentations, an extra space between paragraphs).
- Put your name and contact information at the top of your letter, centered, or in your letterhead.
- Keep the query to one page.
- Single-space the body of the letter and double-space between paragraphs.
- Catalog every item you're sending in your enclosures.

Other Dos and Don'ts

- Do state any previous publishing credits.
- Do tell if you're sending simultaneous submissions to other agents and editors.
- Do address your letter to a specific agent or editor. Call to get the appropriate name and gender.
- Don't fax your query.
- Don't mention that you're a first-time writer or that you've never been published.
- Don't spend much time trying to sell yourself. Your manuscript will stand on its own.
- Don't state that some other agent or editor has rejected your novel.
- Don't ask for advice or criticism—that's not the agent's or editor's job at this stage.
- Do summarize any relevant experience you have.
- Don't mention anything about yourself not pertinent to the novel.
- Don't bring up payment expectations.
- Don't mention copyright information.
- Don't staple your query letter to your manuscript.

ELECTRONIC QUERY LETTER

Submission Tips

Most publishers and agents now accept queries via e-mail. Before you send a query off to a publisher or agent electronically, however, you must either have permission to send it via e-mail or make sure that their guidelines indicate that it is acceptable. Communicating with a publisher or agent via e-mail should be just as formal and respectful as if you were sending it through the mail. The basic tone and format of the electronic query shouldn't be much different from a query sent on paper. Keep your query relatively short. Just because you're communicating via e-mail doesn't allow you to have a long query.

Formatting Specs

- Include the same information you would in a paper query, including your name and contact information. With e-mail queries, it's recommended to put your contact information at the lower left under your signature. Because the window to view the letter on a computer screen is not large, doing this allows the reader to jump right into your query. It isn't necessary to include your e-mail address in the body of the e-mail since the editor can reply easily with the click of a button.
- Put a description of your novel or its title in the subject line.
- Follow the same format you would with a paper query, including the date, salutation to a specific editor, and block paragraph format. See the tips for submitting a paper query on pages 125–126; the same rules apply.

Other Dos and Don'ts

- Don't use all caps or exclamation points in the subject line.
- Don't submit an e-mail query unless specifically requested by the publisher or agent or if it is stated clearly in their guidelines that it is acceptable.
- Don't insert clip art graphics or other images into your query letter.
- Do maintain formal communication, just like you would in a paper query.
- Don't send your query letter as an attachment. Paste it into the e-mail body.

Even though I accept online queries, I still want the query to come in somewhere close to one page. I think that writers often think that because it's online, I have no way of knowing that it's more than a page. Believe me, I do. Queries that are concise and compelling are the most intriguing.

—REGINA BROOKS

literary agent, Serendipity Literary Agency

QUERY LETTER TO AN AGENT: MEMOIR Comments provided by Mollie Glick of Foundry Literary + Media

Dr. Doreen Orion
123 Author Lane
Writerville, CA 95355
(323) 555-0000
janeqwriter@email.com

Contact information

April 5, 2006

Date flushed right

Mollie Glick
Foundry Literary + Media
33 West 17th St. PH
New York, NY 10011

Dear Ms. Glick:

Always address your query to a specific agent.

I am a psychiatrist, published author, and expert for the national media seeking representation for my memoir titled, *Queen of the Road: The True Tale of 49 States, 22,000 Miles, 200 Shoes, 2 Cats, 1 Poodle, a Husband, and a Bus with a Will of Its Own*. Because you are interested in unique voices, I thought we might be a good match.

Books are "titled," not "entitled."

Memoirs are the only kind of nonfiction treated like fiction because they read like novels. Memoirs require a query and synopsis.

When Tim first announced he wanted to "chuck it all" and travel around the country in a converted bus for a year, I gave this profound and potentially life-altering notion all the thoughtful consideration it deserved. "Why can't you be like a normal husband with a midlife crisis and have an affair or buy a Corvette?" I asked, adding, "I will never, ever, EVER live on a bus."

The author has done significant research on agents and chosen one for specific reasons.

1" margin

What do you get when you cram married shrinks—one in a midlife crisis, the other his materialistic, wise-cracking wife—two cats who hate each other and a Standard Poodle who loves licking them all, into a bus for a year? *Queen of the Road* is a memoir of my dysfunctional, multi-species family's travels to and travails in the forty-nine continental states.

Use a quick, catchy hook with an entertaining but professional tone.

A brief overview of the plot

As a psychiatrist, award-winning author (*I Know You Really Love Me*, Macmillan/Dell) and frequent media expert on psychiatric topics (including *Larry King*, *GMA*, *48 Hours*, *The New York Times* and *People* magazine), my life has centered on introspection, analysis, and storytelling. Yet, I count among my greatest accomplishments that last year our bus was featured as the centerfold of *Bus Conversions Magazine*, thus fulfilling my lifelong ambition of becoming a Miss September.

Single-spaced text, block format

Include an author bio that demonstrates your platform and why you're the right author for this project.

I hope you are interested in seeing sample pages. If so, I would be most happy to send them to you via e-mail or regular mail.

Best wishes,

Signature

Dr. Doreen Orion

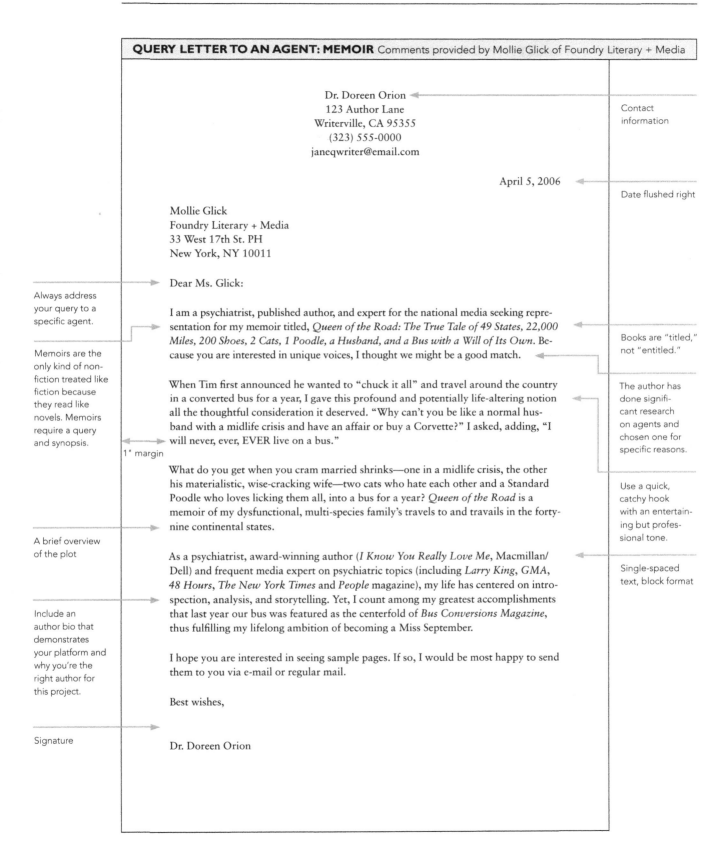

ELECTRONIC QUERY LETTER TO AN AGENT: NOVEL Comments provided by literary agent Jessica Faust

TO: jfaust@email.com
CC: janeqwriter@email.com
SUBJECT: Query – Murder on the Rocks

June 14, 2004

Jessica Faust
BookEnds, LLC
136 Long Hill Rd.
Gillette, NJ 07933

Dear Ms. Faust,

I enjoyed meeting you at the conference in Austin this past weekend. As I mentioned, I have had my eye on BookEnds for quite some time; when I discovered you would be at the conference, I knew I had to attend. We met during the final pitch session and discussed how the series I am working on might fit in with your current line of mystery series. Per your request, I have enclosed a synopsis and first three chapters of *Murder on the Rocks*, an 80,000-word cozy mystery that was a finalist in this year's Writers' League of Texas manuscript contest and includes several bed-and-breakfast recipes.

Natalie Barnes has quit her job, sold her house, and gambled everything she has on the Gray Whale Inn on Cranberry Island, Maine. But she's barely fired up the stove when portly developer Bernard Katz rolls into town and starts mowing through her morning glory muffins. Natalie needs the booking, but Katz is hard to stomach—especially when he unveils his plan to build an oversized golf resort on top of the endangered tern colony next door. When the town board approves the new development. The terns face extinction, and Natalie's Inn might just follow along. Just when Natalie thinks she can't face more trouble, she discovers Katz's body at the base of the cliff and becomes the number one suspect in the police's search for a murderer. If Natalie doesn't find the killer fast, she stands to lose everything—maybe even her life.

I am a former pubic relations writer, a graduate of Rice University, a member of the Writers' League of Texas, and founder of the Austin Mystery Writers critique group. I have spent many summers in fishing communities in Maine and Newfoundland, and escape to Maine as often as possible. The second Gray Whale Inn mystery, *Dead and Berried*, is currently in the computer.

If you would like to see the manuscript, I can send it via e-mail or regular mail. Thank you for your time and attention. I look forward to hearing from you soon.

Sincerely,

Koren Swartz MacInerney
123 Author Lane
Writerville, CA 95355
(323) 555-0000
janeqwriter@email.com

Margin annotations:

Subject line contains the title and that it is a query.

Notes the personal connection and a reason to querying me.

Establishes voice and a feeling for the book.

Karen's credentials are impressive. She's obviously been writing for a while and I really like the addition of her summers in Maine. It's a personal touch, but one that's perfectly related to the book.

In an e-mail query, your contact information should be at the lower left.

The word count is right there with the standards for cozy mysteries. Also, her description fits her genre. All too often submissions name a genre, but the description doesn't match the genre; a romantic comedy, for example, that didn't sound funny, or a thriller that seemed less than thrilling.

You would usually want to pitch only one book, but Karen knew that I liked to handle mystery series, so this worked well in her case.

Polite wrap-up; offers to send more.

QUERY LETTER TO AN AGENT, MISTAKES TO AVOID: NOVEL

123 Author Lane
Writerville, CA 95355

July 24, 2009

Big Time Literary Agency
200 W. Broadway
New York, NY 10125

Dear Agent:

I have just completed my first novel and would like to sell it to a publisher. I have never had a book published but I know this novel will be a bestseller. I'm looking for an agent to help me. I would really appreciate it if you could read over the enclosed chapters and give me some advice on whether you think this a good novel and if it needs any extra work to make it a bestseller.

The Subject of Susan is about 60,000 words long and is geared toward an adult audience. It is all about a headstrong woman named Susan and her trials and tribulations throughout the 1950s and beyond as she makes her way in the legal world after graduating from law school as the only woman in her graduating class.

This is my first novel and while I am not familiar with the legal world, since I'm not a lawyer, I find the subject fascinating and think readers will too. I've written a lot of short stories dealing with women's lives but they were much more romanticized than the story of Susan. Susan is someone you would know in real life. I have spent the last twenty years of my life raising my children and think I have what it takes to become a successful writer.

I own the copyright on this book and would like to discuss possible advances and royalties with you sometime soon.

Thank you very much,

John Q. Writer

Margin notes:

The author's name, phone number, and e-mail are missing. Be sure to include all pertinent contact information.

Always address your query to a specific agent.

Don't ask an agent for advice or criticism—that's not the agent's job nor the purpose of the query letter.

Never mention that you're a first-time writer or that you have never been published—it singles you out as an amateur.

Don't draw attention to your lack of experience as a writer, and don't mention anything about yourself that is not pertinent to the novel. Keep all your information focused on the book itself.

This is vague and tells the agent very little about the book. There is no "hook" to capture the agent's attention.

There is nothing here to indicate how this book will distinguish itself from the thousands of other similar books that have been published.

Don't mention copyright information or payment expectations. This is a query to assess an agent's interest in your novel.

QUERY LETTER TO AN EDITOR: NOVEL

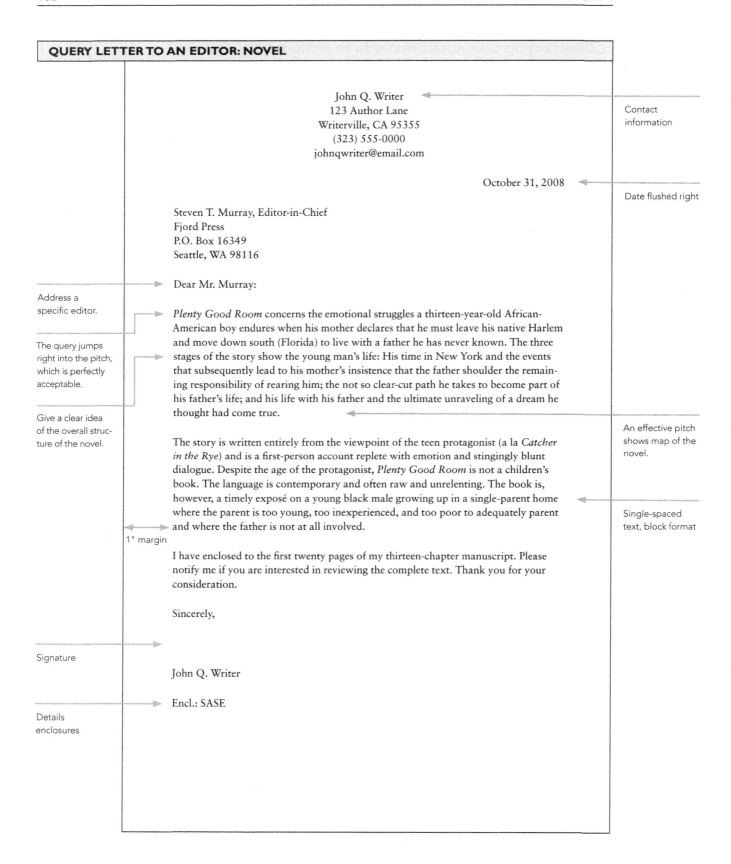

John Q. Writer
123 Author Lane
Writerville, CA 95355
(323) 555-0000
johnqwriter@email.com

October 31, 2008

Steven T. Murray, Editor-in-Chief
Fjord Press
P.O. Box 16349
Seattle, WA 98116

Dear Mr. Murray:

Plenty Good Room concerns the emotional struggles a thirteen-year-old African-American boy endures when his mother declares that he must leave his native Harlem and move down south (Florida) to live with a father he has never known. The three stages of the story show the young man's life: His time in New York and the events that subsequently lead to his mother's insistence that the father shoulder the remaining responsibility of rearing him; the not so clear-cut path he takes to become part of his father's life; and his life with his father and the ultimate unraveling of a dream he thought had come true.

The story is written entirely from the viewpoint of the teen protagonist (a la *Catcher in the Rye*) and is a first-person account replete with emotion and stingingly blunt dialogue. Despite the age of the protagonist, *Plenty Good Room* is not a children's book. The language is contemporary and often raw and unrelenting. The book is, however, a timely exposé on a young black male growing up in a single-parent home where the parent is too young, too inexperienced, and too poor to adequately parent and where the father is not at all involved.

I have enclosed to the first twenty pages of my thirteen-chapter manuscript. Please notify me if you are interested in reviewing the complete text. Thank you for your consideration.

Sincerely,

John Q. Writer

Encl.: SASE

Contact information

Date flushed right

Address a specific editor.

The query jumps right into the pitch, which is perfectly acceptable.

Give a clear idea of the overall structure of the novel.

An effective pitch shows map of the novel.

Single-spaced text, block format

1" margin

Signature

Details enclosures

QUERY LETTER TO AN EDITOR, MISTAKES TO AVOID: NOVEL

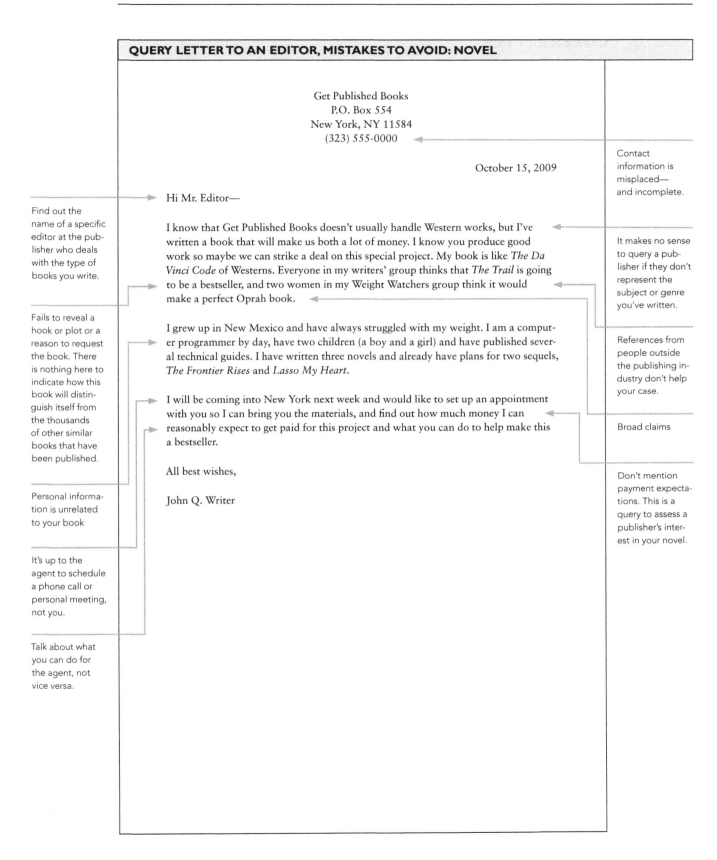

Contact information is misplaced—and incomplete.

Get Published Books
P.O. Box 554
New York, NY 11584
(323) 555-0000

October 15, 2009

Find out the name of a specific editor at the publisher who deals with the type of books you write.

Hi Mr. Editor—

I know that Get Published Books doesn't usually handle Western works, but I've written a book that will make us both a lot of money. I know you produce good work so maybe we can strike a deal on this special project. My book is like *The Da Vinci Code* of Westerns. Everyone in my writers' group thinks that *The Trail* is going to be a bestseller, and two women in my Weight Watchers group think it would make a perfect Oprah book.

It makes no sense to query a publisher if they don't represent the subject or genre you've written.

Fails to reveal a hook or plot or a reason to request the book. There is nothing here to indicate how this book will distinguish itself from the thousands of other similar books that have been published.

I grew up in New Mexico and have always struggled with my weight. I am a computer programmer by day, have two children (a boy and a girl) and have published several technical guides. I have written three novels and already have plans for two sequels, *The Frontier Rises* and *Lasso My Heart*.

References from people outside the publishing industry don't help your case.

I will be coming into New York next week and would like to set up an appointment with you so I can bring you the materials, and find out how much money I can reasonably expect to get paid for this project and what you can do to help make this a bestseller.

Broad claims

All best wishes,

John Q. Writer

Personal information is unrelated to your book

It's up to the agent to schedule a phone call or personal meeting, not you.

Don't mention payment expectations. This is a query to assess a publisher's interest in your novel.

Talk about what you can do for the agent, not vice versa.

COVER LETTER

Submission Tips

A cover letter accompanying a novel package is a tightened version of a query letter.

Like the query, your cover letter lets the editor know who you are and what you have to offer. But, because so much information is included in the rest of the package, and because you should have already queried the agent or editor, the cover letter can be fairly brief.

With a cover letter, there's no need to explain why your book is worthwhile; you just need to introduce the material. Why spend a lot of space synopsizing your novel and telling about yourself when you've included a synopsis, three sample chapters, and an author bio? Of course, you still want to hook the editor or agent, but you don't need to go into as much detail as you would in a blind query letter.

A good rule of thumb is to keep your cover letter to three short paragraphs and organize it in the following order:

- The **introductory paragraph** states the novel's title, then hooks the editor with a brief description of your novel.

- The **biographical paragraph** explains, in one or two sentences, anything about yourself that's pertinent to the novel, such as previous publishing credits, or why you're sending it to this particular agency or publisher.

- The **concluding paragraph** politely closes the letter.

Formatting Specs

- Use a standard font, 12-point type. Avoid bold or italic except for titles.

- Put your name and contact information at the top of the page, centered, or in your letterhead.

- Use a 1" margin on all sides.

- Address the cover letter to a specific editor. Call and get the appropriate editor's name and gender.

- Keep it to one page.

- Use block format.

- Single-space the body of the letter and double-space between paragraphs.

- Catalog every item you're sending in your enclosures.

Other Dos and Don'ts

- Do thank the editor.

- Do provide the novel's word count.

- Do mention whether you're soliciting other agents or editors.

- Do include an SASE or postcard for reply, and state in the letter that you have done so.

- Don't mention that you're a first-time writer, or that you've never been published, or that someone else has rejected your novel.

- Don't start your pitch all over again in the cover letter. If your query made enough of an impression to spark the editor or agent's interest, alluding to his request to see the package is enough. Your novel will stand on its own.

- Don't ask for advice or criticism—that's not the agent's or editor's job at this stage.

- Don't mention anything about yourself that isn't pertinent to the novel.

- Don't bring up payment; it's premature.

- Don't mention copyright information. What you've written is already copyrighted, and you don't need to imply that the editor or agent is out to steal your idea.

- Don't include your social security number.

- Don't staple your cover letter to your novel package. A butterfly or clamp-style paperclip can hold the package elements together, and the cover letter stands alone in front.

- Don't put a page number on the cover letter.

ELECTRONIC COVER LETTER

Submission Tips

If a publisher requests that you submit your book package electronically, don't forget to include the cover letter. Just like a paper cover letter, keep it brief, and stick to the format of an introductory paragraph, a biographical paragraph, and a concluding paragraph. Your cover letter should be pasted inside the e-mail body because it's your initial communication with the agent. Your synopsis and other included materials will be attached, preferably as Microsoft Word files.

Formatting Specs

- Include the same information you would in a paper query, including your name and contact information. The top center position is fine for this, though you can also include this information in a signature line at the end in an e-mail. It isn't necessary to include your e-mail address in the body of the e-mail, however, since the editor can reply easily with the click of a button.

- Put a description of your novel or its title in the subject line.

- Follow the same format you would with a paper query, including the date, salutation to a specific editor, and block paragraph format. See the tips for submitting a paper cover letter on page 134; the same rules apply, with the exception of including an SASE.

Other Dos and Don'ts

- Don't use all caps or exclamations in the subject line.

- Don't submit an e-mail cover letter and package unless specifically requested by the editor.
- Don't insert clip art graphics or other images into your cover letter.
- Do read the Dos and Don'ts listed for a paper cover letter submission on pages 134–135; the same rules apply.

You should send out simultaneous submissions. There is no reason you should be expected to wait on an agent before you send your work to other agents. It's simply not fair. What's the worst that could happen? More than one agent is interested in your work. Call me crazy and unethical, but I am willing to bet this is a problem any writer without representation would welcome.

—PHIL LANG

literary agent, Reece Halsey North

COVER LETTER: NOVEL PACKAGE

John Q. Writer
123 Author Lane
Writerville, CA 95355
(323) 555-0000
johnqwriter@email.com

March 2, 2009

Sam Sertz
A&B Publishing
187 72nd St., 5th Floor
New York, NY 10000

Dear Mr. Sertz:

In my novel, *Officer on the Run*, the town of Little Hills, Ohio, gets a jolt when Police Chief John Murphy's body is found with a bullet between the eyes and deep fingernail scratches down his back. The primary suspects are women, particularly the Chief's seven mistresses (he calls them his "Seven Deadly Sins"). But none of their DNA matches the killer's. Is it possible that the murderer could be none other than the man who's next in line for the Chief's job, Lieutenant Robert Lieberman? It's up to detective David Black to solve the case.

I am a published mystery writer whose short stories have appeared in *Over Your Dead Body* and *A Dime for Crime*. I am also a prosecuting attorney, and I have brought my writing and professional interests together in *Officer on the Run*. The novel weighs in at 70,000 words.

I think it will fit quite well with your successful series by Patty Smith and your current bestseller *The CIA Murders* by Terry Clark, both of which point to the continued popularity of detective novels.

Thank you for considering *Officer on the Run*. I look forward to hearing from you.

Sincerely,

John Q. Writer

Encl.: Contents page
Chapters 1, 2, 3
Synopsis
SASE

Annotations (margin notes):

Addressed to a specific editor—likely the same individual who responded to the initial query and requested the complete package.

Introductory paragraph states the novel's title, sets the hook (grabber), and reels the editor in.

Word count

1" margin

Politely close the letter.

Signature

Catalogs every item being sent in the novel package (including an SASE).

Contact information. You don't need to include your e-mail address here if you are sending your cover letter via e-mail.

Date flushed right

Single-spaced text, block format

State publishing credits and pertinent professional background.

Mention the intended audience and why the book will fit in well on this publisher's list.

I do pretty much all of my business online, and that includes scouting for clients, offering representation, e-mailing back and forth with authors, submitting to editors, doing market research, and more. I do find a lot of clients online. I read pop culture and industry blogs to stay updated on current trends. I read *The New York Times* online. And when I'm browsing, I bookmark reviews, articles, and blogs from new authors I love.

—BRANDI BOWLES

literary agent, Horward Morhaim Literary Agency

COVER PAGE

Submission Tips

The cover page includes the title, an estimated word count, and either your contact information (if you're submitting directly to an editor) or your agent's contact information (if you're submitting through an agent).

Formatting Specs

- If you're using an agent, put the agent's contact information in the bottom right corner and don't put your name and address on the cover. If you're submitting to an editor, put your contact information in place of an agent's.
- Put an estimated word count (for the entire book, not for the package) in the top right corner.
- Center the title, subtitle, and author's name in the middle of the page.
- Put the title in all capital letters and the subtitle in upper- and lowercase. If you want to use bold for the title and italics for the subtitle, that's fine, too.

Other Dos and Don'ts

- Don't include both your contact information and the agent's. Use one or the other, depending on the situation.
- Don't use a header or number the cover page.
- Don't fax or e-mail your package to a publisher or agent unless they specifically request it.

COVER PAGE: NOVEL PACKAGE

Always include the novel's word count.

70,000 words

OFFICER ON THE RUN
A Novel

by
John Q. Writer

Center the title in the middle of the page.

Author's contact information at the lower right if the package is going to an agent. Use the agent's contact information if the package is going to an editor.

John Q. Writer
123 Author Lane
Writerville, CA 95355
(323) 555-0000
johnqwriter@email.com

SYNOPSIS

Submission Tips

The synopsis supplies key information about your novel (plot, theme, characterization, setting), while also showing how these coalesce to form the big picture. Quickly tell what your novel is about without making the editor or agent read the novel in its entirety.

There are no hard and fast rules about the synopsis. In fact, there's conflicting advice about the typical length of a synopsis. Most editors and agents agree, though: The shorter, the better.

When writing your synopsis, focus on the essential parts of your story, and try not to include sections of dialogue unless you think they are absolutely necessary. (It is okay to inject a few strong quotes from your characters, but keep them brief.) Finally, even though the synopsis is only a condensed version of your novel, it must seem complete.

Keep events in the same order as they happen in the novel (but don't break them down into individual chapters). Remember that your synopsis should have a beginning, a middle, and an ending (yes, you must tell how the novel ends to round out your synopsis).

That's what's required of a synopsis: You need to be concise, compelling, and complete at the same time.

THE SHORT SYNOPSIS VS. THE LONG SYNOPSIS

Since there is no definitive length to a synopsis, it's recommended you have two versions: a long synopsis and a short synopsis.

In past years, there used to be a fairly universal system regarding synopses. For every 35 or so pages of text you had, you would have one page of synopsis explanation. So, if your book was 245 pages, double-spaced, your synopsis would be approximately seven pages. This was fairly standard, and allowed writers a decent amount of space to explain their story. Write this first. This will be your long synopsis.

The problem is that sometime in the past few years, agents started to get really busy and they want to hear your story now-now-now. They started asking for synopses of no more than two pages. Many agents today request specifically just that—two pages max. Some may even say one page, but two pages is generally acceptable. You have to draft a new, more concise synopsis—the short synopsis.

So, which do you submit? If you think your short synopsis (one to two pages) is tight and effective, always use that. However, if you think the long synopsis is much more effective, then you will sometimes submit one and sometimes submit the other. If an agent requests two pages max, send only the short one. If she says simply, "Send a synopsis," and you feel your longer synopsis is superior and your long synopsis isn't more than eight pages, submit the long one. If you're writing plot-heavy fiction, such as thrillers and mysteries, you might really benefit from writing a longer synopsis.

Your best bet on knowing how long to make your synopsis is to follow the guidelines in the agency or publisher's listing.

Formatting Specs

- Use a 1" margin on all sides.

- Justify the left margin only.

- Put your name and contact information on the top left corner of the first page.

- Type the novel's genre and word count, and then the word "Synopsis" on the top right corner of the first page.

- Do not number the first page (but it is considered page one).

- Put the novel's title, centered and in all caps, about one-third of the way down the page.

- Drop four lines below the title and begin the text of the synopsis.

- The text throughout the synopsis should be double-spaced (unless you intend to keep your synopsis to one or two pages, then single-spaced is okay).

- Use all caps the first time you introduce a character.

- After the first page, use a header on every page. The header contains your last name, slash, your novel's title in all capital letters, slash, the word "Synopsis": Name/TITLE/Synopsis.

- Also after the first page, put the page number in the top right corner of every consecutive page, on the same line as the header. You can include this in the header.

- The first line of text on each page after the first page should be three lines below the header.

Other Dos and Don'ts

- Do keep in mind that this is a sales pitch. Make it a short, fast, exciting read.

- Do establish a hook at the beginning of the synopsis. Introduce your lead character and set up a key conflict.

- Do introduce your most important character first.

- Do provide details about your central character (age, gender, marital status, profession, etc.), but don't do this for every character, only the primary ones.

- Do include the characters' motivations and emotions.

- Do highlight pivotal plot points and reveal the novel's ending.

- Don't go into detail about what happens; just tell what happens.

- Don't inject long sections of dialogue into your synopsis.

- Do write in the third person, present tense, even if your novel is in the first person.

ELECTRONIC SYNOPSIS

Submission Tips

Some editors or agents might ask you to submit your synopsis via e-mail or on a disk or CD. The editor or agent can provide you with specific formatting guidelines indicating how she wants the outline sent and the type of files she prefers.

Formatting Specs

- Follow the same formatting specs as for a paper synopsis submission (see page 140).
- When sending your synopsis via e-mail, put the name of your novel in the subject line.
- Send the synopsis as an attachment to your e-mail unless the editor or agent requests otherwise.
- Include your cover letter in the body of your e-mail and your cover page and table of contents in the file along with the synopsis.

With a synopsis, do not intrude in the narrative flow with authorial commentary, and do not let the underlying story framework show. Don't use headings such as "Setting" or phrases like "At the climax of the conflict..." or "The next chapter begins with..." In short, do not let it read like a nonfiction outline.

—IAN BESSLER
former Writer's Digest Books editor

Other Dos and Don'ts

- Don't use all caps in your subject line.
- Don't submit a synopsis electronically unless the editor or agent requests it.
- Don't justify text or align the right margin.

SYNOPSIS, PAGE 1: NOVEL PACKAGE

Contact information on the top left corner of first page

John Q. Writer
123 Author Lane
Writerville, CA 95355
(323) 555-0000
johnqwriter@email.com

Mystery
70,000 words

Novel's genre and word length

Do not number the first page.

OFFICER ON THE RUN
Synopsis

Title is centered and in all caps.

Use all caps the first time a character is introduced.

Investigative officer DAVID BLACK doesn't know where to begin when he gets word Police Chief JOHN MURPHY is found dead on his bed—with a silver bullet between his eyes and half-inch nail marks running down his back. Black has to answer two questions: Who would kill the Chief, and why?

Establish a good hook, introduce important characters, and set up a key conflict

It turns out quite a few people aren't too pleased with the Chief. He'd been on the force for twenty-three years and no doubt made some enemies. All the townspeople called him Bulldog because he looked like a pit bull, and certainly acted like one.

Double-spaced text

Countless stories passed through City Hall about how the Chief wouldn't hesitate to roll up his cuffs and beat suspects into submission until they would confess to a crime. That was his method and it worked. He could take control of any person and any situation.

1" margin

Except his wife and his marriage. On that front, the Chief was completely out of control. He'd lost all affection for his wife, MARY, who was once the apple of his eye but now weighs in at 260 lbs. That was fine with the Chief—the less he had to see Mary, the more time for his own pursuits. But he really had only one pursuit: younger women. That fact he didn't hide. He'd often brag to guys on the force about being the only Chief in the history of law enforcement to "burn through seven dispatchers in just as many years." He even called them his "Seven Deadly Sins." Little did he know that one day they'd all be suspects for his murder.

Justify left margin only.

SYNOPSIS, PAGE 2: NOVEL PACKAGE

Writer/OFFICER ON THE RUN/Synopsis   2

Black interviews all seven women and finds no leads until MARLENE PRES-TON, the Chief's "Seventh Deadly Sin," reveals how the Chief repeatedly would handcuff her arms and legs to four metal poles under the bleachers at the school football stadium. Marlene says she's never told anyone about any of it. Black then interrogates the six other "sins" to see if they had also been physically mistreated. They all say the Chief never tried anything like that with them.

Black drinks himself into a stupor and pours out his problems to a young barmaid, SARAH, who just happens to be the best friend of the Police Lieutenant's daughter, KELLY LIEBERMAN. Sarah tells Black the Chief deserved to die and that he was a jerk, especially to Kelly when she'd baby-sit for the Chief and his wife. According to Sarah, the Chief used to talk dirty to Kelly and then warn her not to tell her father because LIEUTENANT LIEBERMAN was in line for a promotion.

Black interviews Kelly. She denies the Chief did anything but make a few lewd comments on occasion. When Black approaches Kelly's father, Lieutenant Lieberman says Kelly never mentioned a word about the Chief. Black returns to talk with Kelly and asks why she's never mentioned anything to her father. She says she's afraid he'd get upset at her for bringing it up. Black presses further, asking Kelly if the Chief ever did anything other than verbally harass her. Kelly says no.

Black decides to walk back under the bleachers to the spot where Marlene says the Chief repeatedly handcuffed her. There, he notices two sneaker shoestrings on the ground by the four poles Marlene pointed out. The strings had been tied in knots and then cut. Black shows the strings to Marlene and asks if the Chief ever tied her to the poles with them. "Not once," she says. "Handcuffs every time."

Header includes your name, the title, the word "Synopsis," and the page number.

Text begins three lines below the header.

In a long synopsis, a new scene or twist begins with the start of a new paragraph. There is not enough room to do this in a short synopsis.

Synopsis should be in third person, present tense.

Paragraphs are short and fast reads, mentioning only the essentials of the story.

SYNOPSIS, MISTAKES TO AVOID: NOVEL PACKAGE

John Q. Writer
123 Author Lane
Writerville, USA 95355

The genre of the novel is not mentioned here, nor is the word length. These elements should be included in the synopsis.

Phone number and e-mail address are missing.

Officer on the Run

The title of the book should be in all caps, or at least bold and italicized.

Investigative officer David Black doesn't know where to begin when he gets word Police Chief John Murphy is found dead on his bed—with a silver bullet between his eyes and half-inch nail marks running down his back. Black has to answer two questions: Who would kill the Chief, and why?

The text should be double-spaced.

The first time a character is introduced, the name should be in all caps.

It turns out quite a few people aren't too pleased with the Chief. He's been on the force for twenty-three years and no doubt made some enemies. On the home front, the Chief was completely out of control. He'd lost all affection for his wife, Mary, who was once the apple of his eye.

A shorter synopsis is preferable, but this is too short and doesn't give enough information about the characters or the plot to make it compelling.

Black interviews all of the women that the Chief had affairs with, whom he called his "Seven Deadly Sins," and finds no leads until Marlene Preston, the Chief's seventh "sin." She reveals how the Chief repeatedly would handcuff her arms and legs to four metal poles under the bleachers at the school football stadium. Black drinks himself into a stupor and pours out his problems to a young barmaid, who tells him that the Chief deserved to die.

Pivotal plot points are glossed over—they should be highlighted.

Black continues investigating the Chief and uncovers all kinds of sordid details. The killer is revealed at the end, and it is a total shock and surprise to all, especially Black.

Be sure to reveal your novel's ending.

The characters' motivations and emotions aren't conveyed at all in this synopsis, leaving the editor or agent to think, "Why should I care about these characters?"

OUTLINE

Submission Tips

An outline is often used interchangeably with a synopsis, but for most editors and agents, there is a distinction. Whereas a synopsis is a brief, encapsulated version of the novel at large, an outline makes each chapter its own story, usually containing a few paragraphs per chapter. In short, an outline is a breakdown of the novel with a synopsis of each individually chapter.

Never submit an outline unless an agent or editor specifically asks for it. Fewer and fewer agents and editors want outlines these days. Most just request a cover letter, a few sample chapters, and a short synopsis or sometimes the entire manuscript. However, it's still something you will probably have to write sometime. Genre fiction editors often request outlines because genre books run for many pages and have numerous plot shifts (see more on genres in chapter six).

Formatting Specs

- Use a 1" margin on all sides.
- Justify the left margin only.
- At the top left of every page, use a header with your last name, slash, your novel's title in all capital letters, slash, the word "Outline": Name/TITLE/Outline.
- Put the page number in the top right corner of every page. This can be part of your header.
- Drop four lines below the header, then put the words "Chapter-by-Chapter Outline" centered and bold or underlined.
- Drop four more lines and type the chapter number (Chapter 3).
- Drop two lines and put the chapter's title (if applicable) on the left margin and the number of manuscript pages that chapter runs on the right margin.
- Drop two lines and begin the text of the outline.
- Double-space the text throughout the outline.
- Use all caps the first time you introduce a character.
- Use a separate page for each chapter.

Other Dos and Don'ts

- Do keep in mind that your outline is an extended, more detailed, and structural version of your synopsis.
- Do explain the gist of each chapter.
- Do highlight pivotal plot points.
- Do provide a hook for each chapter.
- Do reveal how the chapter begins and ends.
- Do make sure each succeeding chapter picks up where the previous chapter left off.
- Don't include extended dialogue.

If your query letter is more than one page long, there are things in there that are superfluous. The most common unnecessary addition is a description of the writer's family/personal life, if the book is not a memoir. Some personal background is good, but I would much prefer to know about the amazing novel you wrote.

—ABIGAIL KOONS

literary agent, The Park Literary Group

ELECTRONIC OUTLINE

Submission Tips

Some editors or agents might ask you to submit your outline via e-mail or on a disk or CD. The editor or agent can provide you with specific formatting guidelines indicating how he wants the outline sent and the type of files he prefers.

Formatting Specs

- Follow the same formatting specs as for a paper outline submission (see page 146).
- When e-mailing your outline, put the name of your book in the subject line.
- Send the outline as an attachment to your e-mail unless the editor or agent requests otherwise.
- Include your cover letter in the body of your e-mail and your cover page and table of contents in the file along with the outline.

Other Dos and Don'ts

- Don't use all caps in your subject line.
- Don't submit an outline electronically unless the editor or agent specifically requests it.

OUTLINE: NOVEL PACKAGE

Header includes your name, the title, the word "Outline," and the page number.

Writer/OFFICER ON THE RUN/Outline   3

CHAPTER-BY-CHAPTER OUTLINE

Indicate that this page is part of the chapter-by-chapter outline.

Chapter number

Chapter 3

Chapter's title and number of pages it runs

Under the Bleachers at Campbell Field   14 pages

Justify left margin only.

Marlene takes Detective Black to a dark, concealed spot under the bleachers at the school football field, the same spot where the Chief used to take her. Marlene tells Black it was here that the Chief first came on to her, eventually handcuffed her, and threatened her to keep silent (which she did). Sure, everyone suspected they were having an affair, but nobody had a clue that it was entirely against her wishes.

Reveal how the chapter begins.

Explain the gist of the chapter and highlights pivotal moments.

Double-spaced text

This all comes as a surprise to Black, who just assumed all the Chief's affairs were mutual. Black presses Marlene to tell him everything. She does. She even shows him where the chief would handcuff her arms and legs to the poles. About six inches from the ground around all four poles were rings showing where the paint chipped from the handcuffs grinding against them.

1" margin

Dismayed, Black asks Marlene if she's ever told anyone else about this. She says, "Not a soul." Black wonders, could there be more?

Reveal how the chapter ends.

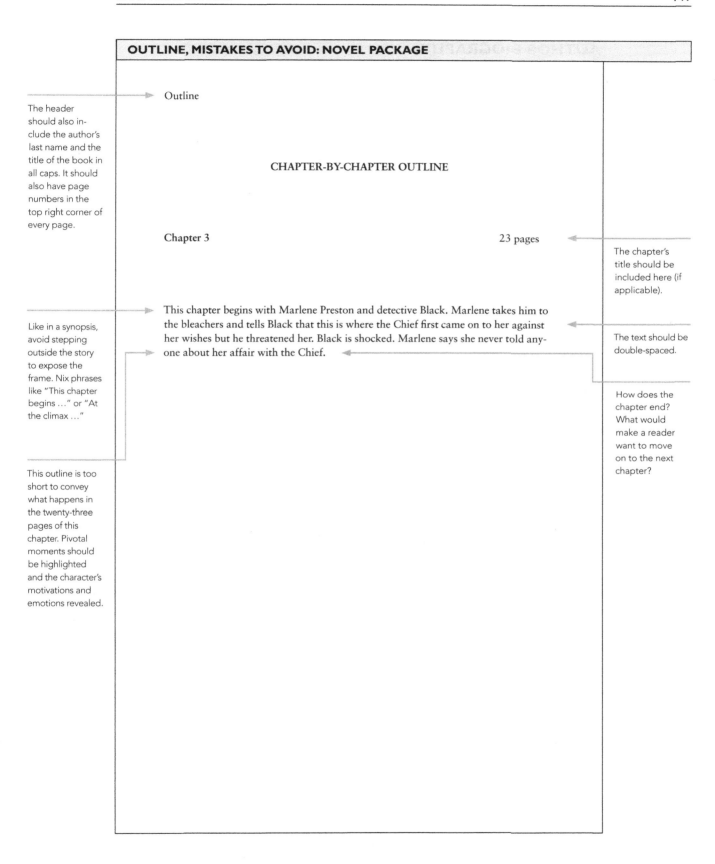

OUTLINE, MISTAKES TO AVOID: NOVEL PACKAGE

Outline

The header should also include the author's last name and the title of the book in all caps. It should also have page numbers in the top right corner of every page.

CHAPTER-BY-CHAPTER OUTLINE

Chapter 3   23 pages

The chapter's title should be included here (if applicable).

Like in a synopsis, avoid stepping outside the story to expose the frame. Nix phrases like "This chapter begins ..." or "At the climax ..."

This chapter begins with Marlene Preston and detective Black. Marlene takes him to the bleachers and tells Black that this is where the Chief first came on to her against her wishes but he threatened her. Black is shocked. Marlene says she never told anyone about her affair with the Chief.

The text should be double-spaced.

How does the chapter end? What would make a reader want to move on to the next chapter?

This outline is too short to convey what happens in the twenty-three pages of this chapter. Pivotal moments should be highlighted and the character's motivations and emotions revealed.

AUTHOR BIOGRAPHY

Submission Tips

Your author bio is about you, but only in the context of what makes you the perfect person to tell this story. Don't include any information that doesn't directly help the pitch. You may include educational information if you have an advanced degree, and your profession if it's pertinent to the novel. It's OK to say where you live and to whom you're married, but unless there's something strikingly unusual about your family, don't mention them. Definitely include any previous publishing credits. Keep your bio less than a page.

Formatting Specs

- Use a header with your last name, slash, the novel's title in all caps, slash, the words "Author Biography": Name/TITLE/Author Biography.
- Double-space the text.
- Write in the third person, present tense.
- Keep it to one page. Standard length is 200–250 words.

Other Dos and Don'ts

- Don't mention your membership in any writer's organizations, unless it can help promote your novel (e.g., if you write a mystery, tell that you belong to the Mystery Writers of America).
- Do mention any publicity or promotion you've received, such as appearances on national TV or radio programs, or interviews in national magazines.
- Don't mention any "minor" publishing credits unrelated to your novel (e.g., that you had two poems published in your local paper).
- Don't spend too much time complimenting yourself.
- Do stick to the facts (don't exaggerate or lie).
- Don't include an author bio if you're a beginning writer with no publishing credits, and don't have much to say regarding qualifications or credentials.
- Do have separate bios if you're collaborating with another author, but make sure both bios fit on the same page.

AUTHOR BIOGRAPHY: NOVEL PACKAGE

Header

Writer/OFFICER ON THE RUN/Author Biography

About the Author

Reveal information that's pertinent to the novel.

John Q. Writer has been a prosecuting attorney for Big Lake County, Pennsylvania,

since 1985. He garnered regional media attention during the late 1990s by winning

Double-spaced text

the case that put all-star Pittsburgh Steelers quarterback Warren St. Christofer in

prison for sexually harassing his sports agent.

Mr. Writer's writing credits include stories published in mystery magazines *Over*

1" margin

Your Dead Body and *A Dime for a Crime*, as well as numerous articles in law-

Mention previously published material.

enforcement trade journals, such as *Police Time*, *By the Book*, *Today's Attorney*, and

Beneath the Badge.

He received his B.A. in Comparative Literature from Kent State University and

Write in the third person.

his law degree from Case Western Reserve. Mr. Writer lives with his wife and three

children in Allentown, Pennsylvania. This is his first novel.

Briefly tell a bit about yourself.

Keep the word count between 40 and 400 words.

ENDORSEMENTS PAGE

Submission Tips

An endorsements page is like a dishwasher—it's not essential, but it helps to have one. Putting the page together is simple because it's nothing more than a list of quotes. The trick, however, is that these quotes must come from noteworthy people, typically prominent industry insiders (well-known authors, agents, editors, experts on the topic) who have read your manuscript and have decided to comment favorably on it. Forget about including what your husband or neighbor or writing group said about your novel. While their words of praise matter to you, they don't matter to an agent or publisher—such opinions won't help sell your novel.

Unless you have contacts, it is difficult to obtain a quote from someone noteworthy.

It's best not to include an endorsements page unless you have at least two good quotes from well-known, well-respected sources. Don't fret if you don't have an endorsements page—very few authors include one with fiction manuscripts. Most endorsements will come once the galleys go out to reviewers.

Formatting Specs

- Use a header with your last name, slash, your novel's title in all caps, slash, the word "Endorsements": Name/TITLE/Endorsements.

- Single-space the text within each quote.

- Triple-space between quotes.

- Attribute the quotes. Double-check for correct spelling of names and titles.

- Keep each endorsement short (fifty words or less).

Other Dos and Don'ts

- Don't worry too much about obtaining endorsements; fiction manuscripts stand on their own.

- Don't expect a response if you send your manuscript to some prominent person you don't know. (Certainly don't wait more than a few weeks for a response.)

- Do get the source's permission to include the endorsement.

- Do send a thank-you note if someone provides a laudatory quote.

ENDORSEMENTS: NOVEL PACKAGE

Writer/OFFICER ON THE RUN/Endorsements   84

Header

Advance praise for *Officer on the Run:*

Tell what this
page contains.

"Writer transfers the realities of an investigation from the street to the page better
than any writer I've read."

Single-spaced
text within
each quote

—Sgt. Martin Yadd, Cincinnati Police Department

Keep each
endorsement
short (fifty words
or fewer).

"Stunning!"

—*The New York Times*

Attribute the
quotes and get
them from repu-
table sources.

NOVEL MANUSCRIPT

Your novel manuscript is easy to format and submit. What's most important is that you know when and what to submit. Never send an entire manuscript until you've been requested to do so. Unsolicited manuscripts are often ignored and returned (and sometimes even recycled or thrown away) when sent to an agent or publisher who does not accept them. Don't waste your time, energy, paper, and postage; check the particular agent or publisher's requirements to see if unsolicited manuscripts are accepted.

Submission Tips

When a request for your manuscript does come, you'll need to know precisely what to send and how to organize it.

Package

If an agent or editor wants to consider representing or publishing your manuscript, here's what to send:

- Cover letter
- Title or cover page
- Table of contents
- Chapters
- SASE or postcard reply (regular mail submissions only)

Optional Front Matter:
- Author biography (see page 150)
- Endorsements page (see page 152)
- Epigraph (see page 171)

Accepted Package

If a publisher agrees to publish your novel, submit:

- Cover letter
- Title or cover page
- Table of contents
- Chapters
- SASE or postcard reply (regular mail submissions only)

Optional Front Matter:
- Acknowledgments (see page 165)
- Author biography (see page 150)
- Dedication page (see page 169)
- Endorsements page (see page 152)

- Foreword (see page 173)
- Preface (see page 175)

MANUSCRIPT PAGES

Formatting Specs

- Use a 1" margin on all sides.
- Use a title page, set up the same as the title page in your package (see page 159).
- Don't number the title page. Begin numbering with the first page of the text of the book, usually the introduction, prologue, or chapter one.
- Use a header on each page, including your name, the title of your novel in all caps, and the page number.
- Start each new chapter on its own page, one-third of the way down the page.
- The chapter number and chapter title should be in all caps, separated by two hyphens: CHAPTER 1--THE BODY.
- Begin the body of the chapter four to six lines below the chapter title.
- Indent five spaces for each new paragraph.
- Double-space the entire text.
- Use a standard font, 12-point type. Times New Roman, Arial, or Courier is fine.
- Use 20-lb. bond paper.

Other Dos and Don'ts

- Don't staple anything.
- Don't punch holes in the pages or submit it in a three-ring binder.
- Don't number the page or use a header on the title or cover page.
- Don't justify or align the right margin.
- Don't put any copyright information on the manuscript. It's copyrighted when you write it, and the editor or agent knows this.
- Do find out what file format the editor or agent prefers if they request that you send the manuscript on a disk or CD.

ELECTRONIC NOVEL MANUSCRIPT

Submission Tips

If an editor or agent is interested in your novel package, they might ask you to submit your manuscript via e-mail or on a disk or CD. The editor or agent can provide you with specific formatting guidelines indicating how she wants the manuscript sent and the type of files she prefers.

Formatting Specs

- Follow the same formatting specs as for a paper manuscript submission (see page 154).
- When sending your manuscript via e-mail, put the name of your book in the subject line.
- Include your cover letter in the body of your e-mail.
- When formatting the manuscript, don't put two spaces after sentences, and don't double-space by using hard returns.

Other Dos and Don'ts

- Don't use all caps in your subject line.
- Don't submit a manuscript electronically unless the editor specifically requests it.
- Do ask for specific file format guidelines to make sure the editor can open your files.
- Don't justify text or align the right margin.
- Don't put any copyright information on the manuscript. It's copyrighted when you write it, and the editor is aware of this.
- Do call after you've sent a file to make sure the editor has received it.

COVER LETTER

Submission Tips

A cover letter accompanying a finished novel is brief. All you must do is let the editor know what's enclosed and how to contact you. Be cordial and feel free to thank the editor for working with you on the project, but don't go into great lengths about the novel or anything else. At this point in the game your editor is focused on one thing: grabbing your novel and reading it in its entirety. So get to the point in your cover letter and let the editor proceed at will.

Formatting Specs

- Use a standard font, 12-point type. Avoid bold or italics unless called for.
- Put your name and contact information in the top right corner.
- Use a 1" margin on all sides.
- Keep it to one page. A short paragraph will be fine.
- Use block format (no indentations, an extra space between paragraphs).
- Single-space the body of the letter and double-space between paragraphs.
- Catalog every item you're sending in your enclosures (manuscript, reply postcard, etc.)

Professionalism is just as important as being a good writer. When agents decide to represent writers' work, they are also representing the writers. Also, don't lose focus on the purpose of writing. The purpose needs to be the love of writing, the expression and the art, so that the best writing can come forth. Keep this in mind, and then think about the goal of publishing. When submitting work to an agent, make sure that you are sending a finished product that has been edited and proofread.

—VERNA DREISBACH

literary agent, Dreisbach Literary Agency

Other Dos and Don'ts

- Do address the cover letter to the editor who requested it.
- Do thank the editor.
- Do tell the novel's exact word count
- Do include a postcard for reply, and state in the letter that you have done so (but you'll probably already have a phone relationship with the editor at this point).
- Don't tell how much time you've spent on the novel.
- Don't bring up payment.
- Don't staple your cover letter to your novel.
- Don't put a page number on the cover letter.

COVER LETTER: NOVEL

Simple return address with phone and e-mail

John Q. Writer
123 Author Lane
Writerville, CA 95355
(323) 555-0000
johnqwriter@email.com

September 28, 2009

Date flushed right

Sam Sertz
A&B Publishing
187 Seventy-second St., 5th Floor
New York, NY 10000

Address a specific editor.

Dear Sam Sertz:

Enclosed is the manuscript for *Officer on the Run*.

1" margin

Also enclosed is a self-addressed, stamped postcard. Would you please indicate that you received this material in good condition and return the postcard to me? Feel free to call or e-mail me as well if either of these modes of communication is more convenient for you.

Single-spaced text

Brief and to the point

Politely close the letter.

I look forward to hearing from you.

Sincerely,

Signature

John Q. Writer

Encl.: Manuscript, *Officer on the Run*
SASE

Catalog every item being sent with the manuscript submission package (omit the SASE if you're sending the manuscript via e-mail).

Give agents exactly what they ask for. If they ask for a one-page synopsis, don't give them a page and a half. If they ask for the submission to be sent as a Microsoft Word attachment, don't send a submission in the body of the e-mail.

—PHIL LANG

literary agent, Reece Halsey North

TITLE PAGE

Submission Tips

The title page includes the title, an estimated word count, and either your name and contact information (if you're submitting directly to an editor) or your agent's name and contact information (if you're submitting through an agent).

Formatting Specs

- Put the word count in the top right corner of the page.
- Center the title of your novel, in bold and in all caps, halfway down the page.
- Drop a line, then type "A Novel" or "A Memoir" (without quotation marks).
- Drop another line, then type your name (if your novel is written with another person, use an ampersand between your names).
- In the lower right corner, put your name and contact information, single-spaced, in regular text (not all caps).
- If you have an agent, put the agent's name and contact information in the lower right corner instead and put your name and contact information in the top left corner.

Other Dos and Don'ts

- Don't use a header or number the title page.
- Don't e-mail your manuscripts to a publisher or agent unless she specifically requests it.

TITLE PAGE: NOVEL

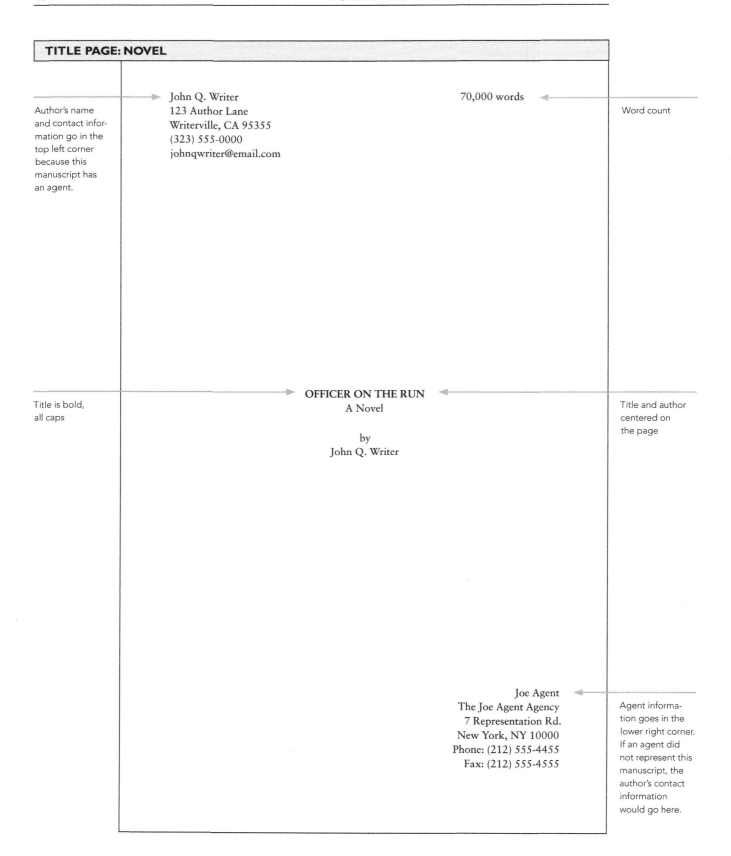

Author's name and contact information go in the top left corner because this manuscript has an agent.

John Q. Writer
123 Author Lane
Writerville, CA 95355
(323) 555-0000
johnqwriter@email.com

70,000 words

Word count

Title is bold, all caps

OFFICER ON THE RUN
A Novel

by
John Q. Writer

Title and author centered on the page

Joe Agent
The Joe Agent Agency
7 Representation Rd.
New York, NY 10000
Phone: (212) 555-4455
Fax: (212) 555-4555

Agent information goes in the lower right corner. If an agent did not represent this manuscript, the author's contact information would go here.

MANUSCRIPT, PAGE 1: NOVEL

Writer/OFFICER ON THE RUN   1

CHAPTER 1--THE BODY

Chapter number and chapter title in all caps, separated by two hyphens, one-third of the way down the page

Justify left margin only.

Marlene Preston walked like a freak but sang like a bird. With aspirations to become a star, she sang in a band on weekends but was a nightshift dispatcher during the week. She was the Chief's latest affair, his Seventh Deadly Sin. He would joke about her with the other officers and refer to her as Lucky No. 7. To her face he only called her Lucky. She never figured out why. She just wanted him to call her Marlene.

Indent five spaces for each new paragraph.

Marlene grabbed the Chief's attention her second day on the job, when she arrived at work after a rare midweek gig. Because the band played until 11:30 and she had to start her shift at midnight, Marlene didn't have time to change into suitable work clothes. To everyone's surprise, she showed up at the station in skin-hugging black leather tights, six-inch silver pumps and a white halter top. Her long, dark, untamed hair wrapped around her shoulders, and her perfume smelled like a rose. Marlene Preston blazed a trail of lust.

1" margin

Every officer on the force was checking out Marlene. That was for her one of the perks of the job—being the only woman in the company of men. She loved the attention, especially from the Chief. He was, after all, The Man—the guy all the other officers aspired to be. Marlene was flattered by his flirtations. She knew she was looking good, and it pleased her that the Chief noticed. And notice he did.

Double-spaced text

MANUSCRIPT, PAGE 2: NOVEL

Writer/OFFICER ON THE RUN   2

Header with
the novel's title
in all caps

At 12:50, a call came in about a robbery. Two guys held up a 24-hour conve-

nience store and shot a clerk in the shoulder. The Chief immediately directed all four

officers on duty to hit the streets, two at the crime scene and two to find the getaway

car. As soon as the station cleared, the Chief was alone with Marlene. And he let her

know he liked that.

"So, Marlene, this is your first major dispatch, isn't it?"

"Well, yeah."

"You handled that call really well, Marlene. Like a pro."

"Thanks."

"But then again you look like you could handle just about anything. You're

so calm."

"Thanks."

"You gotta admit it's kind of exciting, isn't it?"

"Yeah. But it's really sad somebody would go and shoot a poor clerk just for

some cash register change."

"People do crazy things for personal gain, Marlene. Stay on this job and it won't

take you long to figure that out."

"I guess not. I mean it's only my second day and already a robbery. What's next?"

"Oh, who knows. Maybe it could be something really exhilarating . . . like a

murder. Like maybe an angry wife murdered her husband because he was having an

affair with a colleague. Now that sounds fun."

The Chief then walked out the door and left Marlene to ponder such a scenario.

She was nervous. What did he mean by that? Marlene thought about that for a while

but decided she was probably just reading too much into it. Everyone knew the Chief

was a happily married man, a father of two lovely children and well respected in the

community. Surely she must have misunderstood.

Start each change
of dialogue on a
new line, with a
five-space para-
graph indent.

White space
on a page is a
good thing.

Mistakes in grammar, spelling, word usage, or sentence structure—anything like that is going to put me right off. Also, I dislike it when authors don't say what the book is about right away. I am only able to spend a minute at most reading your query letter—tell me exactly what I should know immediately because I may not read all the way to the end.

—ELLEN PEPUS

literary agent, Signature Literary Agency

REPLY POSTCARD

If you're a bit worried about whether your novel actually makes it to the publisher, enclose a reply postcard to be signed by the editor (or someone on the staff) and sent back to you. Two caveats: (1) Not all editors are gracious enough to send your reply postcards back, but most are. (2) Just because you receive a postcard reply from an editor, you cannot assume your novel has been read or will be read in the next few days or even weeks. The only function of your reply postcard is to let you know your package has been received.

Your best bet to ensure an editor will return your reply postcard is to make it neat and simple to use. That means typing your postcard and not asking the editor to do anything other than note your submission has been received. Although it's okay to leave a small space for "Comments," keep the space small and don't expect it to be filled in—most editors don't have the time or a reason to write anything in it. You'll turn off an editor if you ask him to do too much.

Follow the example here to create a suitable and functional reply postcard. Remember to keep things short and sweet—and, of course, always supply the postage.

REPLY POSTCARD: NOVEL

Front of card:

John Q. Writer
123 Author Lane
Writerville, CA 95355

Back of card (query):

John Q. Writer, 123 Author Lane, Writerville, CA 95355, (323) 555-0000
Date: _____
Your novel *Officer on the Run* was received in my office on:

_____

Other comments:_____
_____
Company _____

Fill in the company name before mailing out the reply postcard so that you will know who's sending what to you.

ACKNOWLEDGMENTS PAGE

Submission Tips

The acknowledgments page, which is optional, is the place where you spend time thanking everybody who helped you throughout the process of writing the book. Most people thanked in an acknowledgments page are friends who gave you ideas and offered criticisms, family and friends who supported you, an institution that awarded you a grant or sabbatical, and, of course, your agents and editors. Sometimes, what would normally go into an acknowledgments page ends up in a preface.

Formatting Specs

- Put the acknowledgments page on its own page.
- Do not number the page. Use a header and double-space the text.
- Be sure to drop about one-third of the way down the page and use a centered heading that says, "Acknowledgments" underlined.
- At the end of your acknowledgments, sign your initials and indicate the place and date.

Other Dos and Don'ts

- Don't forget anyone who helped in preparation of the book when you write acknowledgments, unless they don't want to be mentioned.
- Do keep a running file of names and ways that people helped so you don't have to scramble for this information at the end.

> Do not call if you haven't heard back from an agent after a week, or even a month. I wish it weren't true, but it takes time to get through submissions. If you haven't heard back in a few months, then drop a polite e-mail.
>
> **—PHIL LANG**
> literary agent, Reece Halsey North

ACKNOWLEDGMENTS: NOVEL

Header, with no page number

Writer/OFFICER ON THE RUN/Acknowledgments

Acknowledgments

Heading is centered and underlined, one-third of the way down the page.

Double-spaced text

Completing and publishing a novel of this magnitude is no easy task, and there are

many to thank. Without the following, this book would not be in your hands today.

    First and foremost, I would like to thank my editor, John Doe, whose insightful

comments and criticisms vastly improved this book after I turned it in. Although we oc-

casionally wrestled a bit over which chapters, pages, paragraphs, sentences, and words

to keep and which to do away with, in the end John was usually right. In my moments

1" margin

of bullheadedness, I'm glad he took me by the horns. I also want to thank my agent,

Joe Agent, who believed in this project from the beginning, has guided me through ev-

ery stage in the process, and has handled all the business aspects of publishing.

    The Cincinnati police department deserves a big thanks for allowing me access

to the workings of a top-notch investigative team. Numerous car trips, conversations,

and boxes of jelly donuts have gone into this book.

    Finally, and above all, I am indebted to my beloved wife, Breanna, for giving me

Keep this to one page.

the idea to write this book and supporting me throughout. Her enduring love and pa-

tience did as much—if not more—to make this book complete than did the sweat of

my own brow.

TABLE OF CONTENTS

Submission Tips

The table of contents for fiction manuscripts is pretty spare. Those that are included merely list the chapter title and page numbers.

Formatting Specs

- Center the heading "Table of Contents" or "Contents" at least one-third of the way down the page.
- Provide an extra-wide margin, at least 1.5".
- Use a header.
- At the very least, include the chapter titles.
- Include such front-matter elements as prefaces, forewords, and prologues.
- Don't include acknowledgments, dedications, and other short bits of front matter.

Other Dos and Don'ts

- Don't include page numbers with front matter elements.
- Do capitalize all the important words in chapter titles.
- Do skip four lines between "Table of Contents" and the list of chapters unless it will cause you to go over a page.

TABLE OF CONTENTS: NOVEL

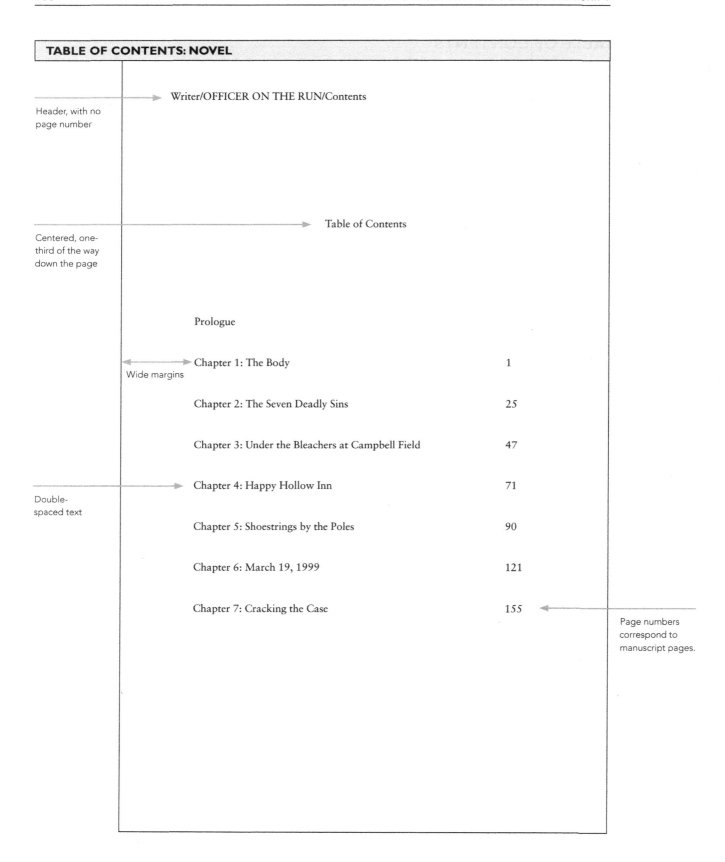

Header, with no page number

Writer/OFFICER ON THE RUN/Contents

Centered, one-third of the way down the page

Table of Contents

Prologue

Wide margins

Chapter 1: The Body   1

Chapter 2: The Seven Deadly Sins   25

Chapter 3: Under the Bleachers at Campbell Field   47

Double-spaced text

Chapter 4: Happy Hollow Inn   71

Chapter 5: Shoestrings by the Poles   90

Chapter 6: March 19, 1999   121

Chapter 7: Cracking the Case   155

Page numbers correspond to manuscript pages.

The surefire way of tempting a literary agent into reading you work is by sending them a fabulous query letter. Note how this method doesn't involve calling an agent. It also doesn't involve a referral. A great query letter trumps all, every time.

—DANIEL LAZAR

literary agent, Writers House

DEDICATION PAGE

Submission Tips

The dedication page, which is optional, is a brief inscription in which you express affection or respect for a person (or persons) who may or may not be directly related to the subject matter of your book. This is the place for you to write things like, "For Jennifer—the light of my life."

Formatting Specs

- Keep your dedication short (only a few lines).
- The dedication gets its own page and must have a header that should look like this: Writer/OFFICER ON THE RUN/Dedication. Do not number the page.
- The dedication should be centered about a third of the way down the page.
- Do not put a heading that labels this page a "Dedication."

DEDICATION: NOVEL

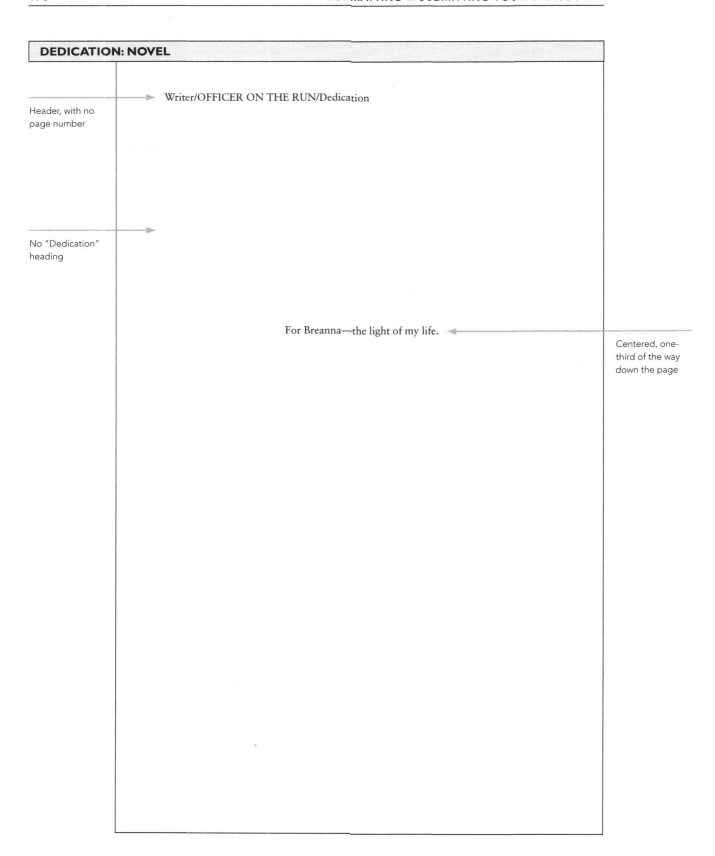

Writer/OFFICER ON THE RUN/Dedication

Header, with no
page number

No "Dedication"
heading

For Breanna—the light of my life.

Centered, one-
third of the way
down the page

EPIGRAPH

Submission Tips

The epigraph, which is optional, is a short quotation used at the beginning of the novel or at the beginning of each chapter. Its content should have relevance to the contents of the book.

Formatting Specs

- Be sure to cite the source of the epigraph.
- When used at the beginning of the novel, type the epigraph on a separate page. Do not number the page.
- If the epigraph is on its own page, be sure to use a header that should look like this: Writer/OFFICER ON THE RUN/Epigraph.
- The epigraph should be centered about a third of the way down the page.
- Do not put a heading that labels this a page and "Epigraph."
- When used at the beginning of a chapter, type the epigraph on the same page as the chapter begins.

EPIGRAPH: NOVEL

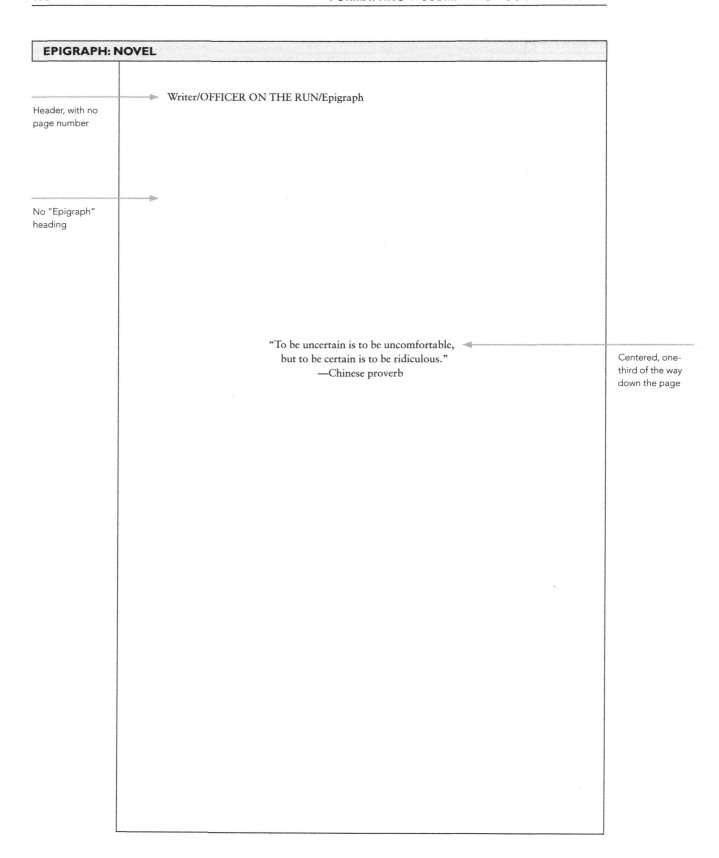

Writer/OFFICER ON THE RUN/Epigraph

Header, with no page number

No "Epigraph" heading

"To be uncertain is to be uncomfortable,
but to be certain is to be ridiculous."
—Chinese proverb

Centered, one-third of the way down the page

FOREWORD

Submission Tips

The foreword, which is optional, is a brief commentary included in a book's front matter in which someone remarks on the book's contents. The foreword is sometimes written by a well-known author or authority to add credibility and sales appeal to the work.

Although the publisher often makes arrangements for the foreword to be written, the author's suggestions about experts in the book's particular subject field are usually welcome.

Formatting Specs

- Like the rest of the front matter, the foreword has a header but no page numbers.
- Use a 1" margin on all sides.
- Use a heading that explicitly states "Foreword" about one-third of the way down the page.
- The name of the foreword's author goes flush right at the end of the text, followed by title and affiliation.
- The foreword's author may want to indicate the city, year, and place the foreword was written.

FOREWORD: NOVEL

Header, with no
page number

Writer/OFFICER ON THE RUN/Foreword

Foreword

Heading is cen-
tered and under-
lined, one-third
of the way down
the page.

I will never forgive John Writer for sending me a copy of *Officer on the Run*. I was

1" margin

staring down a deadline for my latest manuscript, *Can't Find Solace*, and I ended up

paying more attention to John's manuscript. I had a few spare seconds to read the

first sentence, so I did. Then I decided I could take a well-deserved break and finish

Double-
spaced text

the chapter. Before I knew it, I was reading "The End," and the only mystery left was

how to explain why my manuscript wouldn't be on my agent's desk the next morning.

Meg Hanson
San Francisco, California
June 28, 2008

Name, place, and
date go in bot-
tom flush with the
right margin.

In a synopsis, don't concentrate so much on the plot that the characters don't come alive. Show us the major characters' goals (what they want), motivations (why they want it), and conflicts (why they can't have it).

—PAM MCCUTCHEON

author of *Writing the Fiction Synopsis: A Step by Step Approach*

PREFACE

Submission Tips

The preface, which is optional, is usually written if the author feels the need to explain why he wrote the book. It's rarely done with fiction, so talk with your agent or editor about it. The preface can also be used as an acknowledgments page, to thank the people and institutions that helped you bring the book to fruition. You, the author, write the preface.

Formatting Specs

- Type the preface on a separate page and double-space the text.
- Do not number the page.
- Use a 1" margin on all sides.
- Use a header.
- Use a heading, starting about one-third of the way down the page that reads, "Preface," centered and underlined.
- Sign your initials, tell the place you're writing from, and include the date.

PREFACE: NOVEL

Header, with no page number

Writer/OFFICER ON THE RUN/Preface

Preface

Heading is centered and underlined, one-third of the way down the page.

Double-spaced text

This book would not have been possible without generous assistance from Detective Dan Bedilion and her top-notch staff at the Heartland police department. They helped me brainstorm ideas and made sure I got every last detail right. Also, many thanks to my coworkers at the Heartland prosecuting attorney's office for keeping the hot coffee and unconditional encouragement flowing.

1" margin

John Q. Writer
Allentown, Pennsylvania
July 12, 2008

Name, place, and date go in bottom flush with the right margin.

CHAPTER 6:
GENRE NOVELS

Genre fiction refers to distinct types of stories, such as romance, mystery, science fiction, fantasy, thriller, suspense or horror. The stories themselves have certain expectations, and often one story is part of a larger series. If your novel falls within a genre, take careful note of how best to query an agent or editor in that market. The formatting guidelines detailed in chapter five are acceptable for most novels, but different genres have different format specifications that are important to note and keep in mind.

ELECTRONIC SUBMISSIONS

Formatting e-mail queries for genre works follows the same rules and guidelines as with any novel. Reference chapter five on novels to learn more.

ROMANCE

The romance novel is a category of fiction in which the love relationship between a man and a woman pervades the plot. The story concerns the heroine and the hero, who fall in love, encounter a conflict that hinders their relationship, and resolve the conflict. Though marriage is not necessarily the outcome of the story, the ending is always happy.

The couple's relationship determines the plot and tone of the book. Despite all this emotion, however, both the characters and plot must be well developed and realistic. Contrived situations and flat characters are unacceptable. Throughout a romance novel, the reader senses the sexual and emotional attraction between the heroine and hero. Lovemaking scenes, though sometimes detailed, are generally not too graphic; more emphasis is placed on the sensual element than on physical action.

There are many different categories of romances; they run the gamut from historical to humorous to hot and heavy. Today's adult romance novel differs from its counterpart of the past in that it reflects a respect for independent, strong women. "Bodice-rippers" and "rape sagas," though still being published here and there, are becoming less popular than category romances, as authors and readers increasingly subscribe to the values fostered by the women's movement.

Each publisher of romances has detailed, specific guidelines regarding its specific lines. The publisher will stipulate, for example, whether the heroine may engage in sex outside of marriage, whether marriage will occur at the novel's end, and whether the heroine is in her twenties, thirties, or another age group. In addition, publishers specify lengths for romances, which usually range from 50,000 to 60,000 words.

ROMANCE QUERY

Submission Tips

The most important thing to remember about submitting to romance publishers is to make sure your story or novel fits the exact category of the publisher you are submitting to. For instance, don't send your historical romance set in England in the 1730s to an imprint that only looks for stories about finding love in the contemporary United States. Also, know the length of specific lines; don't send a 50,000-word novel to a publisher who looks for much shorter or longer works. The romance market has many more subgenres than other fiction genres, so you have to do your homework to make sure you are submitting to a publisher that works with the type of story you have.

Here are several subgenres of romance:

- **Christian:** The main characters are either devout Christians or follow a journey toward embracing Christianity. Sex is reserved for after marriage.

- **Contemporary:** A general term for a story using modern characters and settings.

- **Erotica:** Sometimes broken down further into "elegant erotica" or "romantica," this subgenre addresses sex openly and in candid terms.

- Historical: Takes place in the past. Although the setting, characters and language are different, the passion of the heroine must shine through.

Formatting Specs

To submit and format your short stories and novels in the romance genre, consult the appropriate pages for fiction submissions (see page 110 for short stories and page 124 for novel packages).

The word count for a romance should range from 50,000 to about 100,000 words. There is a formula to write a good romance. The hero must be a man the reader would like to date and the heroine should be the type of girl that is bigger than life that the reader would like to be like. They should meet, overcome obstacles, and in the end, get together.

—MARY SUE SEYMOUR

literary agent, Seymour Literary Agency

A romance is a pretty specific type of book. At its core, a romance is story about people falling in love and it always ends on an optimistic, emotionally satisfying note. A book can absolutely be romantic though, and not be a romance, per se. I think a novel ceases to be a romance whenever the focus of the book shifts away from the romantic relationship and starts to be more about the other plot elements (finding the serial killer, stopping the alien invasion, making peace with the death of the character's father). If a book strays too far from traditional romance rules, it just isn't a romance anymore and that is fine.

—LAURA BRADFORD

literary agent, Bradford Literary

Other Dos and Don'ts

- Don't believe the myth that romance novels don't have to be as well written as mainstream novels. Today's romance novels are meticulously crafted, character-driven stories that are continually on the top of the best-seller lists.

- Do obtain a copy of a publisher or agent's guidelines. Romance guidelines are extremely specific as to characters, plotlines, and page length, so make sure your story or novel fits the guidelines before sending.

- Do indicate which series you think your novel will be perfect for if you are submitting to a publisher that has several different series of romances.

- Do indicate in your query letter the names of authors that your work is similar to in order to give the editor or agent a point of reference; if possible, reference an author who is published or represented by the publisher or agent you are sending your query to. This shows your familiarity with the publisher's work and that you've done your homework and know the market.

- Don't send a query or package via e-mail or fax unless the editor or agent specifically requests it.

QUERY: ROMANCE

Contact information, including phone number and e-mail

> Jane Q. Writer
> 123 Author Lane
> Writerville, CA 95355
> (323) 555-0000
> janeqwriter@email.com

January 2, 2009

Date flushed right

Robin Roman
Leisure Books
276 Fifth Ave., Suite 1008
New York, NY 10001

Dear Robin Roman:

Address the letter to a specific editor at a publisher that deals with the type of book the writer is submitting—a historical romance.

1" margin

Is there a twelve-step program for Romance Addicts? A "Dear Abby" column for those who promise they'll read "just one" romance this week and end up on an all-night binge? Please, just say "No." As a confessed RA (Romance Addict), I don't want to be cured!

A "grabber" sentence to get the attention of the editor. It's clear from this paragraph that the writer loves the romance genre, and her enthusiasm is infectious.

Single-spaced text

I want all RAs to experience the "high" of falling in love with Cedric of Murtane, a ruthless warlord capable of stealing any woman's heart. Imagine a "trip" to 13th-century England. Put yourself in the trembling shoes of Morgan Steele, a feisty heiress destined to marry a man known best as the "Killer of Kent." Yet think of your relief when you discover that the man has been horribly misjudged by others and needs you as much as you need him. The only trouble lies in an evil stepmother and an illicit connection to the throne. Yet there's never a dull moment. *The Warrior* will give no one a "bad trip."

A nice, brief paragraph gives a quick outline of the novel yet gives a good idea of the novel.

Indicate the length of the novel, and that it's completed. The length is consistent with similar books.

I've enclosed a sample of *The Warrior*, hoping the first three chapters will whet your appetite for more, along with a synopsis. There are twenty-two chapters in this completed novel, a total of 75,000 words to satisfy the RA craving completely. Your response to *The Warrior* would mean a great deal to me.

Sincerely,

Signature

Jane Q. Writer

Encl.: Chapters 1, 2, 3
Synopsis
SASE

Details enclosures in the body of the letter. They are exactly what Leisure Books' guidelines indicate they want.

ELECTRONIC QUERY, MISTAKES TO AVOID: ROMANCE

June 24, 2009

Editor
Love Spell
276 Fifth Avenue
New York, NY 10001

Dear Romance Editor,

I've written a romance novel that I think you'll like. It's all about a contemporary woman, a doctor, who has been unlucky in love. She meets a wonderful doctor at the hospital she works at and they fall in love and get married, hoping to start a family.

This is the first book I've ever written, but I think it will be very popular. My mother, sister, and sister-in-law have all read it and loved it. If you are not interested, please let me know by next week so I can send it on to another publisher.

Thank you for you time.

Jane Q. Writer
(323) 555-0000

Never address a letter to "Editor." Find out the name of a specific editor and address your submission to her.

Don't mention that you're a first-time writer or that you've never been published.

Never say that family members, friends or co-workers enjoyed your book. Their opinions, though meaningful to you, mean nothing in the publishing world.

Watch out for typos!

Love Spell publishes time travel, paranormal, and futuristic romance novels. This novel is a contemporary romance—be sure the publisher you are submitting to works with the kind of books you write.

This tells the editor very little about the book and why it is different from other romances on the market. Who are the characters? What are their motivations? What is the conflict? What is the length of the book?

Don't give the editor an unrealistic deadline to get back to you. If she's interested, you'll hear from her.

Author contact information is missing. Name, address, phone, and e-mail should be included. And it should be at the top of the letter.

MYSTERY

The mystery is a form of fiction in which one or more elements remain unknown or unexplained until the end of the story. The modern mystery story contains elements of the literary novel: a convincing account of a character's struggle with various physical and psychological obstacles in an effort to achieve his goal, good characterization, and sound motivation. Publishers of mysteries, from short stories in mystery publications such as *Ellery Queen's Mystery Magazine* to complete novels, often look for one or more of these categories:

- **Amateur sleuth:** The main character does the detection but isn't a professional private investigator or police detective. Often two amateur detectives, such as a husband and wife, who work together in a bickering team or cohort mystery series. The crime is the main focus, but the relationship is also developed.
- **Caper:** A crime story usually told from the viewpoint of the perpetrator. The tone may be lighthearted and the crime is often theft rather than murder.
- **Cozy:** A murder mystery set in a small English or New England town that features an amateur sleuth. The "detective" is usually a genteel old lady or gentleman.
- **Gothic:** A mystery with a dark and brooding tone. It contains elements of romantic suspense and is usually set at an old estate.
- **Hardboiled:** Features a streetwise and hardened detective. This character type was popularized in the 1940s and 1950s.
- **Heist:** More serious than a caper, a heist focuses on solving the theft, as well as on the planning and execution of the theft.
- **Malice domestic:** A mystery involving a family member's murder.
- **Police procedural:** A mystery featuring a police detective or officer who uses standard professional police practices to solve a crime.
- **Romantic suspense:** A suspense story with strong elements of romance, usually between the detective and the victim or the detective and the suspect.
- **True crime:** Nonfiction about real murders and serial killings.
- **Whodunit:** The focus is on discovering the identity of the murderer.

MYSTERY QUERY

Submission Tips

The mystery market has quite a few subgenres, so you have to research to make sure you are submitting to a publisher that works with the type of story you have written. Do your homework! You wouldn't send your hardboiled crime novel to a publisher that is known for only publishing English cozy mysteries.

Formatting Specs

To submit and format your short stories and novels in the mystery genre, consult the appropriate pages for fiction submissions (see page 110 for short stories and page 124 for novel packages).

Other Dos and Don'ts

- Do obtain a copy of a publisher or agent's guidelines before submitting.

- Do indicate in your query letter the names of authors that your work is similar to in order to give the editor or agent a point of reference; if possible, reference an author who is published or represented by the publisher or agent you are sending your query to. This shows your familiarity with the publisher's work and that you've done your homework and know the market.

- Don't send a query or package via e-mail or fax unless the editor or agent specifically requests it.

> The mystery is a tightly told tale in which every action, every nuance, every shade of character must contribute to the story. If it doesn't, it doesn't belong ... In the mystery, it is the story that matters. Why? Because the mystery novel is a game between author and reader, the goal of which is Find the Villain.
>
> **—HILLARY WAUGH**
>
> mystery author

QUERY: MYSTERY

Contact information, including phone number and e-mail

John Q. Writer
123 Author Lane
Writerville, CA 95355
(323) 555-0000
johnqwriter@email.com

June 29, 2009

Date flushed right

Steven Sleuth
Silver Dagger Mysteries
P.O. Box 1216
Johnson City, TN 37605

Address letter to a specific editor.

Dear Mr. Sleuth:

1" margin

In my novel, *Mystery Lake*, the sleepy southern town of Hathaway, Louisiana, is shocked when the dismembered body of its most prominent citizen washes up on the shores of Mystery Lake. Miriam Linnel was well loved by all the citizens of Valley Mills, and a motive for the murder can't be found. However, everyone has noticed a mysterious drifter who arrived in town just days before the murder. Could he have done it? Or is the secret hidden in Miriam's will? It's up to detective Joshua Dunham to find out.

Good introductory paragraph. It states the novel's title, sets the hook (grabber), and makes the editor want to read the novel.

State publishing credits and pertinent professional background.

I have had short stories published in several mystery magazines, including *Hardboiled*, *Alfred Hitchcock's Mystery Magazine*, and *Ellery Queen's Mystery Magazine*. I have also been a police detective on the Lake Charles, Louisiana, police force for fifteen years.

Tell the exact word count. The author has done his homework, as Silver Dagger's guidelines state that they are looking for books of 60–80,000 words.

The novel is 65,000 words. I think it will fit in well with the other police procedural books you publish, such as *Killer Looks* by Laura Young and *Justice Betrayed* by Daniel Bailey.

Mention the intended audience and why the book will fit in well on this publisher's list. The work is compared to others, but not in a tactless way.

Thank you for your time in considering *Mystery Lake*. I look forward to hearing from you.

Sincerely,

Signature

John Q. Writer

Catalogs every item being sent in the package. This is exactly what the publisher requests in its guidelines.

Encl.: Outline
Chapters 1, 2, 3
Synopsis
Author bio
SASE

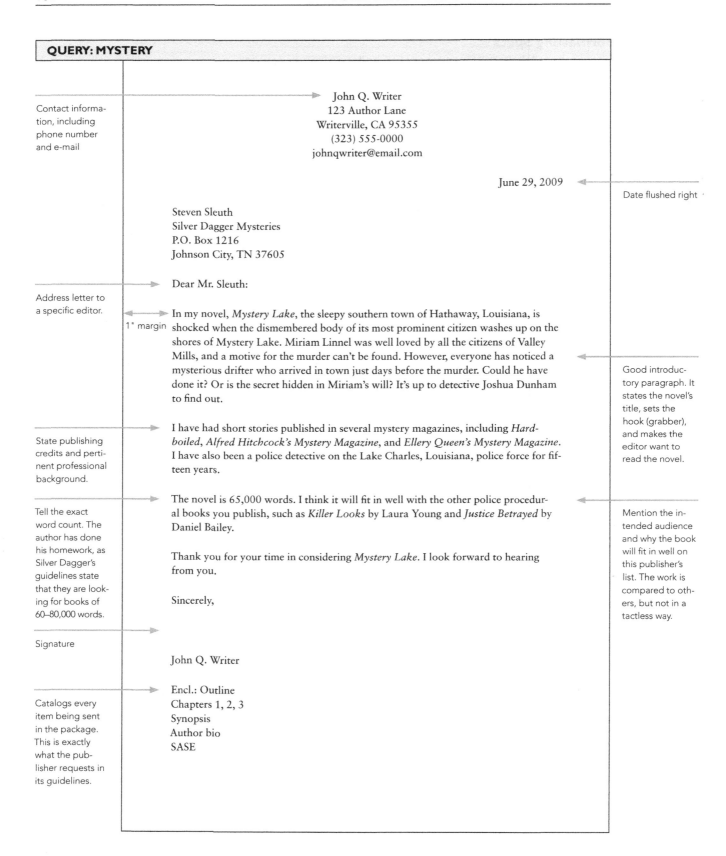

QUERY, MISTAKES TO AVOID: MYSTERY

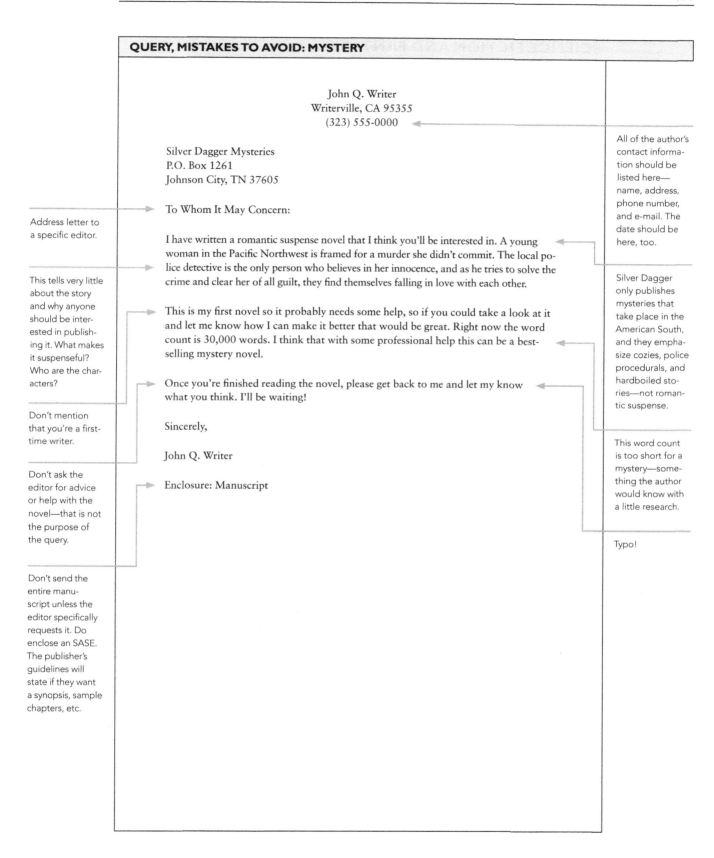

John Q. Writer
Writerville, CA 95355
(323) 555-0000

All of the author's contact information should be listed here—name, address, phone number, and e-mail. The date should be here, too.

Silver Dagger Mysteries
P.O. Box 1261
Johnson City, TN 37605

Address letter to a specific editor.

To Whom It May Concern:

I have written a romantic suspense novel that I think you'll be interested in. A young woman in the Pacific Northwest is framed for a murder she didn't commit. The local police detective is the only person who believes in her innocence, and as he tries to solve the crime and clear her of all guilt, they find themselves falling in love with each other.

Silver Dagger only publishes mysteries that take place in the American South, and they emphasize cozies, police procedurals, and hardboiled stories—not romantic suspense.

This tells very little about the story and why anyone should be interested in publishing it. What makes it suspenseful? Who are the characters?

This is my first novel so it probably needs some help, so if you could take a look at it and let me know how I can make it better that would be great. Right now the word count is 30,000 words. I think that with some professional help this can be a best-selling mystery novel.

Don't mention that you're a first-time writer.

Once you're finished reading the novel, please get back to me and let my know what you think. I'll be waiting!

This word count is too short for a mystery—something the author would know with a little research.

Don't ask the editor for advice or help with the novel—that is not the purpose of the query.

Sincerely,

John Q. Writer

Enclosure: Manuscript

Typo!

Don't send the entire manuscript unless the editor specifically requests it. Do enclose an SASE. The publisher's guidelines will state if they want a synopsis, sample chapters, etc.

SCIENCE FICTION AND FANTASY

Science fiction is literature that involves elements of science and technology as a basis for conflict, or as the setting for a story. The science and technology are generally extrapolations of existing scientific facts, and most (though not all) science-fiction stories take place in the future. There are other definitions of science fiction, and much disagreement in academic circles as to what constitutes science fiction and what constitutes fantasy. In some cases the line between science fiction and fantasy is virtually nonexistent. Despite the controversy, it is generally accepted that, to be science fiction, a story must have elements of science. Fantasy, on the other hand, rarely utilizes science, relying instead on magic, mythological and neo-mythological beings and devices, and outright invention for conflict and setting.

Other than the emphasis either on science or magic, science fiction and fantasy have similar roots. Some of the basic elements of science fiction have been in existence for thousands of years. Fortune-tellers, prophets, and clairvoyants have always sought to foretell the future, and a grand adventure in an exotic setting, a recurring story theme in science fiction, goes back to the dawn of time. Tales of mythological gods and their involvement with humans are echoed by modern-day encounters with alien beings. The heroic quest, occurring so often in mythology, is paralleled by stories of pioneering space explorers.

Contemporary science fiction, while maintaining a focus on science and technology, is more concerned with the effects that technology on people. Since science is a key component in science fiction, accuracy with reference to scientific fact is important. Most of the science in science fiction is hypothesized extrapolations from known facts. Science-fiction writers may make their own rules for future settings, but the rules require consistency and logic based in scientific fact.

As with all forms of fiction, science fiction and fantasy are dependent upon the standard elements of storytelling—plot, characterization, theme, motivation, etc.—for success. Many would-be science fiction writers miss this fact and attempt to dazzle readers with gimmicks and gadgets, to no effect. Beyond inconsistency and an overabundance of gadgetry in place of a good story, there are few taboos in science fiction and fantasy.

There are several subgenres of science fiction, including sociological science fiction, space opera, military science fiction, alternate history, and cyberpunk, each having its own peculiarities. Extensive reading in the field can aid in identifying these subcategories and is recommended for anyone wishing to write science fiction.

Fantasy is a genre that typically takes place on a separate plane of reality—in a made-up world or on a fictional planet. Strange creatures and races are often involved. This is a world of dragons, new languages, swords of destiny, and more. Some subgenres of fantasy include urban fantasy, wuxia, sword and sorcery, epic fantasy, dark fantasy, and Arthurian fantasy. Thanks to the popularity of the Harry Potter books as well as the *Lord of the Rings* films, fantasy is a more mainstream genre than in decades past.

I prefer authors follow up on their submissions by not following up! We're pretty prompt around here and always respond to submissions in a very timely manner—as long as it's not between Christmas and New Year's!

—HARVEY KLINGER

literary agent, Harvey Klinger, Inc. Literary Representation

Submission Tips

The most important thing to remember about submitting to science-fiction and fantasy publishers is to make sure your story or novel fits the exact category of the publisher you are submitting to. The science-fiction and fantasy market has different subgenres, so you really have to do some research to make sure you are submitting to a publisher that works with the type of story you have written.

Formatting Specs

To submit and format your short stories and novels in the science-fiction and fantasy genres, consult the appropriate pages for fiction submissions (see page 110 for short stories and page 124 for novel packages).

Other Dos and Don'ts

- Do obtain a copy of a publisher or agent's guidelines. Some publishers or fiction magazines only publish certain types of science fiction and fantasy, so make sure your story or novel fits their guidelines before sending.

- Do indicate in your query letter the names of authors that your work is similar to in order to give the editor or agent a point of reference; if possible, reference an author who is published or represented by the publisher or agent you are sending your query to. This shows your familiarity with the publisher's work and that you've done your homework and know the market.

- Don't send a query or manuscript via e-mail or fax unless the editor or agent specifically requests it.

HORROR

H.P. Lovecraft, the master of the horror tale, wrote, "The oldest and strongest emotion of mankind is fear, and the oldest and strongest kind of fear is fear of the unknown. These facts few psychologists will dispute, and their admitted truth must establish for all time the genuineness and dignity of the weirdly horrible tales as a literary form."

Lovecraft distinguishes horror literature from fiction based entirely on physical fear and the merely gruesome. "The true weird tale has something more than secret murder, bloody bones, or a sheeted form clanking chains according to the rule. A certain atmosphere of breathless and unexplainable dread of outer, unknown forces must be present; and there must be a hint, expressed with a seriousness and portentousness becoming its subject, of that most terrible concept of the human brain—a malign and particular suspension or defeat of the fixed laws of Nature which are our only safeguard against the assaults of chaos and the daemons of unplumbed space." It is that atmosphere—the creation of a particular sensation or emotional level—that, according to Lovecraft, is the most important element in the creation of horror literature.

Some horror writing has elements of science fiction and fantasy, and the lines between these genres can get blurred. Dark fantasy is a horror genre that combines the traditional elements of horror with the fantastical elements of fantasy. A good way to research current trends in horror is to study anthologies such as *The Year's Best Fantasy and Horror*, published yearly by St. Martin's Press.

Submission Tips

Before you submit your query, story, or package, be sure that your story fits the type of horror stories or novels that the publisher works with. Do your homework! Don't send your traditional ghost story to a publisher that only publishes dark fantasy.

Formatting Specs

To submit and format your short stories and novels in the horror genre, consult the appropriate pages for fiction submissions (see page 110 for short stories and page 124 for novel packages).

Other Dos and Don'ts

- Do obtain a copy of a publisher or agent's guidelines. Make sure your story or novel fits their guidelines before sending.

- Do indicate in your query letter the names of authors that your work is similar to in order to give the editor or agent a point of reference; if possible, reference an author who is published or represented by the publisher or agent you are sending your query to. This shows your familiarity with the publisher's work and that you've done your homework and know the market.

- Don't send a query or package via e-mail or fax unless the editor or agent specifically requests it.

Suspense is emotional. It's surprise and confusion and fear and anticipation. And suspense is danger. Immediate danger. It's worrying about what's going to happen, not about the action taking place at that moment.

—T. MACDONALD SKILLMAN

author, *Writing the Thriller*

QUERY: SCIENCE FICTION OR HORROR

Contact information, including phone number and e-mail

John Q. Writer
123 Author Lane
Writerville, CA 95355
(323) 555-0000
johnqwriter@email.com

April 24, 2009

Date flushed right

Kathy Kirk
DAW Books, Inc.
375 Hudson St., Third Floor
New York, NY 10014

Address the letter to a specific editor.

Dear Ms. Kirk:

Good introductory paragraph. States the novel's title, sets the hook (grabber), introduces the main character, and makes the editor want to read the novel.

1" margin

In *Colony Out of Time*, the year is 2624. On the seemingly serene ocean world of Aquataine, a colony of humans fights for its very existence, for their new home planet harbors a secret—a fatal water-borne disease that is killing everything that comes in contact. As this relentless disease decimates the population of Aquataine, Artemis Chase, a marine biologist, races against time to defeat the disease before it wipes out the entire human race. Can he do it before time runs out?

States publishing credits and pertinent professional background.

I have had short stories published in several science-fiction and fantasy magazines, including *Asimov's Science Fiction*, *Starlog*, and *Artemis Magazine*. I am also a marine biologist, working in my field for over twenty-five years, and have brought my writing and professional interests together in *Colony Out of Time*. The novel is 80,000 words. I think it will fit in well with the other science-fiction books you publish, such as *Explorer* by C.J. Cherryh and *The Burning Heart of Night* by Ivan Cat.

Word count

Thank you for your time and consideration, and I look forward to hearing from you.

Sincerely,

Mention other authors the publisher works with who are similar, indicating that the book will fit in well on this publisher's list.

Signature

John Q. Writer

Encl.: SASE

Publisher's guidelines ask for a query with an SASE.

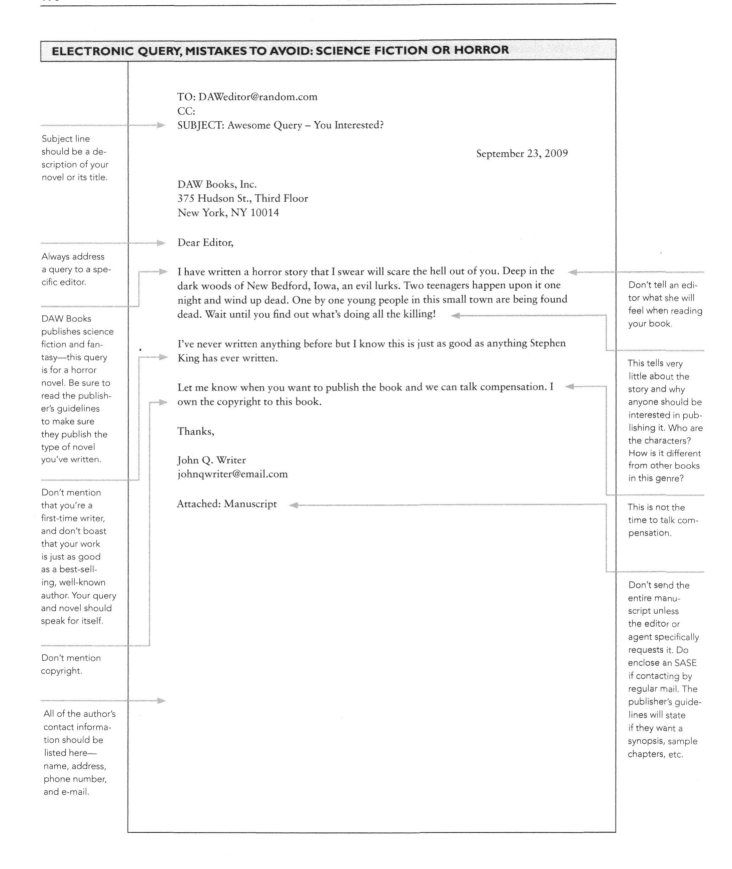

ELECTRONIC QUERY, MISTAKES TO AVOID: SCIENCE FICTION OR HORROR

TO: DAWeditor@random.com
CC:
SUBJECT: Awesome Query – You Interested?

September 23, 2009

DAW Books, Inc.
375 Hudson St., Third Floor
New York, NY 10014

Dear Editor,

I have written a horror story that I swear will scare the hell out of you. Deep in the dark woods of New Bedford, Iowa, an evil lurks. Two teenagers happen upon it one night and wind up dead. One by one young people in this small town are being found dead. Wait until you find out what's doing all the killing!

I've never written anything before but I know this is just as good as anything Stephen King has ever written.

Let me know when you want to publish the book and we can talk compensation. I own the copyright to this book.

Thanks,

John Q. Writer
johnqwriter@email.com

Attached: Manuscript

Subject line should be a description of your novel or its title.

Always address a query to a specific editor.

DAW Books publishes science fiction and fantasy—this query is for a horror novel. Be sure to read the publisher's guidelines to make sure they publish the type of novel you've written.

Don't mention that you're a first-time writer, and don't boast that your work is just as good as a best-selling, well-known author. Your query and novel should speak for itself.

Don't mention copyright.

All of the author's contact information should be listed here—name, address, phone number, and e-mail.

Don't tell an editor what she will feel when reading your book.

This tells very little about the story and why anyone should be interested in publishing it. Who are the characters? How is it different from other books in this genre?

This is not the time to talk compensation.

Don't send the entire manuscript unless the editor or agent specifically requests it. Do enclose an SASE if contacting by regular mail. The publisher's guidelines will state if they want a synopsis, sample chapters, etc.

CHAPTER 7:

COMICS AND
GRAPHIC NOVELS

Although many use the terms comics and graphic novels interchangeably, there are a few key differences. Comic books are magazine-sized periodicals, while graphic novels are book-sized volumes of material generally not previously published in comic book form. Their plot accessibility is also different. Comic periodicals are generally part of a lengthy, ongoing series, so a new reader might have to read a few back issues to understand the story. Graphic novels, on the other hand, are usually self-contained, novel-length books that stand alone. To further confuse things, the term graphic novel is also often applied to respected works that are reprinted in the book-sized format but were originally published as comic books, such as *Watchmen* by Alan Moore and Dave Gibbons and Neil Gaiman's Sandman series. Even though they're called graphic "novels," graphic novels do not have to be works of fiction. Graphic novel is a format, not a genre; it can encompass nonfiction as well. Graphic novels and comics are a unique fusion of art and text that are arranged together in such a way to create a compelling story. It's not uncommon for a screenwriter to crossover to these media, as a screenwriter is already adept at composing for a visual medium. In the media of graphic novel and comics, the key is to be a visual storyteller, and reveal information and emotion through action and gesture, rather than a block of prose or monologue.

> Graphic novels are such a fresh format. That said, not all novelists are natural graphic novelists. You need to be a visual storyteller. You need to be able to reveal information via image and gesture, rather than dialogue. You need to be a tight, swift, and sparse plotter who favors action over exposition. Common mistakes I've seen: too much text, humdrum rather than spectacular illustrative opportunities, and a graphic novel that doesn't "need" to be one.
>
> **—MICHELLE ANDELMAN**
>
> literary agent, Lynn C. Franklin Associates, Ltd.

COMIC AND GRAPHIC NOVEL MANUSCRIPT

Submission Tips

Before you submit to any comics or graphic novel publisher, read their submission guidelines carefully. You should also become familiar with techniques and terminology used in comics and graphic novels. You might want to consult *Comics & Sequential Art* and *Graphic Storytelling*, both by Will Eisner (Poorhouse Press).

Each agent or publisher will have different submission guidelines or whether they only want "packages" where the writer and illustrator come together, or whether they will review work that is only a script or only art, in the hopes of pairing professionals up to compose a work.

For a graphic novel, you may approach either an agent or the publisher, but comic books submissions are usually sent directly to a publisher, unless you are already have an agent representing you.

If you're submitting the script only, you can include plenty of information on how each panel should look.

- What's the shape?
- How many panels on a page?
- What's the action inside the panel?
- What's the viewpoint of the observer (e.g., bird's-eye view)?

A comic is short enough that you should complete the text of at least one sample issue before submitting. A graphic novel, however, is typically a lot longer, and you may not need to submit a full script. An agent or publisher may want a query letter followed by a treatment. Check a publisher or agent's submission guidelines to see exactly what she is looking for.

TREATMENTS

Much like a film treatment, a graphic novel treatment is a detailed explanation of a story from front to back. It can be broken down by chapters (or in sections), but it does not have to be. As always, the more concise you can make a treatment the better, but as a general rule of thumb, do not go over twelve pages.

In a graphic novel, I'm looking for stylized, professional artwork, but more than that—a fresh, compelling story. My mind was opened to graphic novels after reading Marjane Satrapi's incredible *Persepolis*. I myself hadn't realized how emotional and powerful a graphic novel could be as a medium to tell a tale until the moment I opened that book.

—LILLY GHAHREMANI

literary agent, Full Circle Literary

The success of a comic is all in the execution. The story, or the subject matter, should be served by the marriage of illustration and writing. It is a huge letdown to read a comic and feel no influence from the illustration. On the other end of that, a well-executed comic can provide some of the most poignant, satisfying reading I have ever experienced. For each comic, there must be a reason to tell the story in sequential art style, an advantage that you gain only by telling the story in comic format.

—BERNADETTE BAKER

literary agent, Baker's Mark Literary Agency

If you're the artist yourself or if you are collaborating with someone prior to submission, know you that you should turn in at least ten pages of sample art that will be in the graphic novel, if not more. The editor doesn't need to see the whole publication upfront, but he does need the entire story front to back and a thorough representation of the art (as the latter is such a crucial component).

QUERY LETTER

A query letter for a comic or graphic novel is very similar in formatting and contents to a script query (see page 229). The crucial part of the letter is the pitch, which is sometimes called a "springboard." It's the hook, the concept, the words you envision on the back of the DVD box when the story is adapted to film. It gives the reader a reason to want to look over the treatment and see what happens.

Formatting Specs

If a publisher requests art, follow their guidelines meticulously. Never send original art—send copies, slides, or photographs (whatever is requested) and make sure they are clean, sharp, and easy to read.

Comic scripts are blueprints for the artwork, so they can be detailed or bare bones with only dialogue or action described. A lot of what is included depends on who the artist is and whether you are already collaborating at the stage the submitted script is completed. Instead of using word counts, script lengths are determined by the number of pages in the published work. Full-length comic stories usually run from twenty-two to twenty-five pages, depending on the publication and the required format. Graphic novels are novel-length; the publisher's guidelines will indicate the length of the books they usually publish, usually 120–180 pages.

In a comic or graphic novel manuscript, your dialogue will resemble script formatting, with character cues in the center and indented (see "Parts of a Script" in chapter 11). Each panel will be clearly labeled with a number (e.g., 1.1, 1.2, 2.1), pushed left. If you move on to a new page in the story, but are still writing on the same page of your Word document, feel free to put a line across the page, so that the reader can "feel" an imaginary page break.

Other Dos and Don'ts

- Do include your name and contact information on each page of your submission and on each piece of art.
- Don't send original artwork!
- Do include an SASE for a reply with enough return postage.
- Do type your material and use only one side of the paper.
- Do make your submission professional (neat, typed, spell-checked, brief).
- Do include a short cover letter that briefly states your background in comics or graphic novels, or any related information.
- Don't send portfolios or other expensive packages.
- Don't call an editor to check on your submission.
- Don't send a résumé along with your submission.
- Don't staple pages together.

ELECTRONIC COMICS AND GRAPHIC NOVEL SUBMISSION

It is rare for a publisher to request comics or graphic novels via e-mail, but it might happen. If it does, make sure you get detailed guidelines as to how the script and art should be submitted and follow them meticulously. Find out how they want the art submitted (via e-mail, on a CD) and make sure the art is saved in the proper file format and resolution that the publisher requests.

Writing a good script for comics is extremely difficult. With film, the writer leaves an awful lot up to the director and the director isn't obligated to stick to the script. This is not the case in comics. In comics, the writer tells the artist a story and lays it out in detail. The artist does have leeway, but the artist's job, in most cases, is to clarify and intensify what the writer has written.

—ANDY SCHMIDT

senior editor, IDW Publishing (*G.I. Joe* and *Star Trek* comics)

COVER PAGE: COMIC OR GRAPHIC NOVEL

The name of the comic should be bold in all caps and centered. Next to the name, use a number sign (#) to show what issue it is.

LIGHT CITY # 1
"City Hall"

by

John Q. Writer

Put the name of the issue in quotes, centered.

If the comic or graphic novel is adapted from another medium, skip four lines under your name and say so.

Adapted from the novel *Light City*
by David Lamay

John Q. Writer
123 Author Lane
Writerville, CA 95355
(323) 555-0000
johnqwriter@email.com

Author's name and contact information at the lower right

SCRIPT, PAGE I: COMIC OR GRAPHIC NOVEL

Writer/Light City/"City Hall"   1

<u>PAGE ONE</u>
              (Three Panels)

Panel Layout: Three bands each occupying the full width of the page; each panel decreases in height, one after the next.

Panel 1.1
Wide view of LIGHT CITY in all its grandeur—skyscrapers, majesty, power, sun reflecting off glass and metal. Many, many buildings. The center of the world right here.

                              CAPTION
                         Light City. Yesterday.

Panel 1.2
Straight on—one building in particular: CITY HALL. It's a towering behemoth of a building. The outside is old brick, and the structure seems to command respect. In the background, the sun is rising on the horizon. It's morning.

Panel 1.3
Close on a RECTANGULAR SECURITY ID BADGE. It's clipped to a suit lapel. The badge reads:

            MAYOR HERBERT I. MAGHIS
            LIGHT CITY
            SECURITY CLEARANCE: BLACK

_____

<u>PAGE TWO</u>
              (Five Panels)

Panel 2.1
Small panel. A figure—a man, bathed in shadow—stands at the front doors of City Hall about to enter. His hand is on the front door.

Panel 2.2
Up shot: Large panel of City Hall's MAIN LOBBY. A huge spectacle of people. We finally see the man with the badge: MAYOR MAGHIS. The lobby is four stories high and the walls are intricately designed with angelic images. It's a jaw-dropping kingdom, and the king is walking in. A SECURITY GUARD is closest to the door.

                         SECURITY GUARD
                         Mr. Mayor, sir.

Panels 2.3–2.5
Small panels of Mayor Maghis weaving through all the people on his way to the elevator.

Side annotations:

After the cover page, use a header containing your name, the comic name, the script name (in quotes), and the page number. Feel free to shorten and abbreviate if space is an issue.

Break the script down into pages like a comic book. Bold and underline each new page marking.

The first number of a panel is the page number; the second number is the panel number on the page.

You don't have to start each new page on an actual page. Use a thin gray or black line to separate pages on your manuscript.

Capitalize key actions and objects.

Dialogue follows the same format as movie script dialogue.

If multiple panels act as a mini-montage, feel free to say so. Explain in detail where necessary, but skip the detail when you can.

Though not necessary, you can add a "panel layout" explaining how each panel fits together in the page.

Format captions like dialogue.

Below each new page heading, tell how many panels are on the page.

Explain how the panel should look.

Capitalize characters as they are introduced.

Feel free to give directions when scripting an image. For example: "Keep it rated PG," or "The image should be goofy—this man looks like a buffoon right now." If you are a writer/artist and include the actual images, you will not need to describe them in the script text.

PART 3:
CHILDREN'S BOOKS

CHAPTER 8:
PICTURE BOOKS

Picture books are written for very young children to read or have read to them. They usually have very little text, but plenty of illustrations to engage children. The text of a picture book is well organized and carefully constructed, since its audience has little experience with stories. Because picture books are often read aloud, and because children have an instinctual fondness for rhythm, poetic techniques such as alliteration, consonance, assonance, and onomatopoeia can enhance a picture book's story. Other techniques that appeal to children is a repeated anecdote, which is used in *The Three Little Pigs*, and a refrain, used in *The Gingerbread Man*. Vocabulary in picture books is simple, and sentence construction is likewise uncomplicated. It often uses the active voice and mimics speech patterns. Though picture books may rhyme, most publishers are not looking for rhyming books.

WHAT YOU NEED TO SUBMIT

A typical picture book contains around 150–1,000 words, running around thirty-two pages, with twenty-eight pages of text and illustrations. The rest of the book contains front and back matter, such as the copyright page and the title page.

The primary difference between submitting a picture book and an adult book is that you generally send the entire manuscript of your picture book, not just a proposal or a few sample chapters. Picture books are generally so short in length that it takes very little time to read the entire text and make a decision. Some publishers do accept and want query letters, though.

A common misconception among many new writers of picture books is that they must find illustrators for their work before they submit. This is absolutely not the case; in fact, most editors frown upon a writer and illustrator teaming up on a submission. Once a publisher accepts your material, the editor will select an appropriate illustrator for your project. So even if your sister-in-law or coworker is an illustrator, it's best not to send their illustration samples with your manuscript. Most likely a publisher will not be interested in the whole package, and including those illustrations will only hurt your chances of getting published. Also, if you enclose unprofessional art samples with your manuscript, you're destined for rejection.

Even worse, the biggest taboo in picture book publishing is submitting finished artwork with the proposal. This is the unmistakable mark of an amateur—worse, an amateur who has not researched the field. The size, color, and method of printing the art can only be determined after a book is budgeted and designed. Your best bet is to write a great story, forget about the illustrations, make your query or cover letter professional, and submit your manuscript.

QUERY LETTER AND MANUSCRIPT

Submission Tips

Check each publisher or agent's specific guidelines before you send anything. An agent who represents "children's" or "juvenile" work may not present picture books, as well; she may just take on middle-grade and young adult work. Make sure before you send a submission.

The cover letter accompanying your manuscript should be brief and professional, yet friendly. It should interest the reader but not overdo it on cuteness or cleverness. Mention the title of the work you are sending, a few sentences about the material, and a brief summary of previous writing experience. If you don't have any previous experience, don't mention it and simply thank the editor or agent for her consideration.

And, even though the text for a picture book is short, publishers do not want you to submit more than one manuscript at a time.

Formatting Specs

Submit your picture book lines as double-spaced text, pushed left. If you have multiple lines on pages (rather than simply one line per page), feel free to use a blank line to signify page changes.

Other Dos and Don'ts

- Do obtain a copy of the publisher or agent's guidelines and follow them carefully.
- Don't include a sentence that says, "I read my work to my kids/grandkids/second-grade class and they loved it." This definitely does not sway an editor's opinion, and seems amateurish.
- Don't include unnecessary personal information in your query letter.

I suspect the common thinking goes that if a writer "knows" children, she can write for them. But a successful children's author doesn't simply "know" children—what makes them tick, what their internal and emotional lives are like—but she also knows children's literature. She's an avid reader, so she's familiar with what's age-appropriate and authentic to her category of the market. If she's writing a picture book, she's a skilled visual storyteller and can offer up a plot, character, relationship, or emotional arc in miniature—but still, and this is the difficult part, in full.

—MICHELLE ANDELMAN

literary agent, Lynn C. Franklin Associates, Ltd.

- Don't say, "I've always wanted to write for children." Although this may be true, it doesn't really help your cause.

- Do research the publisher you are querying to make sure you are sending the type of book they publish (fiction, nonfiction, certain age groups, etc.).

- Don't recommend an illustrator for your manuscript. The editor will decide which illustrator she wants to use if she is interested in your book.

- Do indicate in your query letter any previous writing experience or credits you may have, as well as memberships in children's writing organizations such as the Society of Children's Book Writers & Illustrators (SCBWI).

- Don't send a query or manuscript via e-mail or fax unless a publisher or agent specifically requests it.

- Do include an SASE when sending a query or manuscript through the mail.

- Don't indicate page breaks and don't type each page on a new sheet of paper.

ELECTRONIC SUBMISSIONS

Before you send a query or manuscript to a publication via e-mail, make sure they accept electronic submissions by contacting the publication directly or checking out their writers' guidelines. Never send a query or manuscript via e-mail unless you have permission from the editor or if the submission guidelines state it is acceptable.

I feel that picture books are more like poems than anything else, so it's especially important to me to be aware of every single detail in them. Each syllable, each line break, each sentence's placement on the page and where those critical page-turns occur—all of these are massively important.

—ALLYN JOHNSTON

former Harcourt Children's Book editor

QUERY: CHILDREN'S PICTURE BOOK

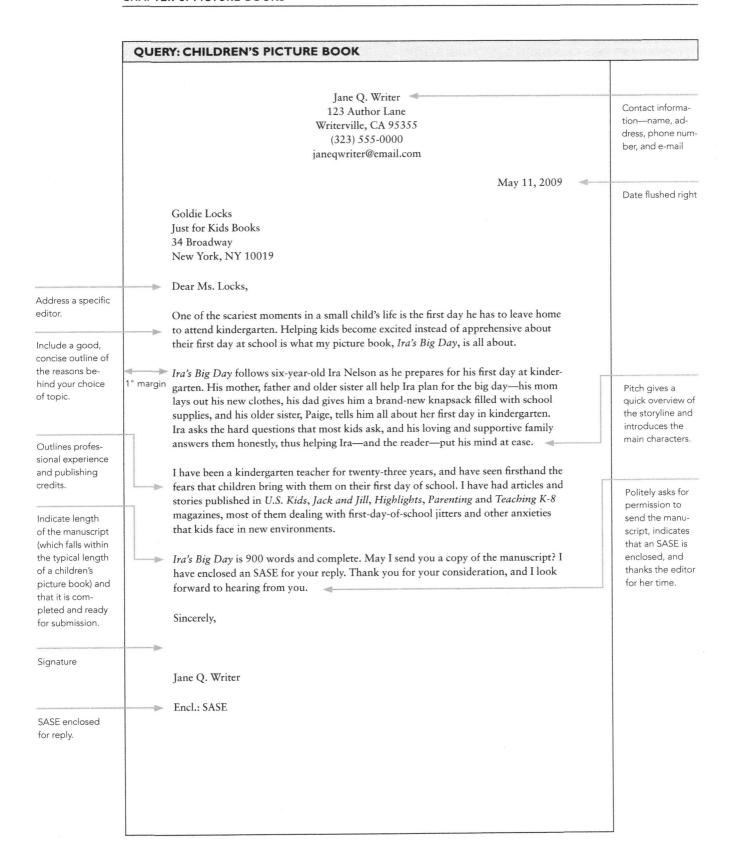

Jane Q. Writer
123 Author Lane
Writerville, CA 95355
(323) 555-0000
janeqwriter@email.com

Contact information—name, address, phone number, and e-mail

May 11, 2009

Date flushed right

Goldie Locks
Just for Kids Books
34 Broadway
New York, NY 10019

Dear Ms. Locks,

Address a specific editor.

One of the scariest moments in a small child's life is the first day he has to leave home to attend kindergarten. Helping kids become excited instead of apprehensive about their first day at school is what my picture book, *Ira's Big Day*, is all about.

Include a good, concise outline of the reasons behind your choice of topic.

1" margin

Ira's Big Day follows six-year-old Ira Nelson as he prepares for his first day at kindergarten. His mother, father and older sister all help Ira plan for the big day—his mom lays out his new clothes, his dad gives him a brand-new knapsack filled with school supplies, and his older sister, Paige, tells him all about her first day in kindergarten. Ira asks the hard questions that most kids ask, and his loving and supportive family answers them honestly, thus helping Ira—and the reader—put his mind at ease.

Pitch gives a quick overview of the storyline and introduces the main characters.

Outlines professional experience and publishing credits.

I have been a kindergarten teacher for twenty-three years, and have seen firsthand the fears that children bring with them on their first day of school. I have had articles and stories published in *U.S. Kids*, *Jack and Jill*, *Highlights*, *Parenting* and *Teaching K-8* magazines, most of them dealing with first-day-of-school jitters and other anxieties that kids face in new environments.

Indicate length of the manuscript (which falls within the typical length of a children's picture book) and that it is completed and ready for submission.

Ira's Big Day is 900 words and complete. May I send you a copy of the manuscript? I have enclosed an SASE for your reply. Thank you for your consideration, and I look forward to hearing from you.

Politely asks for permission to send the manuscript, indicates that an SASE is enclosed, and thanks the editor for her time.

Sincerely,

Signature

Jane Q. Writer

Encl.: SASE

SASE enclosed for reply.

COVER LETTER: CHILDREN'S PICTURE BOOK

Contact informa-
tion—name, ad-
dress, phone num-
ber, and e-mail

Jane Q. Writer
123 Author Lane
Writerville, CA 95355
(323) 555-0000
janeqwriter@email.com

June 23, 2009

Date flushed right

Sandra Bernie
The Sandra Agency
111 Broadway
New York, NY 10001

Address a
specific editor.

Dear Ms. Bernie:

Enclosed is my 900-word picture book, *Ira's Big Day*, which follows six-year-old Ira
Nelson as he prepares for his first day at kindergarten. His mother, father and older
sister all help Ira plan for the big day—his mom lays out his new clothes, his dad
gives him a brand-new knapsack filled with school supplies, and his older sister, Paige,
tells him all about her first day in kindergarten. Ira asks the hard questions that most
kids ask, and his loving and supportive family answers them honestly, thus helping
Ira—and the reader—put his mind at ease.

1" margin

Introductory para-
graph includes
the book's title,
the word count,
the central char-
acters, and tells
what the story
is about.

I have been a kindergarten teacher for twenty-three years, and have seen firsthand the
fears that children bring with them on their first day of school. I have had articles and
stories published in *U.S. Kids*, *Jack and Jill*, *Highlights*, *Parenting*, and *Teaching K-8*
magazines, most of them dealing with first-day-of-school jitters and other anxieties
that kids face in new environments.

Mention perti-
nent personal
information and
past publishing
credits.

Thank you for considering *Ira's Big Day*, and I look forward to hearing from you.

Politely close
the letter.

Sincerely,

Jane Q. Writer

Signature

Encl.: Manuscript, *Ira's Big Day*
SASE

Detail everything
that is included
in the submission
package. Omit
the SASE if you
are sending your
manuscript via
e-mail.

MANUSCRIPT: CHILDREN'S PICTURE BOOK

Writer/IRA'S BIG DAY   1

Header with the author's name and the novel's title in all caps

Page number (on the same line as the slug line)

When Ira Nelson woke up on Sunday morning, he knew this day was different.

What was it? Was it his mother's birthday? No, her birthday was the day after the

Fourth of July. Was it his dad's birthday? No, his birthday was just last month. His

big sister Paige's birthday? No, her birthday was easy to remember—it was on New

Year's Day. So what was so different about this day? As Ira sat up in bed trying to fig-

ure it out, he heard his mother calling him from downstairs.

Justify left margin only.

1" margin

Don't indicate page breaks.

"Ira, time for breakfast!" she said in a sing-song voice.

"We've got your favorite, eggs and bacon and bagels!"

"Come on Ira, we're hungry," yelled his big sister Paige.

"Woof," said Ira's dog Sparky.

Ira jumped out of bed and headed downstairs to the kitchen.

His mother would know what was so different about this day.

"Here's our sleepyhead," said Ira's dad. "Just in time for breakfast." Ira took his

seat at the end of the table, and

Sparky sat down at his feet.

"Mom," Ira said as he took a gulp of orange juice. "What is today?"

"Sunday," his mother said.

"I know," said Ira as he took a bite of his bagel. "But what's different about today?"

"Different?" said his mom. "Oh, Ira, today's the day before you start kindergarten!"

Ira felt funny. That's what was so different.

"I don't want to go to kindergarten," Ira said. "I want to stay here with you

and Sparky."

Double-spaced text

CHAPTER 9:

MIDDLE GRADE AND YOUNG ADULT BOOKS

Books written for children ages 9–15 are divided into two groups according to the readers' ages: books written for children 12 and younger are called middle grade (MG), and those written for children older than 12 are called young adult (YA). Nonfiction books for middle grade and young adults should reflect the age of the intended reader; obviously a book on science geared toward fifth-graders would be much more simplistic than one written for high school freshmen. Make sure you know the educational level of the book's intended audience and write specifically for them.

The main character in a children's novel should be no younger than the age group of the book's intended audience. In fact, the character is typically a year or two older than the novel's oldest reader. Children like to read about the adventures of older kids.

MG novels tend to focus on topics such as friendships, neighborhood adventures, school rivalries, and bullying. These novels usually run between 20,000 and 45,000 words. YA novels revolve around characters involved in more complex plots and show more depth than those characters in mid-grade novels. YA books can deal with more adult subjects—such as violence, sex and drugs—whereas MG cannot. Also, YA novels employ a more sophisticated writing style, vocabulary, subject matter, and general treatment. They are typically 45,000–65,000 words.

In writing a YA novel, remember that this work will be read predominantly by young teenagers, since older teenagers are likely to read fiction written for an adult audience. Therefore, the plot and situations of the characters should be identifiable to the child of junior high school age. Reading children's novels and talking to public or school librarians are important steps toward understanding your audience.

WHAT YOU NEED TO SUBMIT

Middle grade and young adult novels should be the submitted as a novel package, the same as an adult novel. Your MG or YA novel package should include a query letter and sample chapters, along with an outline and an SASE for a reply. See the discussion on "The Novel Package" in chapter five for more on the requirements. For nonfiction books, follow the guidelines outlined the "Book Proposal" section in chapter two.

In young adult writing, I would say this: No subject is taboo if it's done well. Each scene needs to matter in a novel. I've read a number of "edgy" young adult books where writers seem to add in scenes just for shock value and it doesn't work with the flow of the rest of the novel. "Taboo" subjects need to have a purpose in the progression of the novel—and of course, need to be well written!

—JESSICA REGEL

literary agent, Jean V. Naggar Literary Agency

QUERY LETTER AND MANUSCRIPT

Submission Tips

Check each publisher's specific guidelines before you send anything, and make sure that the children's publisher you are submitting to is interested in a mid-grade or YA book. Some children's publishers only work with picture books.

The query or cover letter accompanying your manuscript should be brief and professional, yet friendly. It should interest the reader but not overdo it on cuteness or cleverness.

Mention the title of the work you are sending, a sentence or two about the material, and a brief summary of previous writing experience. If you don't have any previous experience, don't mention it and simply thank the editor or agent for her consideration.

Don't send the entire manuscript at this point. Like with other novels, include an outline and sample chapters unless the editor or agent requests more.

Formatting Specs

To submit and format your mid-grade or young adult manuscript, see page 124 for the section on novel packages.

Other Dos and Don'ts

- Do obtain a copy of the publisher's guidelines and follow them carefully.
- Don't include a sentence that says anything such as, "I read my work to my grandkids and they loved it." This definitely does not sway an editor's opinion, and seems amateurish.
- Do indicate how your book is different from similar books on the market.
- Do indicate the word count of the book in your query letter.
- Do indicate the age group that your book is intended to reach.
- Do cite works from the publisher that you are sending your query to, if possible, to indicate where your work falls in the publisher's line. This shows your familiarity with the publisher's work and that you've done your homework and know the market.

- Do indicate in your query letter any previous writing experience or credits you may have, as well as memberships in children's writing organizations such as the Society of Children's Book Writers & Illustrators (SCBWI).

- Do indicate where you see your nonfiction book being used and marketed, if relevant (in the classroom, at home, sold through bookstores, museum stores and catalogs, etc.).

- Don't send a query or manuscript via e-mail or fax unless an editor or agent specifically requests it.

- Do include an SASE unless you are sending it via e-mail.

ELECTRONIC SUBMISSIONS

Before you send a query or manuscript to a publisher or an agent via e-mail, make sure they accept electronic submissions by checking out their writers' guidelines on-line. Never send a query or manuscript via e-mail unless you have permission from the editor or agent or if the submission guidelines state it is acceptable.

> If someone wanted to write for children, I would tell that person to go to their local bookstore, browse extensively and read everything that they can before they start a project. They need to understand the categories of children's books, as well as the differences in writing style between adult and children's writing.
>
> **—CARYN WISEMAN**
>
> literary agent, Andrea Brown Literary Agency

ELECTRONIC QUERY: MIDDLE GRADE AND YOUNG ADULT NONFICTION BOOK

TO: submissions@williamson.com
CC: johnqwriter@email.com
SUBJECT: Query: Geology Rocks! A juvenile nonfiction submission

September 23, 2009

Pamela Potter
Williamson Publishing Company
Church Hill Road
P.O. Box 185
Charlotte, VT 05445

Dear Ms. Potter,

Try to find fun, easy-to-understand geology activities that go beyond making baking soda and vinegar volcanoes. Imagine constructing your own periodic table while cooking *Igneous Edibles* or understanding how fossils by creating *Sponge Stones.*

For ten years I have researched, developed, and field-tested many hands-on geology activities. My experience is the basis for *Geology Rocks!* This manual of interconnected activities addressing conceptual geology:

- features innovative activities and uses inexpensive, everyday materials like candy and building blocks

- offers levels of information from beginning to advanced

- furnishes multiple, flexible ways to learn the same concept

- involves users in simulated geologic processes like cave formation

Geology Rocks! emphasizes learning-by-doing. This single-subject book, aimed at children ages 7–12, would fit well with your Kaleidoscope Kids series. It would be appropriate for kids to use at home, for teachers planning lessons, and for professionals designing enrichment programs.s.

The enclosed section, *Make Mine Metamorphic*, highlights the type of activities and information included throughout the book. I have also attached an outline. I look forward to hearing from you.

Sincerely,

John Q. Writer
123 Author Lane
Writerville, CA 95355
(323) 555-0000
johnqwriter@email.com

Encl: Section One and Outline

Subject line includes a brief description and the title of the book.

This paragraph shows that the author knows the publisher's mission and did his homework. He is offering something different from what's already on the market.

Briefly outlines the author's experience in the subject.

Quickly outline on the content and goals of the book

Mention the age group the book is intended for.

Contact information is at the bottom left in e-mail correspondence.

Detail enclosures.

Address a specific editor.

References books in the publisher's line where this book would fit in—this shows that the author knows the market.

Outline potential uses and markets for the book.

ELECTRONIC QUERY: MIDDLE GRADE NOVEL

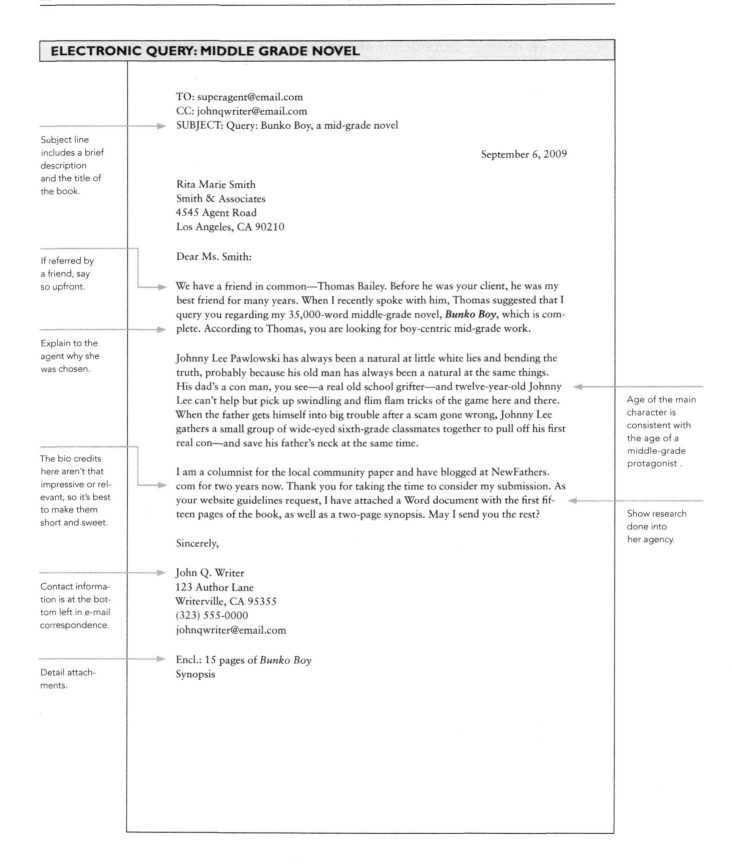

Subject line includes a brief description and the title of the book.

TO: superagent@email.com
CC: johnqwriter@email.com
SUBJECT: Query: Bunko Boy, a mid-grade novel

September 6, 2009

Rita Marie Smith
Smith & Associates
4545 Agent Road
Los Angeles, CA 90210

Dear Ms. Smith:

If referred by a friend, say so upfront.

We have a friend in common—Thomas Bailey. Before he was your client, he was my best friend for many years. When I recently spoke with him, Thomas suggested that I query you regarding my 35,000-word middle-grade novel, *Bunko Boy*, which is complete. According to Thomas, you are looking for boy-centric mid-grade work.

Explain to the agent why she was chosen.

Johnny Lee Pawlowski has always been a natural at little white lies and bending the truth, probably because his old man has always been a natural at the same things. His dad's a con man, you see—a real old school grifter—and twelve-year-old Johnny Lee can't help but pick up swindling and flim flam tricks of the game here and there. When the father gets himself into big trouble after a scam gone wrong, Johnny Lee gathers a small group of wide-eyed sixth-grade classmates together to pull off his first real con—and save his father's neck at the same time.

Age of the main character is consistent with the age of a middle-grade protagonist.

The bio credits here aren't that impressive or relevant, so it's best to make them short and sweet.

I am a columnist for the local community paper and have blogged at NewFathers. com for two years now. Thank you for taking the time to consider my submission. As your website guidelines request, I have attached a Word document with the first fifteen pages of the book, as well as a two-page synopsis. May I send you the rest?

Show research done into her agency.

Sincerely,

Contact information is at the bottom left in e-mail correspondence.

John Q. Writer
123 Author Lane
Writerville, CA 95355
(323) 555-0000
johnqwriter@email.com

Detail attachments.

Encl.: 15 pages of *Bunko Boy*
Synopsis

QUERY, MISTAKES TO AVOID: MIDDLE GRADE AND YOUNG ADULT BOOK

February 2, 2009

No contact information

Editor
Random House Inc.
Juvenile Books
201 E. 50th St.
New York, NY 10022

Should be addressed to a specific editor.

Dear Sir,

Being professionally involved in the funeral industry through contract work and having kids of my own has brought an interesting twist to my children's writing.

This is vague. What is "contract work" in the funeral industry? What children's writing? Has the author been published before?

What age is specifically being targeted?

These experiences have allowed me to approach the subject of death without being threatening to young readers. I have developed a series of stories involving the interaction of different dogs with morticians and undertakers in a vast array of situations, including embalming, funeral planning, grief, and mourning, etc.

What is this series? How long is each book in the series? Needs a lot more detail.

Publisher's guidelines state that they request a copy of the complete manuscript with a query.

If you are interested in a manuscript copy of one of these stories, please contact me.

Thank you for your time.

Sincerely,

John Q. Writer

At the very least, a SASE should have been included.

These are completely inappropriate subjects for children's books, which indicates that the author knows nothing about the market.

CHAPTER 10:
CHILDREN'S MAGAZINES

Writing articles for children's magazines is similar to writing articles for any other magazine—you have to know what audience a magazine serves and then write for that audience. There are hundreds of children's magazines for sale on newsstands and distributed in schools that are aimed at children of all ages and interests.

WHAT YOU NEED TO SUBMIT

Read as many back issues as you can of a magazine that you're thinking of submitting to so you can identify the magazine's "voice." Make sure you know what a publication's focus is before you submit anything. Don't send a short story or poem to a magazine that only publishes news stories for kids. In this and any other magazine market, you have to study what's out there so you don't waste your time submitting inappropriate articles and stories. Whether you are sending a story, article, or poem, your submission should be age-appropriate and follow the publication's guidelines meticulously.

Submitting stories to children's magazines is much the same as submitting short stories; all you need to send in is a cover letter and the story in its entirety.

QUERY LETTER AND MANUSCRIPT

Submission Tips
Be sure to check each publisher's specific guidelines before you send anything. The query or cover letter accompanying your manuscript should be brief and professional, yet friendly. It should interest the reader but not overdo it on cuteness or cleverness.

Mention the title of the work you are sending, a sentence or two about the material, and a brief summary of previous writing experience. If you don't have any previous experience, don't mention it and simply thank the editor for her consideration.

Formatting Specs
To submit and format your story to a children's magazine, see page 120 for specifications on short story submissions.

Other Dos and Don'ts

- Do obtain a copy of the publisher's guidelines and follow them carefully.

- Don't include a sentence that says, "I read my work to my kids/grandkids/second-grade class and they loved it." This definitely does not sway an editor's opinion, and seems amateurish.

- Do indicate your familiarity with the publication. It's okay to make a positive comment, if it's sincere and appropriate.

- Do indicate in your query letter any previous writing experience or credits you may have, as well as memberships in children's writing organizations such as the Society of Children's Book Writers & Illustrators (SCBWI).

- Do indicate if you are sending simultaneous submissions to other publications.

- Don't send a query letter or manuscript via e-mail or fax unless a publisher or agent specifically requests it.

- Don't discuss payment terms. This will be discussed if your manuscript is accepted.

- Do include an SASE if you're not using e-mail.

ELECTRONIC SUBMISSIONS

Before you send a query or manuscript to a publication via e-mail, make sure they accept electronic submissions by contacting the publication directly or checking out their writers' guidelines.

> The fundamental thing children's writers should remember is that their readers deserve the very best. Children's writers should set the quality bar high and believe that "good enough" is never good enough for children. I think the writing has to be tighter and livelier than before. Kids have so many distractions pulling them away from reading.
>
> **—CHRISTINE FRENCH CLARK**
>
> editor, *Highlights*

QUERY: CHILDREN'S MAGAZINE

Contact information, including phone number and e-mail

John Q. Writer
123 Author Lane
Writerville, CA 95355
(323) 555-0000
johnqwriter@email.com

April 2, 2009

Date flushed right

Address a specific editor.

Lewis Romanoski
U.S. Kids
P.O. Box 567
Indianapolis, IN 46205

Dear Mr. Romanoski:

Word count

Enclosed please find a 500-word nonfiction manuscript titled "The First Horse," which is about the first horse to go into battle in the Civil War. I would appreciate it if you'd consider it for publication.

Fits right in with the article requirements for *U.S. Kids.*

Opening paragraph is straightforward and to the point. The author doesn't waste time telling the editor how much kids will enjoy reading his article—the editor will be the judge of that.

I'm a professional archaeologist and freelance writer whose most recent publications include articles in the September 2008 and 2009 issues of *America's Civil War*, the June 2007 issue of *True West*, and the autumn 2007 issue of *Persimmon Hill*, a publication of the National Cowboy Hall of Fame.

Briefly outline your experience in the subject and previous publications.

1" margin

I have enclosed an SASE for your reply. Thank you for your consideration. I look forward to hearing from you on this matter.

Sincerely,

Signature

John Q. Writer

List what is enclosed.

Encl.: Manuscript
SASE

The ending is polite and business-like.

QUERY LETTER, MISTAKES TO AVOID: CHILDREN'S MAGAZINE

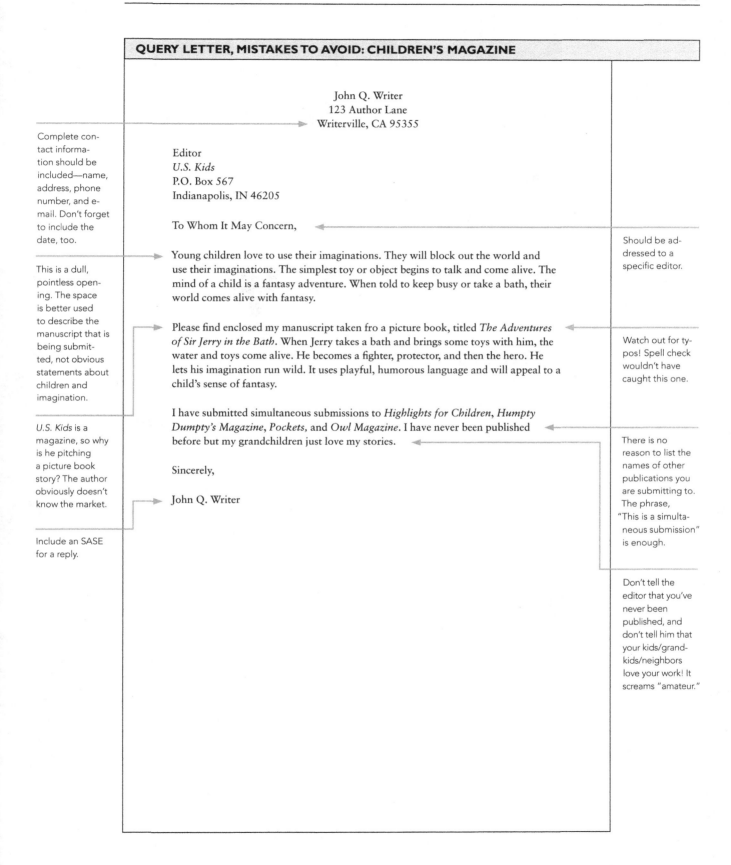

John Q. Writer
123 Author Lane
Writerville, CA 95355

Editor
U.S. Kids
P.O. Box 567
Indianapolis, IN 46205

To Whom It May Concern,

Young children love to use their imaginations. They will block out the world and use their imaginations. The simplest toy or object begins to talk and come alive. The mind of a child is a fantasy adventure. When told to keep busy or take a bath, their world comes alive with fantasy.

Please find enclosed my manuscript taken fro a picture book, titled *The Adventures of Sir Jerry in the Bath*. When Jerry takes a bath and brings some toys with him, the water and toys come alive. He becomes a fighter, protector, and then the hero. He lets his imagination run wild. It uses playful, humorous language and will appeal to a child's sense of fantasy.

I have submitted simultaneous submissions to *Highlights for Children*, *Humpty Dumpty's Magazine*, *Pockets*, and *Owl Magazine*. I have never been published before but my grandchildren just love my stories.

Sincerely,

John Q. Writer

Complete contact information should be included—name, address, phone number, and e-mail. Don't forget to include the date, too.

This is a dull, pointless opening. The space is better used to describe the manuscript that is being submitted, not obvious statements about children and imagination.

U.S. Kids is a magazine, so why is he pitching a picture book story? The author obviously doesn't know the market.

Include an SASE for a reply.

Should be addressed to a specific editor.

Watch out for typos! Spell check wouldn't have caught this one.

There is no reason to list the names of other publications you are submitting to. The phrase, "This is a simultaneous submission" is enough.

Don't tell the editor that you've never been published, and don't tell him that your kids/grandkids/neighbors love your work! It screams "amateur."

PART 4:
SCRIPTS

PART 4: INTRODUCTION

FORMATTING SOFTWARE FOR SCRIPTWRITERS

Fortunately for scriptwriters, there are several highly competitive stand-alone and add-on software programs to help format scripts. All will save you time and all will make your writing easier on both Macs and PCs. They don't take up much disk space on your hard drive, either. You should also be able to download a demo of the product from the retailer's website (don't buy unless you try). Find out more about these programs by checking the individual websites. Below, we list several popular and efficient stand-alone software programs, and offer information about each program.

STAND-ALONE PROGRAMS

A stand-alone script processor does it all. Essentially, it works without a word processor and requires just a few keystroke commands from you and minimal hardware space from your computer. Costs vary, but all programs offer screenplay, sitcom, and stage play formats. While there are individual differences among them, they all make writing scripts and organizing ideas unbelievably easy.

Final Draft (www.finaldraft.com) offers formatting capabilities for screenplays, sitcoms, or stage plays. The "enter" and "tab" keys can handle most of the commands in Final Draft. You can easily change your script from one format to another (in case you write a sitcom but change your mind and want to turn it into a screenplay). Final Draft offers an outline view and an index card view, as well as a great spell-checker and thesaurus. It even has a "voice" option where you can hear your words read aloud by voices through the program. If you start your screenplay in a Word on Text (Notepad) document, it can easily be imported. Pop-up screens can help with a "to-do" list, as well.

Movie Magic Screenwriter (www.screenplay.com) offers formatting for screenplays, sitcoms, stage plays, and multimedia scripts. You can do almost all your work with the "tab" and "enter" keys. You get a spell-checker, a thesaurus, and a Character Name Bank containing thousands of names (in case you need some). Perhaps the most impressive part is its electronic index card system that lets you build your script scene by scene. The program also controls your script length. All production features (revisions, breakdown sheets, etc.) are in one menu. Screenwriter also includes templates with preset margins, sets, character lists, and script styles for most of the television shows on the air. It offers several tools for outlining, if that's your style, and has a "bookmarks" file so you can flag certain scenes or instances you want to examine and rewrite later. Using the bookmarks and color-coded notes allows you to seamlessly collaborate on a project with other writers. Movie Magic can export your screenplays in PDF form, allowing anyone to read or print your work.

ScriptWare (www.scriptware.com) has formatting capabilities for screenplays, television shows, sitcoms, and stage plays. ScriptWare also contains Scriptype, the interface now copied by most other programs, which keeps track of and fixes all margin changes, spacing changes, capitalization and punctuation. All you need to do is control the "tab" and "enter" keys. ScriptWare takes care of page breaks and scene and page numbering. You can create scene cards that let you rearrange your scenes in index card mode. You can export and import a range of files, too. The program's thesaurus and spell-checker are excellent.

Celtx (www.celtx.com) is a newer program that has gained attention because it's free and easy to use. Though not as detailed as its expensive competitors, Celtx allows you to format and create a screenplay, mark notes, collaborate with other screenwriters and more. Since the program is free, it lacks backend customer support, and video tutorials are hard to come by. One of the best parts of Celtx is its online community aspect, which allows you to share (or not share) your work with other writers if you want to, and where you can make comments and provide helpful critiquing.

If you want your script to stand out from the crowd in a good way, you want to make sure it doesn't stand out from the crowd just because of how it looks. If your script looks like you know what you're doing, you'll pass the first "smell" test and, with luck, you can hook people with your story.

—GREGORY K. PINCUS

screenwriter of *Little Big League*

Concerning Add-On Programs

Certain software programs are called "add-on" programs, and they complement your existing word processor software (usually Microsoft Word). Generally, these programs—such as Script Wizard (www.warrenassoc.com)—are helpful, but there are some significant downsides, as well:

- Add-on programs are more likely to become outdated more quickly than stand-alone programs.
- It's true that add-on programs are cheaper than stand-alone programs, but if it's a matter of money, know that it's probably worth investing twice as much to get a more efficient stand-alone program, or just to download Celtx for free.

CHAPTER 11:

SCREENPLAYS

A screenplay is a script for a motion picture. They can be feature-length scripts for a typical movie, or a shorter script for a short film.

We all know what a novel looks like; we've been reading them most of our lives. But a screenplay is a different matter. You can't write a script in prose and then worry about the format later, once you are ready to submit. The format is such an integral part of a screenplay that it is necessary to first learn to use the parts of a script with a vocabulary of its own.

PARTS OF A SCRIPT

Screenplays have a specific industry-standard format; see "Automatic Formatting Software Programs for Scriptwriters" on page 215 for software help on screenplay formatting. Most motion picture scripts run from 100 to 120 pages. Especially if you're a new writer, try to stick to that average page count. Figure on one minute of screen time for each manuscript page, in a Courier 12-point type (hence a 120-page script will run two hours). Scripts should include dialogue and action descriptions but few to no camera directions, no soundtrack suggestions, and no casting suggestions. Do not number your scenes, and always leave 1–1.5" margins at the top and bottom of each page.

A screenplay can be broken down into six basic parts. Here they are in the order they are likely to appear in your script:

- Transitions
- Slug line
- Action description
- Character cue
- Dialogue
- Parenthetical comment

Now let's take a closer look at each of these.

Transitions

Transitions simply indicate that a shot or scene is either beginning, ending, or shifting to another shot or scene. These include such directions as FADE IN:, FADE TO:, CUT

TO:, and DISSOLVE TO:. Transitions appear in all caps and are flush with the right margin, except FADE IN:, which is flush with the left margin.

Slug Line

The slug line, also called a scene heading, sets the scene. It begins on the left margin and is written in all caps, with a double-spaced line before and after it. Most slug lines begin with either EXT. (exterior shot) or INT. (interior shot). After you determine whether the shot is outside or inside, identify the specifics of the shot, such as a particular building or house, and then if necessary, precisely where the shot takes place. With the slug line, organize the details by going from the general to the more specific. End each slug line is typically ended by indicating whether it's day or night. For example:

> INT. WOODROW WILSON ELEMENTARY SCHOOL—
> PRINCIPAL'S OFFICE—DAY

Note that there is no ending punctuation for slug lines.

Action Description

The action descriptions, also called narrative, are sentences or very short paragraphs that describe what happens during the scene. They should always be written in present tense. The text within the action descriptions begins on the left margin and is single-spaced, with regular capitalization. Do not justify the right margin. There should be one double-spaced line before and after the action text. If you have a lot of description, break up the text to leave some white space. Try not to allow a block of text to run more than five or six lines without a double-spaced break for the eyes (the more white space in a script, the better).

Character Cue

The speaking character's name—the character cue—should be typed in all caps, and should appear approximately 2.5 inches (or 5 tabs) from the left margin, quite close to the center. A double-spaced line should appear before the character's name, but there should be no double-space between the name and the dialogue, or between the name and the parenthetical comment (see below).

Dialogue

Dialogue should be in regular text (not all caps) and begin on the line below the speaking character's name. The left margin for dialogue is at at about 1.5 inches (or 3 tabs) from the left margin of the page, and the right margin is at about 2 inches from the right edge of the paper. This means dialogue will not touch the left or right edges of the page. Try to avoid large blocks of dialogue that run seven or more lines. If your character needs to say more than can be fit in seven lines, try adding some narrative—such as a visual cue—to break up the long speech. That will make the text more visually pleasing.

Parenthetical Comment

Parenthetical comments, also known as parentheticals, help the speaker of the dialogue know what emotion you intend for the delivery. Parenthetical comments are typically short (often a word or two), typed in regular text (not all caps), and set in parentheses. They appear one line below the character's name (and thus one line above dialogue). Parentheticals should look like this:

                           CRAIG
                      (panicking)
                 I don't want to fight you, Russ.

                           CRAIG
                      (re: Craig's nervousness)
                 You should be scared.

Some screenwriters prefer not to use parentheticals and instead detail the emotion in a descriptive action line instead.

   Craig paces back and forth.

                           CRAIG
                 I've never been in a fight. Somebody tell me
                 what to do.

Parentheticals are acceptable in a screenplay, but don't overuse them; try a descriptive line or an action beat to show emotion instead.

   In addition to the aforementioned regular elements of your screenplay, you will probably find situations where you need some special formatting and cues. Here are some of the more common script tricks you can inject in your screenplay.

Narrative Voice-Over

Some films have a first-person narrator who relates parts of the story to the viewer. If your script calls for voice narration, indicate it as such by typing "(V.O.)" next to the name of the character who is narrating. A scene with a voice narration should look like this:

INT. ROGER'S CHILDHOOD HOME—LIVING ROOM—DAY

   Young kids are running around the room yelling and screaming at each other. The mother has no control over the situation.

                      ROGER (V.O.)
                 Mine wasn't what you'd call a typical childhood.
                 With ten brothers and sisters running around, I
                 never got the sense that I was unique. I was always
                 just one of the boys. Mom spent her time trying to
                 keep use from killing each other. Feeling special just
                 wasn't possible. But she did the best she could.

Carrying Dialogue From One Page to the Next

Do your best not to make an actor (character) flip a page in the middle of dialogue. If, however, you can't avoid carrying a character's dialogue on to the next page, use the indicator "(MORE)" on the bottom of the first page and "(CONT'D)" next to the speaker's name at the top of the next page:

> ROGER
> I'm sorry, Marcia. I've tried and tried to please
> you but you never appreciate a damn thing I do.
> (MORE)

_____NEW PAGE_____

> ROGER (CONT'D)
> I just can't go on being your slave. You never
> clean up after yourself. Hell, you've never given
> me even a penny for the rent.

Having a Character Speak Off-Camera

In movies, characters often speak off-camera, and you'll probably write at least one scene in which this happens. When you have a character speaking off-camera, use "(O.S.)" (off screen) next to the character's name. Let's say Roger is on camera in the bedroom while talking to Marcia, who is off-camera in the bathroom.

> ROGER
> Marcia, did you just say something? I thought
> I heard you say something.

> MARCIA (O.S.)
> I asked if you would bring me a towel. I'm soaking
> wet for God's sake. Are you deaf?

> ROGER
> What did you say?

Employing Continuing Shots

Although as a screenwriter you should refrain from giving camera directions (that's the director's job), you might want to tell part of your story with a series of camera shots without dialogue or narration. These kinds of "moving pictures" usually tell their own little story. They are often accompanied by a musical score and are used to quickly advance the plot. Try doing it like this:

SERIES OF SHOTS: ROGER AND MARCIA EXPLORE NEW YORK

(A) On a ferry to the Statue of Liberty.

(B) Eating hot dogs from a vendor on Times Square.

(C) Walking arm-in-arm through Central Park.

(D) Kissing outside the Guggenheim.

(E) Driving across the George Washington Bridge.

BACK TO SCENE

Another way to use continuing shots is with a montage. A montage is pretty much the same as a series of shots except it's used for a briefer sequence of shots and doesn't really have to tell its own story. A montage is formatted a little differently, with a double hyphen instead of letters in parentheses:

MONTAGE—ROGER AND MARCIA AT DISNEY WORLD

--They get their pictures taken with Mickey and Minnie.

--They ride Splash Mountain.

--Roger offers Marcia some cotton candy. She makes a mustache out of it and Roger eats it. They laugh.

END MONTAGE

With both a series of shots and montages, be sure to end with either "BACK TO SCENE" or "END MONTAGE."

I think (new writers tend to) overexplain. Unless your script is a parable or something that's not realistic, you shouldn't try to make it too profound or affecting or sentimental. A lot of new screenwriters don't write the way people talk. And often, what's not said is just as important as what is said.

—DIANA OSSANA

cowriter of *Brokeback Mountain*

Other Dos and Don'ts

- Do spell out numbers one through ninety-nine, but use numerals for 100 and over.
- Do spell out personal titles (Father Niehaus, Pastor Karl) except for Mr., Mrs., and Ms.
- Do spell out time indicators: eleven-thirty, not 11:30.
- Do spell out "okay," not OK or o.k.
- Do number your pages and put a period after the number. The page number goes at the top of the page, flush right, about four lines down.
- Do keep dialogue short.
- Don't use special effects directions, such as FX (visual).
- Don't use sound effects directions, such as SFX (sound).
- Don't use camera directions and camera angles.

- Don't number the first page.
- Don't number your scenes.
- Do leave 1–1.5" margin at the top and bottom of each page.

What follows are formatting specifications for your screenplay as well as a sample screenplay title page and a sample first page of a screenplay. Keep in mind you won't need to worry about nitty-gritty spacing format if you have professional screenwriting software.

Tab and Margin Settings

- Left and right margins: 1 inch
- Dialogue left margin: about 3 tabs, or 1.5 inches from left margin of the page
- Parenthetical comments: about 4 tabs, or 2 inches from left margin
- Character cue: about 5 tabs, or 2.5 inches from left margin
- Dialogue right margin: about 2 inches from the right edge of the page
- Transitions: flushed right (except FADE IN, which is flushed left)
- Page number followed by a period: top right corner

All Caps

- Type of shot (INT. and EXT.)
- Setting or scene location (ITALIAN RIVIERA)
- Time of day (DAY or NIGHT)
- The first time you introduce a character (JOHN walks in)
- The speaking character's name (PHIL), followed by dialogue
- Camera directions (PAN, CLOSE-UP, etc.)
- Important sound cues or objects (Ted hears a GUNSHOT in the hallway.)
- Scene transitions (CUT TO:, DISSOLVE TO:, etc.)

Single Space

- within dialogue
- within action/scene descriptions
- within camera directions, sound cues
- within stage directions
- between the character's name and dialogue

Double Space

- between the scene location and action/scene descriptions
- between the action/scene descriptions and the speaking character's name

- between the speeches of the different characters
- between the paragraphs of lengthy dialogue or action descriptions
- between dialogue and a new speaking character's name
- between dialogue and stage or camera directions

TITLE PAGE

Submitting Tips

Your title page will include the script's title, the author, whether or not the script is based on another source, and your contact information (if you have representation, it will include your agent's contact information instead).

Formatting Specs

- The screenplay title should be in all caps, centered, about one-third of the way down the page.
- Double-space twice, and type either "Written by," "Screenplay by," or just "by."
- Double-space again and type your name. (If your script is written with another person, use an ampersand between your names.)
- If your script is based on a novel or another source, drop six lines and type "Based on Novel's Title," drop two more lines and type "by" and "Author's Name."
- In the lower right corner, put your name, address, phone number, and e-mail, single-spaced, in regular text (not all caps).
- If you have an agent, put "Representation:", skip a line and put the agent's name, address, phone number, and e-mail instead of yours. You will need to include your own information if you lack a manager or agent.
- In front of the title page, make sure you include a cover page that includes only the title and author's name.
- Preferred cover page paper is a white, cream, rust, or pale blue cover of card stock, 40 to 60 lb.
- Bind the pages in two brass brads, short enough so they don't cut through an envelope when mailed.
- Although your script should have three holes punched in it, only the first and third holes should have brads in them.
- Use a backing page with the same stock as the cover page.

Other Dos and Don'ts

- Don't type the draft number and the date in the bottom left corner for a spec script. Including the draft number is irrelevant and including the date of a script can show that it has been circulating for a long time.

- Don't put any pictures or artwork on your cover page.

- Don't use spiral or other machine-type bindings.

- Do register your script with the Writers Guild of America (WGA), but you don't need to put the WGA registration number on the cover page.

- Don't put the copyright symbol or even the word "copyright" on your work if you're sending it out. Agents and other professionals know your work is copyrighted.

TITLE PAGE: SCREENPLAY

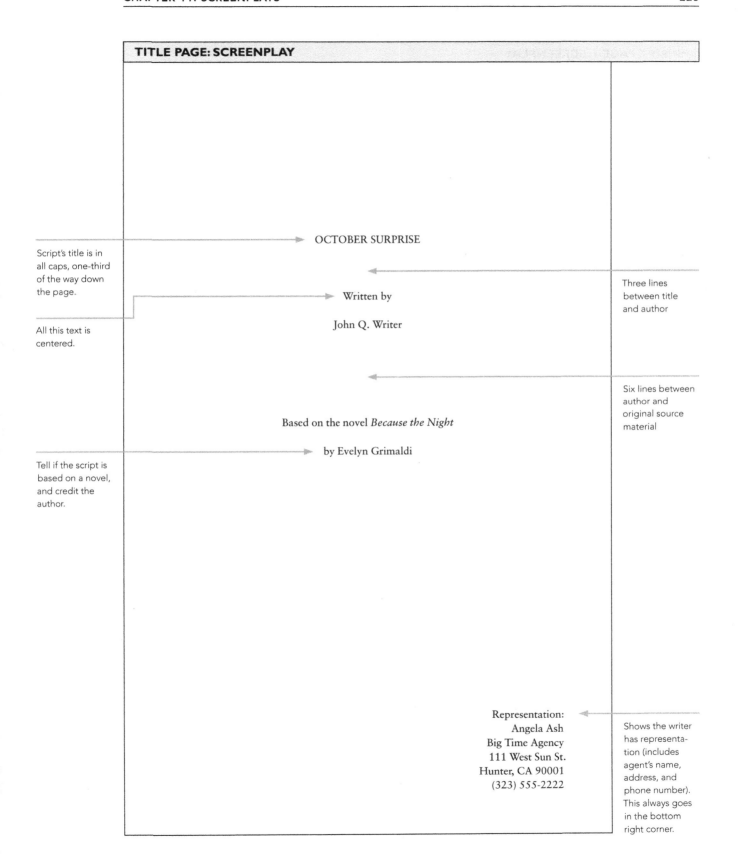

Script's title is in all caps, one-third of the way down the page.

All this text is centered.

OCTOBER SURPRISE

Three lines between title and author

Written by

John Q. Writer

Six lines between author and original source material

Based on the novel *Because the Night*

by Evelyn Grimaldi

Tell if the script is based on a novel, and credit the author.

Representation:
Angela Ash
Big Time Agency
111 West Sun St.
Hunter, CA 90001
(323) 555-2222

Shows the writer has representation (includes agent's name, address, and phone number). This always goes in the bottom right corner.

SCRIPT, PAGE 1: SCREENPLAY

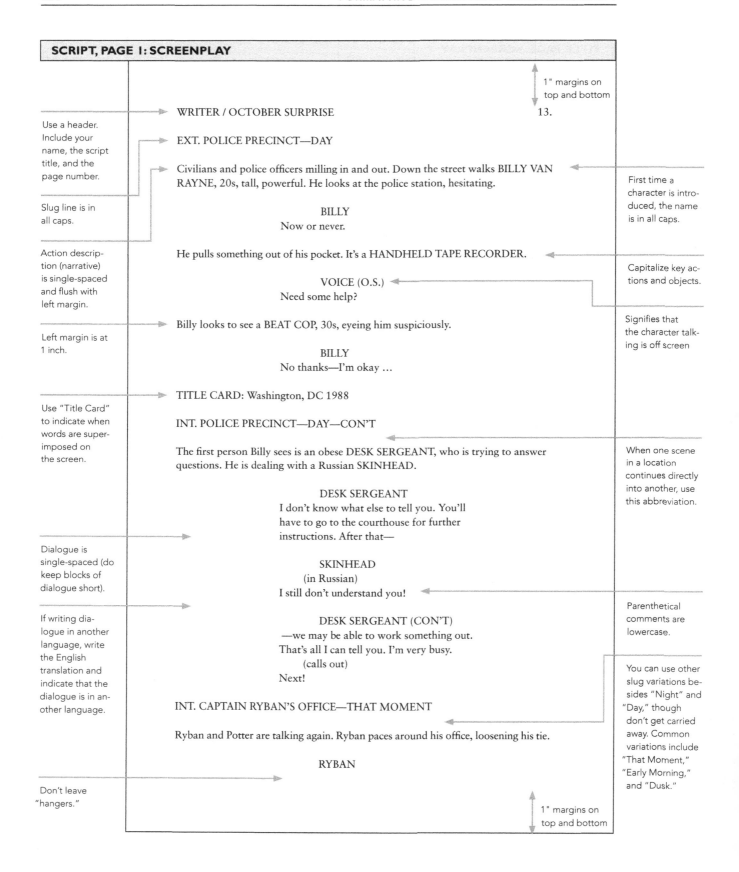

1" margins on top and bottom

Use a header. Include your name, the script title, and the page number.

WRITER / OCTOBER SURPRISE   13.

EXT. POLICE PRECINCT—DAY

Slug line is in all caps.

Civilians and police officers milling in and out. Down the street walks BILLY VAN RAYNE, 20s, tall, powerful. He looks at the police station, hesitating.

First time a character is introduced, the name is in all caps.

                          BILLY
                    Now or never.

Action description (narrative) is single-spaced and flush with left margin.

He pulls something out of his pocket. It's a HANDHELD TAPE RECORDER.

Capitalize key actions and objects.

                       VOICE (O.S.)
                    Need some help?

Left margin is at 1 inch.

Billy looks to see a BEAT COP, 30s, eyeing him suspiciously.

Signifies that the character talking is off screen

                          BILLY
                 No thanks—I'm okay …

Use "Title Card" to indicate when words are superimposed on the screen.

TITLE CARD: Washington, DC 1988

INT. POLICE PRECINCT—DAY—CON'T

The first person Billy sees is an obese DESK SERGEANT, who is trying to answer questions. He is dealing with a Russian SKINHEAD.

When one scene in a location continues directly into another, use this abbreviation.

Dialogue is single-spaced (do keep blocks of dialogue short).

                     DESK SERGEANT
               I don't know what else to tell you. You'll
               have to go to the courthouse for further
               instructions. After that—

                        SKINHEAD
                       (in Russian)
               I still don't understand you!

If writing dialogue in another language, write the English translation and indicate that the dialogue is in another language.

                  DESK SERGEANT (CON'T)
               —we may be able to work something out.
               That's all I can tell you. I'm very busy.
                       (calls out)
               Next!

Parenthetical comments are lowercase.

INT. CAPTAIN RYBAN'S OFFICE—THAT MOMENT

Ryban and Potter are talking again. Ryban paces around his office, loosening his tie.

You can use other slug variations besides "Night" and "Day," though don't get carried away. Common variations include "That Moment," "Early Morning," and "Dusk."

                          RYBAN

Don't leave "hangers."

1" margins on top and bottom

SCRIPT, PAGE 2: SCREENPLAY

Use a header. Include your name, the script title, and the page number.

WRITER / OCTOBER SURPRISE   14.

Include the page number with a period behind it.

What do we know so far?

Don't leave "hangers"

    SGT. POTTER
All we know is that the victim got on the Metro at Foggy Bottom … and she never got off. That's it.

    RYBAN
That's it?

    SGT. POTTER
That's it.

Character cue is in all caps

FADE OUT

Transition is at flush with right margin

***

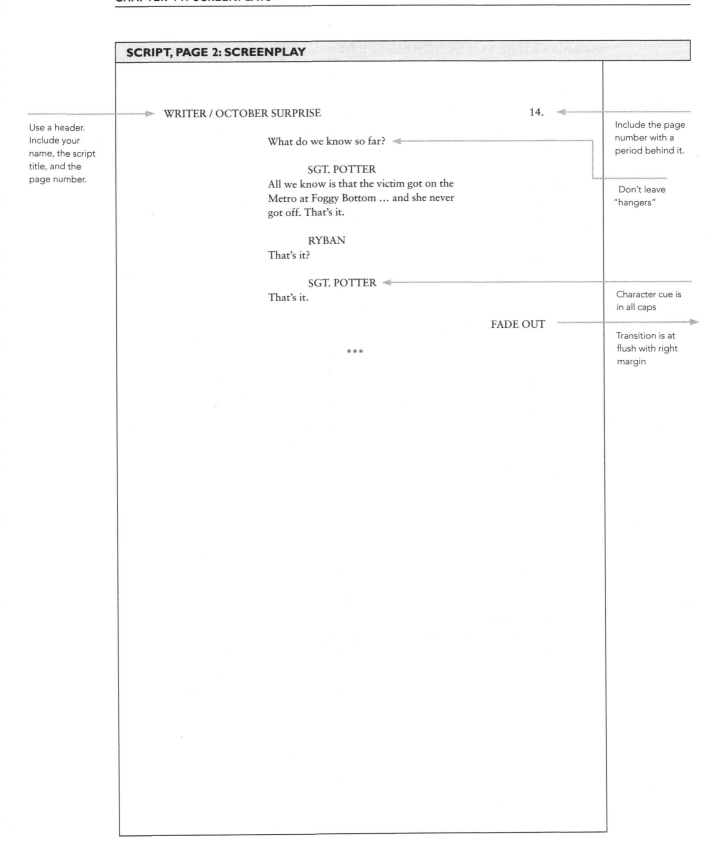

SUBMITTING YOUR SCREENPLAY

After you finish your screenplay, it's time to submit it to a script manager, agent, or a production company. Ideally, you'll find a manager or agent to represent you—someone who knows the ins and outs of Hollywood. Having a good rep who believes in your work and is willing to go to great lengths to get it sold is invaluable. Almost every screenwriter in Hollywood has representation, and so should you.

Managers vs. Agents

Script agents have the ability to sell your work. They're the wheeler-dealers. They get 10 percent of what a writer makes for what they do. The problem is that agents are busy people who usually have a very full list of clients and a full plate of work each day. Getting them to read your work and sign you as a client is difficult. Script managers, on the other hand, specialize in working with new writers and grooming them. A manager will collect an additional 10 or 15 percent of money made by the writer.

Whether you seek a manager or agent, remember that you shouldn't have to pay any upfront fees for them to read your work. They make money when you make money.

If you're indeed a newbie, try targeting people who bill themselves as "managers." A manager is someone who makes herself available to new talent and helps develop and polish a script. She's just as picky as any agent, and yes, she gets a bigger percentage of your take—somewhere around 15 percent. To the writer living outside Tinseltown, she's worth it. Managers nurture new talent with deft coaching, high expectations, and a kick in the pants when needed.

—CANDY DAVIS

screenwriter of *Monsoon Wife*

The Value of a Rep

So, what is a good agent? Aside from being someone who believes in your work, a good agent knows who is working where, who has deals with whom, and who wants what. A good agent will direct your script to the most suitable producer and will negotiate payments on your behalf. Many beginning writers try to become a client at a major agency, but that's not always such a good idea. Newcomers often don't get much attention at major agencies. Your best bet is to find an agent who will appreciate your writing and do his best to champion it—no matter how large or small the agency. Just be sure the agent is a signatory of the WGA: signatory agents have signed and agreed to abide by industry rules and standards. All reputable agencies belong to the WGA; those who do not should be avoided.

Finding the Right Agent for You

A good way to acquire an agent who will appreciate your writing is to find one who already represents material similar to yours. Seek out movies already made that are similar to your screenplay, and pay close attention to the credits. Write down the names of the writers or the story editors.

Once you get these names, call the Writers Guild of America, West (800) 548-4532, request to speak to the agency department, then ask which agency represents those writers or story editors. The agency department will grant your request if you have three names or fewer (no more). After you get the agency's name, consult the WGA's list of signatory agents to make sure that agent is a signatory. The WGA offers the list free on its website (www.wga.org).

Also check the following directories if you wish to do research on agents:

- *Screenwriter's & Playwright's Market*, published by Writer's Digest Books, contains detailed listings of hundreds of script agents and managers. It also includes a variety of insider information (profiles, interviews, articles) on marketing your work and getting your script in the right agent's hands. Its strength is detailed listings explaining what each rep is looking for and how to submit. (www.writersdigeststore.com)

- *Hollywood Representation Directory*, published by the Hollywood Creative Directory, offers probably the most complete list of agents and managers. It boasts 7,000 names and can be purchased as a book or an online directory. Its strength is in its sheer number of Hollywood insider contacts. (www.hcdonline.com)

Selling the Script Yourself

You may wish to shop your script to a studio or production company without first finding an agent. This will likely be difficult but it is still an option, and many first-time writers go this route. Fortunately, a few resources do exist for finding information about producers, studio executives, and other industry insiders. If you do decide to take this route, you should be well educated on who's doing what in Hollywood, because you'll need to make plenty of contacts and know which studies are looking for which properties.

If you want to stay tuned to the day-to-day operations in Hollywood, check out Daily Variety (www.variety.com) and The Hollywood Reporter (www.hollywoodreporter.com), both of which will keep you up on industry news. After you figure out which studio or production company you're interested in, call and ask for the story department, then ask for the name of the story editor. That's it. Don't ask to speak with the story editor—just get her name, then get ready to write your letter of inquiry.

QUERY LETTER

Once you know who to contact (agent, producer, or story editor), send that person a query letter. Do not submit an outline, a treatment, or a script to anyone in the industry unless you've been asked to do so. They will return it because they can't look at anything ("unsolicited material") without a signed release form. In your query letter, say that you have written a script and would like the person you're soliciting to consider it. Don't send a query letter unless you have the script written and polished. If he likes your idea, he may want to see the script immediately. Keep your query letter to a few short paragraphs (less than one page).

When I get a query, I look for some sense of concept and marketing—is the person hitting the commercial side of my brain? Or is the person boring me with unnecessary details about how the main character changes because of a tragedy? If the person's loglines seem to encapsulate a really good movie idea, I will usually ask to see a sample.

—MARC MANUS

script manager, Manus Entertainment

J. Michael Straczynski, in *The Complete Book of Scriptwriting*, suggests mentioning the following:

- That you know the films he produces (or the agency represents, if you're soliciting an agent).
- That you've written an original screenplay that fits in quite well with what he has been producing (or with an agency, representing) over the past few years.
- That you own the rights to the story.
- That you would like to submit your screenplay on a spec basis. (If you go into detail about the contents of your script, you'll ruin your chances of selling it.)
- That when you send your script you will enclose a standard release form or use the production company or agency's preferred release form.
- That you have writing credits or a professional background that qualifies you to write this screenplay. (If you've spent ten years as an attorney and your screenplay is a legal thriller, mention your background. Won awards? Say so.)

Basically, that's all you need to include in your query. Again, never send an unsolicited script, treatment, or synopsis to an agent, producer, or story editor—it will be returned, the package unopened. Producers and agents will not look at unsolicited scripts because they are afraid of getting sued for plagiarism. That's why you need to send the release form. Of course, mention your script idea in your query letter, but do so only in general terms.

Follow these formatting specifications when composing your query letter:

Formatting Specs

- Use a standard font, 12-point type (no bold or italic).
- Put your name and contact information in the top, centered, or in your letterhead.
- Use a 1" margin on all sides.

- Keep it to one page.
- Use block format (no indentations, an extra space between paragraphs).
- Single-space the body of the letter and double-space between paragraphs.
- Catalog every item you're sending in your enclosures.

Other Dos and Don'ts

- Do make the letter pointed and persuasive.
- Do include an SASE or postcard for reply, and state in the letter that you have done so.
- Do offer to sign a release form.
- Do offer to send the script.
- Do address your query to a specific agent, producer, or story editor. Call to get the appropriate name and gender.
- Don't mention that you're a first-time writer or that you've never sold any piece of writing.
- Don't spend much time trying to sell yourself.
- Don't tell how much time you've spent on the script.
- Don't ask for advice or criticism.
- Don't mention anything about yourself not pertinent to the script.
- Don't bring up payment.
- Don't include your social security number.

> Don't call every week to see where your material is or if they have made a decision yet. The process of reading, passing or recommending, and moving to the next level takes time. Don't call unless you haven't heard anything for about six weeks.
>
> **—MICHAEL HERST**
>
> executive director, Knightstar Academy of Screenwriting, and development manager,
>
> Grey Line Entertainment

ELECTRONIC QUERY LETTER

Submitting Tips

Many agents, producers, and story editors now accept queries via e-mail. Before you send a query via e-mail, however, you must have permission to send it. The basic tone and format of the electronic query shouldn't be much different from a query sent on paper. Don't let the medium of e-mail let your query run long. Keep it at the normal length—one page or less.

Formatting Specs

- Include the same information you would in a paper query, including your name and contact information. With e-mail queries, it's recommended to put your contact information at the lower left under your signature. Because the window to view the letter on a computer screen is not large, doing this allows the reader to jump right into your query. It isn't necessary to include your e-mail address in the body of the e-mail, however, since the editor can reply easily with the click of a button.
- Put "Query: (Your Title)" in the subject line.
- Follow the same format you would with a paper query, including the date, salutation to a specific editor and block paragraph format. See the tips on page 229 for submitting a paper query; the same rules apply.

Other Dos and Don'ts

- Don't use all caps or exclamation points in the subject line.
- Don't submit an e-mail query unless specifically requested by an agent, producer or story editor.
- Don't insert clip art graphics or other images into your query letter.
- Do act with humility and professionalism.
- Do read the Dos and Don'ts listed for a paper query on page 231; the same rules apply to electronic queries.

Your pitch is your headline. Write a bad headline for a newspaper story, and we won't read it. Or a misleading headline, or a blurry headline, or a confusing headline. We won't read the article, and that applies to all kinds of things. What's your first point of contact with somebody who isn't standing in your shoes?

—BLAKE SNYDER

author of *Save The Cat! The Last Book on Screenwriting You'll Ever Need*

ELECTRONIC QUERY LETTER TO A SCRIPT MANAGER: SCREENPLAY

TO: mtaylor@hagency.com
CC: johnqwriter@email.com
SUBJECT: Query: October Surprise

June 19, 2009

Michael Taylor
The Hollywood Agency
123 Wilshire Blvd.
Beverly Hills, CA 90210

Dear Mr. Taylor:

My name is John Q. Writer and we crossed paths at the Writer's Digest Books Writers Conference in Los Angeles in May. After hearing the pitch for my feature-length thriller, *October Surprise*, you requested that I submit a query and synopsis. All requested materials are enclosed. This is an exclusive submission, as you requested.

Democratic U.S. Senator Michael Hargrove is breaking ranks with his own party to endorse a Republican for president. At the GOP national convention, he's treated like a rock star—that is, until he's abducted by a fringe political group and given a grim ultimatum: Use your live speech on TV to sabotage and derail the Republican nominee you're supporting, or your family back home won't live through the night.

The spec script was cowritten with my scriptwriting partner, Joe Aloysius. I am a produced playwright and award-winning journalist. I will, of course, send a standard release form with my script submission. May I send you the full screenplay?

Sincerely,

John Q. Writer
123 Author Lane
Writerville, CA 95355
Phone (323) 555-0000
johnqwriter@email.com

It's not a bad to idea to copy (CC or BCC) your queries to keep a record of your e-correspondence.

Address a specific script manager. Use proper greetings and last names.

Some managers and agents want an exclusive look at queries (or most often, at the script itself). If you're submitting exclusively, make sure they know it so they will give your work a quicker look.

Include all contact information—including phone and e-mail. In an e-mail, this should be at the bottom left.

Include a reason for contacting the script manager.

Keep the pitch to one paragraph.

Be concise and honest about your credentials.

QUERY LETTER TO A PRODUCTION COMPANY: SCREENPLAY

John Q. Writer
123 Author Lane
Writerville, CA 95355
(323) 555-0000
johnqwriter@email.com

April 28, 2009

Cynthia Picture
Story Editor
S&T Productions
1111 Movie Road
Hollywood, CA 90120

Dear Cynthia Picture:

I've written a screenplay, *100K*, that I think fits in quite well with pictures recently produced by S&T Productions (namely, *An Uncivil Action*, which shows the popularity of legal thrillers is growing). The script is 118 pages, and I do own the rights to the story.

In *100K*, Cathy McTierney dies after the car she and her husband, John, are traveling in wrecks during a blizzard. After John awakens from his coma, he's faced with another problem: Cathy's mother and father are claiming vehicular homicide.

They think John killed Cathy for the $100,000 dollars she recently inherited from her dying grandfather. A courtroom battle ensues.

I am a published writer whose articles have appeared in *Legal Times* and other trade journals. I am also a prosecuting attorney. I have brought my writing and professional interests together in *100K*. I would like to submit my spec script for *100K* to S&T Productions.

I will, of course, send a standard release form with my script submission. If S&T Productions has its own release form, please send it in the enclosed SASE.

I look forward to hearing from you soon.

Sincerely,

John Q. Writer

Encl.: SASE

Contact information with address, phone number, and e-mail

Date flushed right

Address a specific story editor. Using "Ms. Picture" here is also acceptable.

Briefly tell the gist of the script's story, but only in general terms. The recipient will know quite quickly if the story falls in line with what projects she's looking for.

1" margin

Show you're familiar with other scripts the production company represents, and mention the audience, the script's length, and state that you own the rights to the story in a short space.

Mention writing credits and pertinent professional background.

Single-spaced text, block format

Politely close the letter.

Signature

Note enclosures.

QUERY, MISTAKES TO AVOID: SCREENPLAY

TO: submissions@filmfactory.com
CC:
SUBJECT: Story for you!

123 Author Lane
Writerville, CA 95355

Dear Story Editor:

After working on it for nearly ten years, I've just compleetd my very first screenplay. It's a story of my father's life growing up in the Great Depression on a farm in Iowa. I don't have a name for it yet.

The screenplay follows my father's life from his birth in a barn to raising eleven children on the same farm in Iowa. It is a story of epic proportions with lots of drama.

This is my first attempt at any kind of writing, but my father's life was so interesting that everyone in my family has always said it would make a great movie. Can I send you the script and you can tell me what you think about it?

I can see Haley Joel Osment playing my father as a boy and Russell Crowe playing my father as a man. Jessica Lange would be perfect as my long-suffering mother. Thank you very much for your time and I look forward to hearing from you soon.

Sincerely,

John Q. Writer

Include all your contact information, not just your address. And it should be at the bottom of an e-mail.

This looks like a form letter, as it's not addressed to any particular production company or to a specific person.

Never mention how much time it's taken you to write your screenplay, and don't mention that you're a first-time writer.

Never mention casting suggestions in your query.

Complete contact information should be included here—name, address, phone number, and e-mail.

Typo! Proofread your work.

Tells very little about the screenplay. What is the title of your screenplay? What makes this story compelling?

Don't ask for criticism or advice. The purpose of this query is to gauge interest in your screenplay.

SCREENPLAY MANUSCRIPT

If your query letter does what you want it to, you'll receive a request for your script.

Before you do anything else, register your script with the WGA (you don't need to be a WGA member to do so). To register, contact the WGA (www.wga.org) and ask them to send you an application.

Then you need to get your script ready for submission. Print your script on standard three-hole, 20-lb. paper. Use heavy (40- to 60-lb. bond), colored stock paper (use cream, gray, rust or pale blue paper) for your cover/title page and your back cover. Bind your script with two brass paper fasteners (brads), one in the top hole and one in the bottom. Enclose a simple letter that says the requested script and release form are enclosed. Also include an SASE. Do not forget to sign and include the release form, and on the outside of the package's envelope be sure to write "REQUESTED RELEASE FORM ENCLOSED." Then send your script and wait four to six weeks for a reply.

OUTLINES AND TREATMENTS

Spec scripts are one way of getting noticed by a producer or agent, but outlines and treatments are also stepping-stones on the way to selling your full-length script. Both are summaries of your script, and both share the same format. The outline is a short precursor followed by a longer, more detailed (and more important) treatment. Although your script is composed mostly of dialogue, your outline and treatment cover the overarching story behind (and without) the dialogue and scene descriptions.

Outlines

An outline briefly synopsizes your script. You likely will not have to show anyone your outline, but you could be asked for one—if so, focus only on the major points of your story, keep the outline informal and write it in paragraph form. With an outline, less is more, especially when you use it as a pitch to sell your idea. You don't want to bore anyone, and the rule of thumb in Hollywood is that "high-concept" story ideas can be described quickly (ideally, one sentence) and are the most salable. The outline is an informal but crucial starting point from which you can successfully pitch your story idea, which leads to writing a compelling treatment, which ultimately leads to selling a script. Most outlines run to seven or more pages for a feature film. Rarely should your outline be more than 5,000 words.

Treatments

Unlike outlines, which tend to be a bit informal and more skeletal, treatments are carefully constructed, well-written summaries of your script (in fact, treatments are similar to a novel synopsis). You get to expand on the outline and go into more detail about your characters, settings, and plot twists. You can even weave some samples of dialogue into the narrative. Keep the number of dialogue lines minimal, however, and be sure to inject them only at points where they can tell something significant about the character saying them.

A treatment for a motion picture feature might be ten to fifteen pages. No specific stipulations apply to the length of your treatment, but remember that shorter is usually better. (This is especially true with spec treatments. Keep them to less than ten pages.)

The two imperatives in formatting are that you double-space the text and write in present tense. Capitalize new characters as they are introduced. Tell the entire story front to back, like you're explaining it to your twelve-year-old nephew. Give away the ending. Don't be coy. And don't let the underlying framework show. Keep yourself out of the synopsis writing. Don't say "At the End of Act I ..." or "During the climax ..."

Ideally, your treatment should clearly delineate the major scenes in your script, with a new paragraph devoted to each scene or plot shift. You can break up your treatment by using subheads to denote when a new act begins—motion picture feature films consist of three acts. Doing so shows you've thought out the structure and timing of the script.

Why You'll Need an Outline and Treatment

Whether you're writing for television or the silver screen, to get your foot in the door you will need a sample spec script that showcases your talent as a writer. (That's why you must send a complete script after you have queried. A mere outline or treatment won't do because you still need to prove yourself as a writer.) If that spec script impresses the right person (hopefully, the producer), you might be invited to pitch ideas for other scripts. This is where knowing how to write an outline comes in handy: you use an outline to ensure you cover all the major points in your pitch. If your pitch is successful, you might get an assignment to write a treatment, and if that goes well, you might be asked to write the script.

To make sure you understand the process, let's walk through a hypothetical dream-come-true scenario. You've written a spec motion picture script called *The Summer of Love*, and you've been fortunate enough to get a producer at (since we're dreaming) DreamWorks to read your script. He loves it but he refuses to buy it. Why? Because DreamWorks just bought a similar script called *1967*. However, he was so impressed with your writing that he wants you to come up with a few other movie ideas that he might consider optioning. You agree, come up with three ideas, write pitch outlines for each and make an appointment to pitch your story ideas to him. Your first two ideas don't go over so well, but your third one does. He tells you he'll talk to other producers and get back to you. A few weeks go by, and lo and behold, you get a call from the producer telling you that everybody at DreamWorks loves your idea, and DreamWorks would like to offer you a development deal, or a step deal. Are you interested? Of course.

You then sign a contract for the development or step deal, which means that you get a step-by-step commitment—and payment—from the producer as the deal goes through development. It works like this: The producer can stop the development of your script at any step in the process, but he must pay you for what you've already written. And because he's paid you for what you've done, he owns and can do what he wants with it.

So, what are the steps in a development deal? The first step is a treatment, next comes the first draft of a script, then a second draft, and finally the perfected script. Once the producer asks you to write the initial treatment for your story idea, he must pay you the negotiated fee for that step (step one) of the process. If, unfortunately, you turn in your treatment and DreamWorks doesn't like it, they have the option to drop you from the project and pass it on to other writers (you still, of course, get paid for the treatment).

If they do like it, however, you're asked to write (and get paid for) a complete draft of the script. Even if your final draft goes over well and you get paid lots of money for it, keep in mind that DreamWorks has the right to pass your script on to other writers to make improvements to it—sorry, that's just the way the business works. You'll still get the credit for the screenplay, of course, but your story could get changed quite a bit. Just be prepared.

There's no need to tell an agent or manager that your project is like no other they've ever seen. If it's good, the writing will stand on its own. If it's not solid writing, then there's probably a reason why we've never seen something like it published.

—MARGERY WALSHAW

script manager, Evatopia

Formatting Specs

- Use a 1" margin on all sides.
- Justify the left margin only.
- Type your name and contact information at the top, centered, of the first page.
- Put the script's title, centered and in all caps, about one-fourth of the way down the page.
- Drop one line below the title and type "A Treatment by" or "An Outline by," centered.
- Drop one line and type your name, centered.
- Drop four lines and begin the text of the treatment.
- After the first page, use a header at the top left of every page containing your last name, slash, your script's title in all capital letters, slash, and either the word "Treatment" or "Outline": Writer/OCTOBER SURPRISE/Outline
- After the first page, put the page number in the top right corner of every consecutive page, on the same line as the slug line. Don't number the first page.

- The text throughout the treatment should be double-spaced.
- Use all caps the first time you introduce a character.
- The first line of text on each page after the first page should begin three lines below the header and page number.

Other Dos and Don'ts

- Do use present tense.
- Do write in the first person.
- Do keep in mind that you're writing a sales pitch. Make it a short, fast, exciting read.
- Don't number the first page (although it is considered page one).
- Do establish a hook at the beginning of the treatment. Introduce your lead character and set up a key conflict.
- Do introduce your most important character first.
- Do provide details about your central character (age, gender, marital status, profession, etc.), but don't do this for every character—only the primary ones.
- Do include characters' motivations and emotions.
- Do highlight pivotal plot points.
- Do reveal the story's ending.
- Don't go into too much detail about what happens; just tell what happens (plot twists, etc.).
- Don't insert long sections of dialogue into your treatment.

ELECTRONIC SCRIPT SUBMISSIONS

It is rare for an agent, producer, or story editor to request your script via e-mail, but it might happen. If it does, make sure you get detailed guidelines as to how the script should be submitted and follow them meticulously.

> What I'm looking for, and what every producer, studio, network, and agent I know is looking for, is a killer writing sample—meaning something that we can send out in one day to 30 producers and have them say, "This may not be the exactly the story I'm looking for, but I need to know this writer."
>
> **—KEN SHERMAN**
>
> script manager, Ken Sherman & Associates

OUTLINE, PAGE 1: SCREENPLAY

No page number on the first page

John Q. Writer
123 Author Lane
Writerville, CA 95355
(323) 555-0000
johnqwriter@email.com

Contact information, centered at the top

SUMMER OF LOVE

An Outline by
John Q. Writer

Script's title is in all caps and centered, one-fourth of the way down the page.

Four lines between author and the tex

STEVE JENKEE, UCLA's leading student activist on race relations, finds his

mother, DR. JENKEE (UCLA's Director for Programs in Peace & Justice and avid

1" margin

ally of blacks), has been murdered by an African American. In a rage, Steve kills

the murderer.

There are two major ironies to this script's central story:

Use all caps the first time a character is introduced, and introduces the most important characters first.

Justify left margin only.

1. That Dr. Jenkee, UCLA's Director for Programs in Peace & Justice, who's

been a champion of blacks and fighting against racism since the early 1950s,

would be killed by a black student. Moreover, she must withstand violence (not

peace) and injustice (not justice).

2. That Steve Jenkee, who's been a leading activist against racism, would actu-

Double-spaced text

ally commit the most atrocious act: murdering a person of the race he has been

trying to advance and protect.

Notice how an outline is more informal than a treatment.

TREATMENT, PAGE 1: SCREENPLAY

No page number on the first page

John Q. Writer
123 Author Lane
Writerville, CA 95355
(323) 555-0000
johnqwriter@email.com

Contact information

SUMMER OF LOVE

A Treatment by
John Q. Writer

Script's title in all caps, centered, one-fourth of the way down the page

Four lines between the author and the text

It's 1967 and STEVE JENKEE, UCLA's leading student activist on race relations, doesn't know what to do when a crazed African-American student breaks into his mother's (DR. JENKEE) office and slits her throat, eventually killing her.

The first paragraph establishes a hook by setting up a mystery and a conflict.

Use all caps the first time a character is introduced, and introduces the most important characters first.

Steve can't figure it out and he's angry. Not only did his mother love and care for him, she was also UCLA's Director for Programs in Peace & Justice. She's been fighting for desegregation and against racism since the early 1950s. The murder

Use present tense.

Justify left margin only.

1" margin

just doesn't make sense. A white student murdering her would make sense (she was deemed the white man's enemy and the black man's Aunt Tom, even though she was white herself), but why would an African-American student kill her? After all, thinks Steve, "every African-American student and faculty member on campus loves mom."

Double-spaced text

Incorporates a quote from the script.

All, that is, but one. And now Steve is out to kill him.

Notice how a treatment (like a novel synopsis) tells the story instead of just telling what the story is about, which is what an outline does.

CHAPTER 12:
TELEVISION SCRIPTS

Television scripts used for sitcoms, episodic dramas, soap operas, and television movies are very similar in format to a screenplay and follow many of the same steps to completion. After all, they both serve a visual medium. Although TV scripts follow a similar blueprint of film screenplays, each category of TV show has its own formatting quirks and differences, so it's crucial you observe sample scripts in the vein of the show you're writing or speccing.

SUBMITTING TELEVISION SCRIPTS

To get your television script through the Hollywood maze, you need to put it in the right hands. There are a few ways to go about this. The ideal way is to acquire an agent to represent you, but a few writers sneak through the cracks by contacting the production company first.

Before soliciting anyone, however, you should know a couple peculiarities about submitting scripts for television.

First, have more than one spec script ready to showcase. Some writers actually have a portfolio of scripts for each type of show they want to work on (if they want to write sitcoms, for instance, they'll have one script each for shows like *Two and a Half Men*, *The Office*, and *My Name Is Earl*).

Second, in choosing the shows you write spec scripts for, know that you probably will not be able to submit a script for the exact show you want to work on. It sounds crazy, but that's the way television works. So, if you want to write for *Criminal Minds* for example, you may break in by sending a *Without a Trace* script, or vice versa. You must do this because it reduces the chances of plagiarism lawsuits (plus the show's writers and producers might not be objective enough to fairly evaluate your writing). By submitting a similar type of script, you avert these problems while still demonstrating your writing skills in that medium. Writing a solid spec can also get you a job writing for a similar show. For example, if you write a spec for a fairly new, up-and-coming buddy-cop show, you may get picked up by a new show on another station that is trying to capitalize on the first buddy-cop show's popularity.

Whether you plan to solicit a production company or an agent, you must first target the show you plan to write for, watch it, and pay close attention to the opening and closing credits.

Contacting the Production Company

To contact the production company directly, look at the show's credits for the name of the production company and the producer or story editor. (Tape the show so you can get the correct names and spellings.) Then find the phone number and address of the production company and send the producer or story editor a query letter.

The best way to find a production company's address is to call directory assistance. *The Hollywood Creative Directory* (www.hcdonline.com) is also a great place to locate the person you're looking for. This is the film and television industry bible, with the most complete, up-to-date information about who's who in film and TV development and production. It lists production companies, studios, and networks along with addresses, phone and fax numbers, and e-mail addresses. It also provides cross-referencing.

Contacting Agents

If you don't want to go directly to the production company, contact an agent who represents the show's writers. To do this, pay close attention to the show's credits to find the names of the writers or story editors. Once you get these names, call the Writers Guild of America, West (800) 548-4532, request to speak to the agency department, then ask which agency represents those writers or story editors. The agency department will grant your request if you have three names or less, so don't call with a long list of names.

After you get the agency's name, consult the WGA's list of signatory agents to make sure that agent is a signatory. The WGA offers the list free on its website (www. wga.org). Signatory agents have signed a membership contract agreeing to abide by industry rules and standards. All reputable agents belong to the WGA. A great place to start looking for reps is the book *Screenwriter's & Playwright's Market*, which lists managers and agents.

QUERY LETTER

After you've done your research and know how to contact the right agency, producer ,or story editor, send a query letter. That's all you should send at this point; do not submit your spec script. In your query letter, say you'd like to write for the show and ask if the production company or agency is interested in new writers. J. Michael Straczynski, in *The Complete Book of Scriptwriting* (Writer's Digest Books), suggests mentioning the following:

- That you're enthusiastic about the show and have studied it.

- That you've written a spec script and would like to submit it. (Do not go into detail about the contents of your spec script—you'll definitely ruin your chances of writing for the show.)

- That when you send your spec script, you will enclose a standard release form or will use the production company or agency's release form.

- That you have writing credits or a profession that qualifies you to write for this show.

That's basically all you need to include in your query. Again, never send a spec script to an agent, producer, or story editor unless you are requested to do so. Do not mention any specifics about your story idea in your query letter or it will be returned immediately. They do this for legal reasons. Producers and agents refuse to look at unsolicited spec scripts and story ideas because they are afraid of getting sued for plagiarism. Just keep your query letter to a few short paragraphs and ask for permission to send your spec script.

Formatting Specs

- Use a standard font, 12-point type (no bold or italic).
- Put your name and contact information in the top right corner.
- Use a 1" margin on all sides.
- Keep it to one page.
- Use block format (no indentations, an extra space between paragraphs).
- Single-space the body of the letter and double-space between paragraphs.
- Catalog every item you're sending in your enclosures.

Other Dos and Don'ts

- Do include an SASE or postcard for reply, and state in the letter that you have done so.
- Do offer to sign a release form.
- Do offer to send the spec script.
- Do address your query to a specific agent, producer, or story editor. Call to get the appropriate name and gender.
- Don't mention that you're a first-time writer or that you've never sold any piece of writing.
- Don't spend much time trying to sell yourself.
- Don't tell how much time you've spent writing the script.
- Don't ask for advice or criticism.
- Don't mention anything about yourself not pertinent to the script.
- Don't bring up payment.
- Don't mention copyright information.

ELECTRONIC QUERY LETTER

Submission Tips

Many agents, producers and story editors now accept queries via e-mail. Before you send a query via e-mail, however, you must have permission to send it. The basic tone and format of the electronic query shouldn't be much different from a query sent on paper.

Formatting Specs

- Include the same information you would in a paper query, including your name and contact information. With e-mail queries, it's recommended to put your contact information at the lower left under your signature. Because the window to view the letter on a computer screen is not large, doing this allows the reader to jump right into your query. It isn't necessary to include your e-mail address in the body of the e-mail, however, since the editor can reply easily with the click of a button.

- Put a description of your TV script or its title in the subject line.

- Follow the same format you would with a paper query, including the date, salutation to a specific editor, and block format. See the tips for submitting a paper query on page 244; the same rules apply.

Other Dos and Don'ts

- Don't use all caps or exclamation points in the subject line.

- Don't submit an e-mail query letter unless specifically requested by an agent, producer or story editor.

- Don't insert clip art graphics or other images into your query letter.

- Do read the Dos and Don'ts for a paper query on page 244; the same rules apply.

It's all about who you know. If you don't have any connections, be adamant about making some. Most of the writers I spoke to (in Hollywood) were fortunate to know someone in the industry who helped them get started. Whether it was a showrunner, or simply a writer's assistant on a show, writers took full advantage of connections.

—LIZ LORANG

Denver-based screenwriter

QUERY: TELEVISION SCRIPT

Contact information (don't include the e-mail address if you're sending the query electronically)

John Q. Writer
123 Author Lane
Writerville, CA 95355
(323) 555-0000
johnqwriter@email.com

September 8, 2009

Date flushed right

Thomas Adams
Producer
Stellar Studios
1111 Inquiry Road
Hollywood, CA 90120

Get your query into the right hands.

Dear Mr. Adams:

I have completed a spec script for the show *Fringe*. I am a big fan of the new series and would like to write for the show. My spec script is titled "Perception."

Single-spaced text, block format

I am the author of more than fifty magazines and newspaper articles—for both regional and national publications.

Don't go on too long or gush over how much you enjoy the show. Keep it short and sweet.

1" margin

I will gladly send a signed standard release form with my script. If you would prefer that I use your company's release form instead, please send it in the enclosed SASE.

Politely close the letter.

Thank you for your time.

Sincerely,

Signature

John Q. Writer

Detail enclosures.

Encl.: SASE

ELECTRONIC QUERY, MISTAKES TO AVOID: TELEVISION SCRIPT

TO: submissions@gilliganstudios.com
CC:
SUBJECT: I Love 30 Rock!

Jane Q. Writer
323-555-0000

To Whom It May Concern:

I just love the television show *30 Rock*, and I have a great idea for a story line for an upcoming episode. Can I send it to you? I think you'll really like it. I have a similar relationship with my coworker like Liz Lemon has with Jack, so I really understand what it's like. My husband told me I should write and submit an episode.

The episode I've written is from a real-life adventure that my daughter and I took on a road trip to visit our ailing aunt in the country. Our car trip was filled with witty banter, just like the characters on *30 Rock*, so I based the episode on that. Everyone in my family has read it and thinks it's just wonderful, if not better than the actual episodes that we see every week on *30 Rock*.

I have taken local writing workshops and while I have never been published, I think this is my big break into the land of television writing. Please give me a chance. I will send you the entire script. Since it's my first screenplay, any advice you can give on how to make it even better would be great!

I'm looking forward to working with you on this fabulous script.

Thanks!

Respectfully yours,

Jane Q. Writer

All of your contact information should be included—name, address, phone number, and e-mail. And it should be on the bottom left in an e-mail.

Be sure to address your query to a specific editor that works on the television show you are submitting your script for, and include the editor's address information.

Never say that your friends and family think your script is great. That means nothing to a story editor, and singles you out as an amateur.

You should always mention that you're willing to sign a standard release form.

Don't forget to date your letter.

Briefly state that you would like to write for a show and indicate that you have spec scripts ready to send; your family situation doesn't indicate to a story editor that you're qualified to write for it.

Don't mention that you're a first-time writer, and don't beg a story editor to read your script. And don't ask for advice or criticism!

This paragraph should be used to outline your writing history and pertinent professional background. Explain why you are qualified to write for this show.

OUTLINES AND TREATMENTS

Outlines and treatments are also stepping-stones on the way to selling your script. Both are summaries of your script, and both share the same format. The outline is a short precursor followed by a longer, more detailed treatment. Although your script is composed mostly of dialogue, your outline and treatment cover the overarching story behind (and without) the dialogue and scene descriptions.

Outlines

An outline briefly synopsizes your script. You likely will not have to show anyone your outline, but you could be asked for one—if so, focus only on the major points of your story, keep the outline informal and write it in paragraph form. With an outline, less is more, especially when you use it as a pitch to sell your idea. The outline is an informal but crucial starting point from which you can successfully pitch your story idea, which leads to writing a compelling treatment, which ultimately leads to selling a script. Outlines for a half-hour sitcom run a few pages, while a television movie could be seven or more pages.

Treatments

Unlike outlines, which tend to be a bit informal and more skeletal, treatments are carefully constructed, well-written summaries of your script (in fact, treatments are similar to a novel synopsis). You get to expand on the outline and go into more detail about your characters, settings and plot twists.

A treatment for a half-hour sitcom will probably run from four to six pages, whereas a treatment for an hour episodic drama might run six to nine pages, and one for a television movie might be ten to fifteen pages. No specific stipulations apply to the length of your treatment, but remember that shorter is usually better.

The two imperatives in formatting are that you double-space the text and write in present tense. Capitalize new characters as they are introduced. Tell the entire story front to back, like you're explaining it to your twelve-year-old nephew. Give away the ending. Don't be coy. And don't let the underlying framework show. Keep yourself out of the synopsis writing. Don't say "At the End of Act I ..." or "During the climax ..."

Ideally, your treatment should clearly delineate the major scenes in your script, with a new paragraph devoted to each scene. You can break up your treatment by using subheads to denote when a new act begins.

- Most sitcoms are divided into two acts, although a few are broken down into three acts. Some series use a teaser at the show's beginning or a tag at the show's conclusion.

- One-hour dramas typically have four acts; some shows also use a teaser at the show's beginning or a tag at the ending.

- Television movies contain seven acts. The act breaks coincide with the seven commercial breaks that typically occur during a two-hour time slot for movies on television.

SITCOMS: TWO APPROACHES

Sitcoms are unique in that they have two different formats, and you can tell which format each show will use by observing the show.

Shows that feature laugh tracks and are filmed on video (*How I Met Your Mother*, *Two and a Half Men*) have a distinct format that allows for a lot of white space (for handwritten changes and camera directions). A lot of what's written is in caps and double-spaced. There are good reasons for these differences, most notably that sitcom scripts often get revised up until the taping sessions (there are usually two sessions in front of live audiences, held on the same day), and sitcoms have directions for three cameras written alongside the script.

That said, know that many newer comedies now do not follow the old sitcom rules in that they have no laugh tracks and are shot on film from all angles (*The Office*, *30 Rock*, *My Name Is Earl*). These scripts follow a more screenplay-like approach. The dialogue is single-spaced and the narrative is in lower case, just like a screenplay.

If you're not sure which format to use, it's best to seek sample copies of the show's scripts online. Note: You're looking for scripts, not merely transcripts. This is a good idea in any case. The more scripts you read, the more you'll know how to handle transitions and know one medium from the next.

SCRIPT STRUCTURE

Most sitcoms have only two acts, with three scenes per act (some shows use a teaser or a tag, which we'll discuss later). If your script is double-spaced, plan on about thirty seconds per script page. Consider that the viewing time of the average sitcom is about twenty-two to twenty-four minutes, so your script should be between forty and fifty double-spaced pages. Act titles are in all caps. At the end of the act, type "END OF ACT ONE" (etc.), centered and underlined two or three spaces below the last line of the act. Some sitcoms break up their acts into scenes; some do not.

Teasers and Tags

Many sitcoms today begin with a teaser or end with a tag; some use both. A teaser is a short scene that airs at the beginning of the show, and a tag is a short scene that appears after the final act has been resolved. The tag almost always follows a commercial break and has the show's credits rolling alongside it. Both teasers and tags should run about two pages. Sometimes teasers and tags have little or nothing to do with that episode's story. For example, *The Office* almost always starts with a "cold open"—a short funny scene to get you laughing before introducing the conflict and storyline.

Page Numbers

Page numbers should appear in the top right corner of the page, flush with the right margin (about 75 spaces from the left edge of the page), about four lines from the top of the page, and followed by a period (e.g., 17.).

Transitions

Transitions indicate that a shot or scene is either beginning, ending or shifting to another shot or scene. These include such directions as FADE IN:, FADE OUT, DISSOLVE TO: and CUT TO:. Transitions appear in all caps and are justified with the right margin (about 75 spaces from the left edge of the page), except FADE IN:, which is flush with the left margin (15 spaces from the left edge of the page). FADE OUT is used only at the end of an act and CUT TO: at the end of a scene (to indicate a new scene should begin). Some shows underline transitions.

Slug Line

The slug line (also called a scene heading) specifies the scene. It begins on the left margin (1 inch from the left edge of the page) and is written in all caps and underlined, with a double-spaced line before and after it. Your first slug line should appear two lines below FADE IN:. In sitcoms, the slug line will usually be INT. (interior shot), but occasionally you'll need to use EXT. (exterior shot). With the slug line, organize the details by going from the general to the more specific. End each slug line by indicating whether the action takes place during the day or at night. For almost every sitcom, the slug line typically contains three parts: INT. or EXT., the scene location and DAY or NIGHT. There is no ending punctuation for slug lines.

Your slug line will look like this:

INT. MARSHALL'S LIVING ROOM—NIGHT

Some shows have the character list for that particular scene in parentheses one line below the slug line:

INT. MARSHALL'S LIVING ROOM—NIGHT
(Patty, Marshall, Jane)

Action Direction

The action directions are sentences that describe specifics about what happens, when, where, how, and anything else that's important to the scene. The text within the action sentences begins on the left margin (1 inch from the left edge of the page), is single-spaced, in all caps, and should always be written in present tense (in some scripts, the action is in parentheses). Do not justify the right margin (which is at 75 spaces).

JONATHAN ENTERS THE DINING ROOM.

There should be one double-spaced line before and after the action description. If you have lots of description, break up the text to leave some white space—try not to allow a block of text to run more than four or five lines without a double-spaced break for the eyes (the more white space in a sitcom script, the better).

Character Cue

The speaking character's name (also called the character cue) should be in all caps and should appear approximately 2.5 inches (or 5 tabs) from the left edge of the page. A double-spaced line should appear before and after the character's name. The first time you introduce a character into the script (in the action or narrative), capitalize the character's name. If you're using the sitcom formatting where all narrative is already capitalized, underline the character's name instead.

> JACK
> I think I just saw Susan walk up the steps.
>
> Maybe she's coming up here.

Parenthetical Comment

Parenthetical comments, also known as parentheticals, help the speaker of the dialogue know what emotion or expression you intend with the delivery. A parenthetical is typically short (often a word or two), typed in all caps and appears either on the same line as the first line of dialogue or on a line by itself, not in all caps.

> VERONICA
> (EMBARRASSED) He really said I was cute?

Or:

> VERONICA
> (embarrassed)
> He really said I was cute?

Dialogue

Dialogue is double-spaced, typed in upper- and lowercase text, and begins two lines below the speaking character's name. The left margin for dialogue is at approximately 1.5 inches (or three tabs), and the right margin of the dialogue approximately 2 inches from the right edge of the page. Do not justify the right margin.

Continuations

If you must continue dialogue from one page to the next, use what are called continuations, which are just the words (MORE) and (CONT'D). Use them like this: Put (MORE) under the last line of dialogue on the first page and (CONT'D) to the right of the character's name on the following page:

> PAUL
> Ira, if you don't knock before you come in here,
> (MORE)

NEW PAGE

> PAUL (CONT'D)
> I'm going to sic Murray on you.

Using a Narrative Voice-Over

You will rarely need to use a narrative voice-over with sitcoms, but if you do, make sure you indicate it as such by typing "(V.O.)" to the right of the character's name:

CHARLIE (V.O.)

Wait a minute, now how did that happen?

Having a Character Speak Off-Screen

When you have a character speaking off-camera, type "(O.S.)" (off screen) to the right of the character's name. Let's say Jim is in the office in the hallway talking to Pam who's off hiding behind her desk.

JIM

You gonna stay like that all day?

PAM (O.S.)

Stop talking to me.

Other Dos and Don'ts

- Do keep dialogue short (break it up every four or five lines).
- Do spell out numbers one through ninety-nine, but use numerals for 100 and over.
- Do spell out personal titles except for Mr., Mrs., and Ms.
- Do spell out time indicators: eleven-thirty, not 11:30.
- Do spell out "okay," not OK or o.k.
- Don't use any font other than Courier, 12-point.
- Don't justify right margins.
- Don't date your script.
- Don't include a cast of characters or set list page.
- Don't use camera directions and camera angles.
- Don't use special effects directions, such as FX (visual) or SFX (sound).

What follows are formatting specifications for your sitcom script as well as a sample script title page and sample versions of the first pages of two sitcom scripts.

Tab and Margin Settings

- Left and right margins: 1 inch
- Dialogue left margin: about 3 tabs, or 1.5 inches from left margin of the page
- Parenthetical comments: about 4 tabs, or 2 inches from left margin
- Character cue: about 5 tabs, or 2.5 inches from left margin
- Dialogue right margin: about 2 inches from the right edge of the page
- Transitions: flushed right
- Page number followed by a period: top right corner

All Caps

- Act and scene headings
- Act breaks
- All action/scene/stage directions
- Speech delivery (e.g., SLURRING)
- Transitions (FADE IN:, FADE OUT)
- Tags
- Teasers
- Slug lines (EXT. or INT., DAY or NIGHT)
- All descriptions
- Character names (except when part of dialogue or character list)
- Continuations (MORE or CONT'D)
- Act and show endings (END OF SHOW)

Single Space

- within action directions
- within scene descriptions

Double Space

- between scene heading and first lines of directions or scene descriptions
- between character's name and dialogue
- within dialogue lines
- between dialogue lines and directions or scene descriptions
- before and after transitions

ELECTRONIC SITCOM SCRIPT SUBMISSIONS

It is rare for an agent or story editor to request a sitcom script via e-mail, but it might happen. If it does, make sure you get detailed guidelines as to how the script should be submitted and follow them meticulously.

TITLE PAGE

Submission Tips

The title page includes the series' title, the episode's title, the author, and your contact information (this can be substituted with your agent's name and contact information if you have representation).

Formatting Specs

- The sitcom series should be in all caps, centered, about one-third of the way down the page.

- Drop one line and put the episode title in quotes.

- Drop four lines and type either "Written by" or just "by" (don't type the quotation marks).

- Drop one line and type your name.

- In the lower right corner, put your name and contact information, single-spaced, in upper- and lowercase text. If you have an agent, type "Representation:", double-space, then put the agent's name and contact information instead of yours.

- In front of the title page, be sure to include a cover page that includes only the title and author's name.

- Preferred cover page paper is a white, gray, cream, rust, or pale blue cover of cardstock, between 40 and 60 lbs.

- The pages should be bound by two brass brads, short enough so they don't cut through an envelope when mailed.

- Although your script should have three holes punched in it, only the first and third holes should have brads in them.

- Use a backing page with the same stock as the cover page.

Other Dos and Don'ts

- Don't put any pictures or artwork on your cover page.

- Don't use spiral or other machine-type bindings.

TITLE PAGE: SITCOM

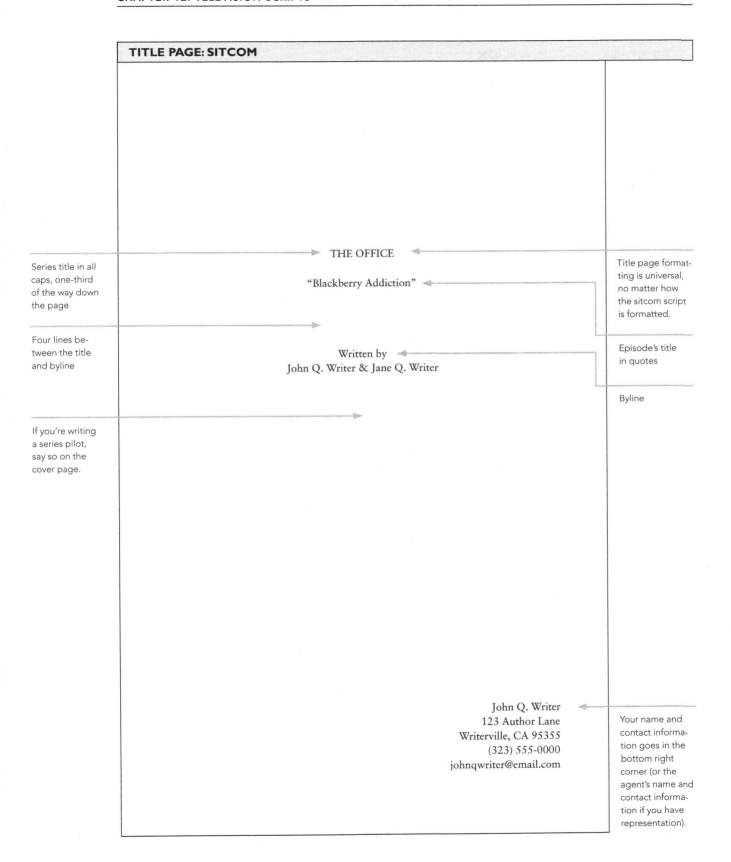

THE OFFICE

"Blackberry Addiction"

Written by
John Q. Writer & Jane Q. Writer

John Q. Writer
123 Author Lane
Writerville, CA 95355
(323) 555-0000
johnqwriter@email.com

Series title in all caps, one-third of the way down the page

Four lines between the title and byline

If you're writing a series pilot, say so on the cover page.

Title page formatting is universal, no matter how the sitcom script is formatted.

Episode's title in quotes

Byline

Your name and contact information goes in the bottom right corner (or the agent's name and contact information if you have representation).

SCRIPT, PAGE 1: SITCOM, VERSION 1

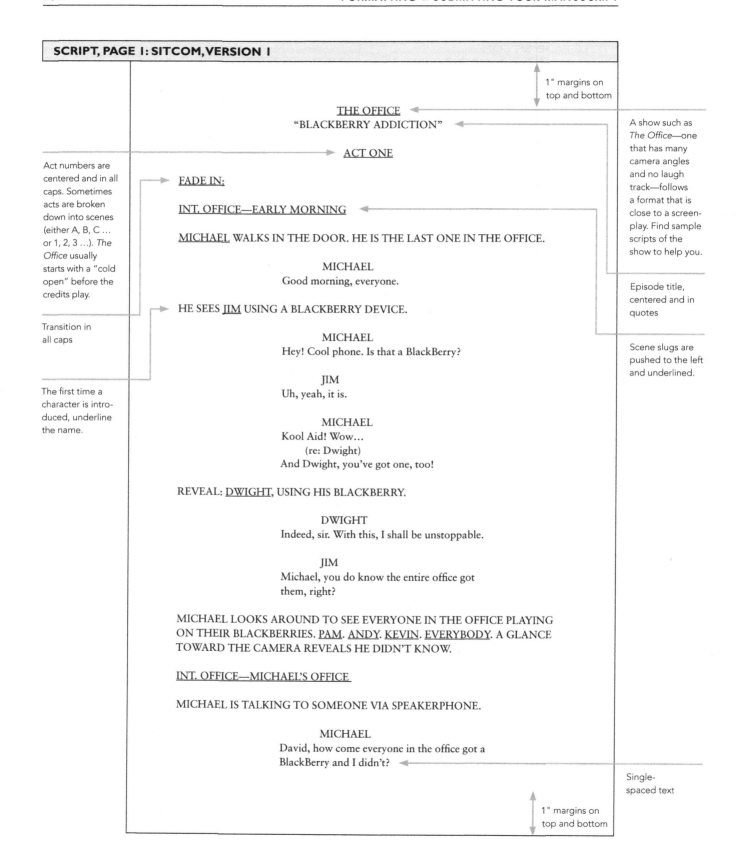

1" margins on top and bottom

THE OFFICE
"BLACKBERRY ADDICTION"

ACT ONE

Act numbers are centered and in all caps. Sometimes acts are broken down into scenes (either A, B, C … or 1, 2, 3 …). *The Office* usually starts with a "cold open" before the credits play.

Transition in all caps

The first time a character is introduced, underline the name.

A show such as *The Office*—one that has many camera angles and no laugh track—follows a format that is close to a screenplay. Find sample scripts of the show to help you.

Episode title, centered and in quotes

Scene slugs are pushed to the left and underlined.

FADE IN:

INT. OFFICE—EARLY MORNING

MICHAEL WALKS IN THE DOOR. HE IS THE LAST ONE IN THE OFFICE.

                    MICHAEL
          Good morning, everyone.

HE SEES JIM USING A BLACKBERRY DEVICE.

                    MICHAEL
          Hey! Cool phone. Is that a BlackBerry?

                    JIM
          Uh, yeah, it is.

                    MICHAEL
          Kool Aid! Wow…
              (re: Dwight)
          And Dwight, you've got one, too!

REVEAL: DWIGHT, USING HIS BLACKBERRY.

                    DWIGHT
          Indeed, sir. With this, I shall be unstoppable.

                    JIM
          Michael, you do know the entire office got
          them, right?

MICHAEL LOOKS AROUND TO SEE EVERYONE IN THE OFFICE PLAYING ON THEIR BLACKBERRIES. PAM. ANDY. KEVIN. EVERYBODY. A GLANCE TOWARD THE CAMERA REVEALS HE DIDN'T KNOW.

INT. OFFICE—MICHAEL'S OFFICE

MICHAEL IS TALKING TO SOMEONE VIA SPEAKERPHONE.

                    MICHAEL
          David, how come everyone in the office got a
          BlackBerry and I didn't?

Single-spaced text

1" margins on top and bottom

SCRIPT, PAGE 2: SITCOM, VERSION I

THE OFFICE / "BlackBerry Addiction" 2.

DAVID WALLACE (V.O.)
Michael, are you serious? We talked about this
six months ago. I told you to buy one for work
purposes and expense it. You told me later that
you already went to the store and got it.

MICHAEL TALKING HEAD

MICHAEL TALKING TO THE CAMERA IN HIS OFFICE.

MICHAEL
The word "blackberry" can mean so many things.
Like maybe a military code name. "Operation Black
Berry." G.I. Joe, I believe that was. Or the food.
Blackberries. Which is what I took it as.
(beat)
They were delicious.

END OF ACT ONE

* * *

Use a header on all pages after the first one. Include page numbers.

Character cue is in all caps.

Properly indent parenthetical.

The end of an act or scene is centered and underlined. The next act or scene should begin on a new page.

V.O. signals voice-over, meaning that the character is speaking, but is not in the room. If someone off-screen is speaking, mark that with the abbreviation (O.S.) by the character cue.

SCRIPT, PAGE 1: SITCOM, VERSION 2

1" margins on top and bottom

HOW I MET YOUR MOTHER
"AND THEN THAT HAPPENED"

Series title in all caps and centered

ACT ONE

Each act or scene begins on a new page.

INT. 2029 LIVING ROOM—EVENING
(NARRATOR, DAUGHTER, SON)

In this version of sitcom formatting, characters in the scene are listed immediately after a scene slug.

THE USUAL SUBURBAN HOME, THE SAME COUCH, THE SAME TEENS.
THE SAME NARRATOR TALKING.

Action line is in all caps and single-spaced.

NARRATOR (O.S.)
I know you've had a long day, but I've got

another great story to tell you.

THE KIDS ARE OBVIOUSLY BORED.

NARRATOR (O.S.)
Just hear me out. Let me tell you about the time

Marshall and I went to the Mets' game.

Left margin is 1 inch.

INT. TED AND MARSHALL'S APARTMENT—NIGHT
(MARSHALL, TED)

The first time a character is introduced, the name is underlined.

TED AND MARSHALL LOUNGE ON THE COUCH. HUGE COUCH
POTATOES. OPEN BAGS OF CHIPS AROUND THEM. THE TV IS ON.

MARSHALL
I've never been more bored.

TED
I'm more bored than you are.

MARSHALL
I'm too tired and bored to argue with you.

I mean, we're still watching *Dog the Bounty*

Hunter. Should I be worried?

Dialogue is double-spaced.

TED
Oh no. I specifically remember the most boring

moment of our lives.

1" margins on top and bottom

SCRIPT, PAGE 2: SITCOM, VERSION 2

HOW I MET YOUR MOTHER / "And Then That Happened"   2.

EXT. SHEA STADIUM—SEATS—DAY
   (MARSHALL, TED)

MARSHALL IS IN THE STANDS WATCHING THE GAME—
EATING POPCORN.

REVEAL: TED, SITTING NEXT TO HIM, WITH HIS WHOLE VIEW
BLOCKED BY A POLE. IN FACT, ONLY TED'S SHOULDER IS VISIBLE.

                         MARSHALL
                (LUCID) Wait a minute. This isn't the most

                boring moment of my life?

                         TED
                (BEHIND POLE) What do you mean?

INT. TED AND MARSHALL'S APARTMENT—NIGHT
   (MARSHALL, TED)

                         TED
                I couldn't see anything!

                       MARSHALL
                That was the most boring moment of *your* life,

                sir. Let me tell you about mine.

                         ***

Slug line is in
all caps.

Character cue
is in all caps.

Page number fol-
lowed by a period,
flush with right
margin

Parentheticals
are all caps. They
can fall within
dialogue or on a
separate line.

ONE-HOUR EPISODIC DRAMAS

Structure

Your hour-long script will be approximately fifty pages long. Most one-hour dramas run forty-eight minutes, and as with the motion-picture format, you can average about one minute of viewing time per manuscript page. Nearly all hour-long dramas contain four acts that occur at roughly twelve- to fifteen-minute intervals (so your script should change acts every twelve to fifteen pages). The act breaks will correspond with the network's commercials, which occur about every thirteen minutes. Because networks want viewers to hang around through the commercial breaks, your story needs to have a cliff-hanger or an emotional moment at the end of each act. Whether or not such a moment needs to be included in the last act depends on the individual show—does it typically end with a neat resolution or with something to carry over to next week?

One-hour episodic dramas share more in common with the formatting of screenplays than of sitcoms.

Transitions

Transitions simply indicate that a shot or scene is beginning, ending or shifting to another shot or scene. These include such directions as FADE IN:, FADE TO:, CUT TO:, and DISSOLVE TO:. Transitions appear in all caps and are justified with the right margin (1 inch from the edge of the page), except FADE IN:, which is flush with the left margin and should appear two lines below the act number. FADE OUT is used only at the end of an act (and is on the right margin).

Teasers and Tags

Many one-hour episodic dramas begin with a teaser or end with a tag; some use both. A teaser is a short scene that airs at the beginning of the show, and a tag is a short scene that appears after the final act has been resolved. The tag almost always follows a commercial break and sometimes has the show's credits rolling alongside it. Both teasers and tags should run about two pages. Sometimes teasers and tags have little or nothing to do with that episode's story.

Slug Line

The slug line sets the scene and specifies the shot. It begins on the left margin and is written in all caps, with a double-spaced line before and after it. Your first slug line should appear two lines below FADE IN:. Most slug lines begin with either EXT. (exterior shot) or INT. (interior shot). After you determine whether the shot is outside or inside, identify the specifics of the shot, such as a particular building or house, and then, if necessary, precisely where the shot takes place. With the slug line, organize the details by going from the general to the specific. End each slug line by indicating whether it's day or night. There is no punctuation at the end of the slug line. For example, your slug line will look like this:

INT. YMCA—MEN'S LOCKER ROOM—NIGHT

Action

The action descriptions (also called narrative) are sentences or very short paragraphs that describe specifics about what happens, location, the time of year, and anything else important to the scene.

The text within the action sentences begins on the left margin (17 spaces from the left edge of the page), is single-spaced (with regular capitalization), and should always be written in present tense. Do not justify the right margin (space 75). There should be one double-spaced line before and after the action text. If you have lots of description, break up the text to leave some white space. Try not to allow a block of text to run more than five or six lines without a double-spaced break for the eyes (the more white space in a script, the better).

Character's Name

The speaking character's name (also called the character cue) should be in all caps and appear approximately 2.5 inches (or 5 tabs) from the left margin. A double-spaced line should appear before the character's name, but there should be no double-space between the name and the dialogue, or between the name and the parenthetical (see below). Note: The first time you introduce a character into the script, put that character's name in all caps. After the character has been introduced, use regular capitalization.

Parenthetical Comment

Parenthetical comments, also known as parentheticals, help the speaker of the dialogue know what emotion you intend for the delivery. Parenthetical comments are typically short (often a word or two), are typed in regular text (not all caps), appear one line below the character's name (and thus one line above dialogue) at space 35, and are set in parentheses. A parenthetical should look like this:

> PATTI HEWES
> (antagonistic)
> What in the hell's going on around here, Ellen?

Dialogue

Dialogue is typed in regular text (not all caps) and begins on the line below the speaking character's name (or one line below the parenthetical). The left margin for dialogue is approximately 1.5 inches from the left margin, and the right margin of the dialogue is about 2 inches from the right edge of the page. Do not justify the right margin. Try to avoid large blocks of dialogue that run seven or more lines. If your character needs to say more than can fit in seven lines, add a blank line space between the text so it's more visually pleasing.

In addition to the regular elements of your one-hour episodic script, you will probably find yourself in situations where you might need some special formatting and cues. Here are some of the more common script elements you might need to inject in your script.

Carrying Dialogue From One Page to the Next

Do your best not to make an actor (character) flip to the next page in the middle of speaking. Sometimes, however, this cannot be avoided, and you must use what's called a continuation. To carry a character's dialogue onto the next page, use the indicator (MORE) on the bottom of the first page and (CONT'D) next to the speaker's name at the top of the next page:

JOE

I swear if I ever see you in this town again I'm going

(MORE)

NEW PAGE

JOE (CONT'D)

to kill you.

Using a Narrative Voice-Over

If your script calls for a narrative voice-over, make sure you indicate it as such by typing "(V.O.)" next to the name of the character who is narrating. A scene with a voice narration should look like this:

CAPTAIN SMITH (V.O.)

Now how did she get into the apartment when the keys are inside?

Having a Character Speak Offscreen

When you have a character speaking off-camera, type "(O.S.)" (offscreen) next to the character's name. Let's say Steve is on camera in the kitchen while talking to Maggie who's offscreen on the back porch.

STEVE

Can you bring that old broom in here?

MAGGIE (O.S.)

What? You want me to put that filthy thing in our kitchen? You're crazy.

STEVE

I need it to sweep up all this flour I just spilled on the floor.

MAGGIE (O.S.)

Oh, you're pathetic.

Other Dos and Don'ts

- Do number your pages and put a period after the number.
- Do keep dialogue short (keep to seven lines per block, then insert a double space).

There are a lot of networks, cable and otherwise, looking for signature shows to distinguish their "brand," so there's a greater openness to considering new concepts from unknown writers.

—RICHARD HATEM

producer and television writer/showrunner

- Do spell out numbers one to ninety-nine, but use numerals for 100 and over.
- Do spell out personal titles except for Mr., Mrs., and Ms.
- Do spell out time indicators: eleven-thirty, not 11:30.
- Do spell out "okay," not OK or o.k.
- Don't use special effects directions, such as FX (visual) or SFX (sound).
- Don't use camera directions and camera angles.
- Don't number the first page.
- Don't number scenes. This is done in the final stages of story editing, before the script moves into preproduction.

What follows are formatting specifications for your one-hour episodic script as well as a sample one-hour episodic script title page and a sample first page of a one-hour episodic script.

Tab and Margin Settings

- Left and right margins: 1 inch
- Dialogue left margin: about 3 tabs, or 1.5 inches from left margin of the page
- Parenthetical comments: about 4 tabs, or 2 inches from left margin
- Character cue: about 5 tabs, or 2.5 inches from left margin
- Dialogue right margin: about 2 inches from the right edge of the page
- Transitions: flushed right (except FADE IN, which is flushed left)
- Page number followed by a period: top right corner

All Caps

- Type of shot (INT. and EXT.)
- Setting or scene location (JOE'S ROOM)
- Time of day (DAY or NIGHT)
- The first time you introduce a character (JOHN walks in)
- The speaking character's name (PHIL), followed by dialogue
- Camera directions (PAN, CLOSE-UP, etc.)

- Important actions, sound cues, or objects (Ted hears a GUNSHOT in the hallway.)
- Scene transitions (CUT TO:, DISSOLVE TO:, etc.)

Single Space

- within dialogue
- within action/scene descriptions
- within camera directions, sound cues
- within stage directions
- between the character's name and dialogue
- between character's name and parenthetical
- between parenthetical and dialogue

Double Space

- between the scene location and action/scene descriptions
- between the action/scene descriptions and the speaking character's name
- between the speeches of the different characters
- between the paragraphs of lengthy dialogue or action descriptions
- between dialogue and a new speaking character's name
- between dialogue and stage or camera directions

ELECTRONIC ONE-HOUR EPISODIC DRAMA SCRIPT SUBMISSIONS

It is rare for an agent, producer, or story editor to request an episodic drama script via e-mail, but it might happen. If it does, make sure you get detailed guidelines as to how the script should be submitted and follow them meticulously.

EPISODIC DRAMA TITLE PAGE

Submission Tips

The title page includes the series' title, the episode's title, the authors, and the author's contact information (this can be substituted with your agent's name and contact information if you have representation).

Formatting Specs

- The one-hour episodic series name should be in all caps, centered, about one-third of the way down the page.
- In the lower right corner, put your name and contact information, single-spaced, in regular text (not all caps).

- If you have an agent, put "Representation:," double-space, then put the agent's name and contact information instead of yours.
- In front of the title page, be sure to include a cover page with the title and author's name.
- Preferred cover page paper is a white, gray, cream, rust, or pale blue cover of cardstock, between 40 to 60 lb.
- The pages should be bound in brass brads, short enough so they don't cut through an envelope when mailed.
- Although your script should have three holes punched in it, only the first and third holes should have brads in them.
- Use a backing page with the same stock as the cover page.

Other Dos and Don'ts

- Don't put any pictures or artwork on your title page.
- Don't use spiral or other machine-type bindings.

You don't write a TV spec with the expectation of selling it to the show. It could happen, but what's more likely … is that you'll write a spec TV episode to prove that you can do the work. It's a writing sample—a portfolio piece. In film, people are looking for a script, but in TV they are looking for a writer.

—ELLEN SANDLER

producer, *Coach* and *Everybody Loves Raymond*

TITLE PAGE: ONE-HOUR EPISODIC DRAMA

DAMAGES

All of this is centered.

Ten lines between the series title and episode title

"He Isn't Laughing Now"

Episode's title in quotes

Four lines between the episode title and the byline

Story and Script

by

John Q. Writer

Byline

John Q. Writer
123 Author Lane
Writerville, CA 95355
(323) 555-0000
johnqwriter@email.com

Your name and contact information (or the agent's name and contact information if you have representation) in bottom right corner.

SCRIPT: ONE-HOUR EPISODIC DRAMA

1" margins on top and bottom

1.

Page number followed by a period (flush with right margin).

Series title, episode title and act number (underlined) are centered near the top margin.

DAMAGES
"He Isn't Laughing Now"

Act One

FADE IN:

Transition in all caps

EXT. DOG PARK—DAY

Slug line is in all caps.

Left margin is 1 inch.

Dogs and owners everywhere. It's October, and many leaves are falling. A YOUNG MAN we haven't seen before is in the park, as well—except he seems to have no dog or purpose there. Behind him appears PATTI HEWES, cool as ice, with her dog in tow.

First time a character is introduced, the name is in all caps.

Action line is single-spaced, upper and lowercase text.

                    PATTI
        You're late.

                    YOUNG MAN
            (startled)
        Patti.

Properly indent character cue.

                    PATTI
        You're late.

                    YOUNG MAN
        I know. I wasn't going to come. But I, uh,
        talked to Tom, and he answered ... most of
        my questions. Listen, do we have to talk here?

Dialogue is single-spaced. Keep blocks of dialogue short.

                    PATTI
        What's wrong with here? You cynophobic?
            (He doesn't get it)
        Afraid of dogs?—

Parentheticals are on a separate line.

Capitalize key actions, sound cues, and objects.

The Young Man LAUGHS.

                    PATTI (CON'T)
        ... No?

Double-space between changes in dialogue and action lines.

                    YOUNG MAN
        Patti, you don't want to know what I'm
        afraid of.

Use this when the same character's dialogue is broken up by action.

                    PATTI
        Well, obviously I do if I'm meeting you here.
        And now you're wasting my time. Do you
        have some information for me or not?

SOAP OPERAS

A finished soap opera script is the result of teamwork. Because soap operas must be cranked out five days week, with multiple stories going at once to carry the drama from episode to episode (seemingly for perpetuity), a number of writers, producers ,and executives are required to get the script in working order. The best way to keep up with such demand is the same way Henry Ford put together cars: division of labor. Soap scripts are an assembly line of sorts.

Here's how that assembly line works. The show's sponsor (usually a corporation, like Procter & Gamble) and the producers will meet with the show's head writer to create a yearlong, roughly sketched outline for the show. Then the head writer breaks that outline into specific weekly and daily outlines. Eventually, a short scene-by-scene synopsis (usually a paragraph or two per scene) is created for each episode; then the head writer sends the synopsis to various associate writers who write all the dialogue for a particular episode.

So, most writers for soap operas are associate writers who pen the dialogue for individual episodes. The best way to become an associate writer is to send a spectacular spec script to the production company or to get an agent who represents the show's writers to also represent you. One other option is to find out if the show has an apprentice program for writers (the show's sponsor usually offers this program) and, if so, enroll in it. To see if the show you wish to write for offers such a program, contact the production company.

> Highly serialized shows—like *24, Lost,* etc.—have constantly evolving plots and characters, so it's very tough to write a spec that has any kind of shelf-life. By the time you've finished it, the stories and people have often changed so much that your script—even if it's only a few weeks old—already feels outdated.
>
> **—CHAD GERVICH**
>
> writer and producer

STRUCTURE

Most soaps run for an hour, with a few that run only a half hour. Either way, you can figure that the viewing time for a soap script is a little more than one minute per page. Therefore, a one-hour show script will run about seventy pages, and a half-hour show will be roughly thirty-five pages. Although commercial breaks will eat up some of this time, ignore them and write as if your show's either an hour or half-hour. Unlike one-hour episodic dramas and sitcoms, which have a set number of acts, soaps work in a different way because they're continually running. A soap episode is more a series of scenes than one story episode delineated into a beginning, a middle, and an end.

Format

The script elements and formatting specifications for soaps are almost identical to those for motion pictures (see page 236). There are, however, a few differences you should be aware of. The primary difference is that all action directions are capitalized, appear in parentheses and get mixed in with the dialogue. Also, a soap script has practically no camera directions and relies heavily on dialogue.

One major problem with writing a spec script for a soap is that the formats vary so much from show to show. Many shows use the "standard" soap format demonstrated on page 270, but some opt for a format that looks more like a radio script:

JOHN: Would you please bring me some water?

MARY: I'm not your maid.

To determine what format the soap you want to write for uses, try to obtain back scripts from the production company. Finding the production company isn't too difficult. Contact them and say you want to write for the show and would like to obtain some back scripts. Offer to send an SASE with adequate postage. Making the call will pay off—it will be to your advantage that you're using the correct format for the show.

ELECTRONIC SOAP OPERA SCRIPT SUBMISSIONS

It is rare for an agent, producer or story editor to request a soap script via e-mail, but it might happen. If it does, make sure you get detailed guidelines as to how the script should be submitted and follow them meticulously.

A pilot can be good ammunition to have in your portfolio. More and more, producers are getting burned out reading spec script after spec script for a particular show, and so they will sometimes ask an agent to send something original. In this case, all the better if you have a pilot script in your back pocket.

—MARTIE COOK

author, *Write to TV*

SCRIPT, PAGE 1: SOAP OPERA

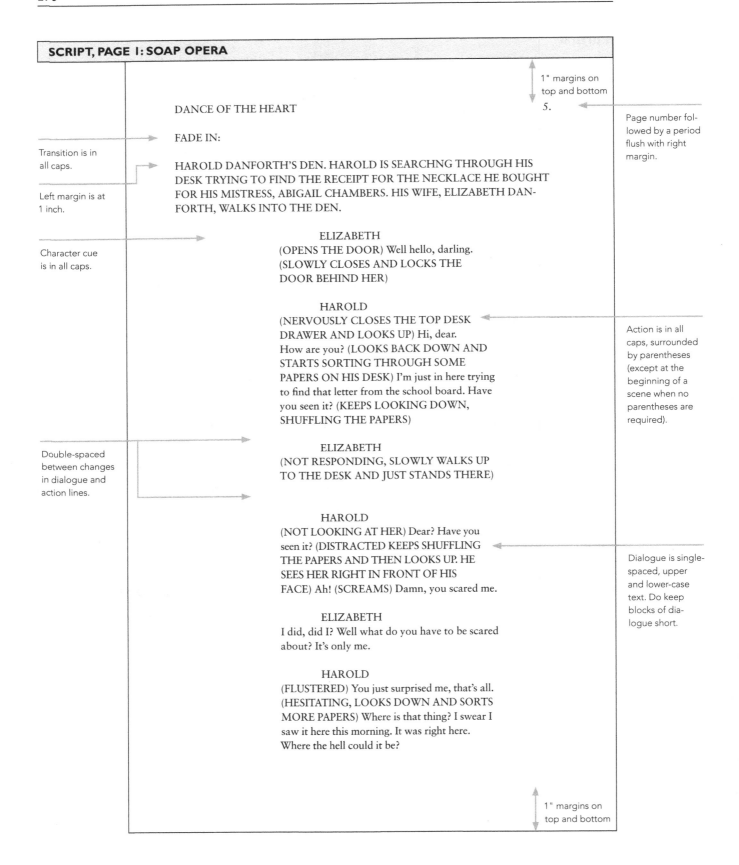

SCRIPT, PAGE 2: SOAP OPERA

DANCE OF THE HEART   6.

                  ELIZABETH
                  (CALMLY PULLS THE RECEIPT FROM HER
                  LEFT SHIRT POCKET) Oh, could this be what

                  you're looking for, darling? (SHE LETS IT HANG
                  IN FRONT OF HIS FACE)

                  HAROLD
                  (LOOKS UP, SEES THE RECEIPT, AND GRABS
                  IT OUT OF HER HAND) Damn you. What the
                  hell is this? (CRUMBLES UP THE RECEIPT)

                  ELIZABETH
                  (STARTS TO CRY) You know damn well what it
                  is Harold. I suppose you bought that necklace for
                  me. But why would you buy me anything? Why,
                  you haven't bought me anything for years.

                  HAROLD
                  (STANDS UP, WALKS AROUND THE DESK)
                  Now dear. (TRIES TO HOLD ELIZABETH'S
                  HAND)

                  ELIZABETH
                  (PUSHES HIS HAND AWAY) Don't "now dear"
                  me, Harold! For God's sake, just admit you're
                  having an affair. Please! I swear, you're nothing
                  but a weak, selfish, lying man. (SLAPS HIM AND
                  WALKS AWAY. SLAMS THE DOOR ON HER
                  WAY OUT)

                                              FADE OUT

Transition to leave scene.

                         * * *

TELEVISION MOVIES

A made-for-TV movie is similar in format to a regular motion picture, but much different when it comes to content. The primary difference is that almost all television movies are geared toward middle-aged and older female viewers. That might not sound too kind or fair, but it's the reality of television movies (especially when aired on Sunday and Monday nights during football season). With that in mind, remember that all television movie scripts have a high level of emotion, are more character driven than plot driven, and contain less action and violence than your average motion picture feature.

Structure

The television movie has seven acts and runs anywhere from 90 to 105 pages, which takes up about 90 to 95 minutes of viewing time. Almost all television movies are granted a two-hour block of time. Aside from the seven-act breaks (for commercials), a television movie has the same format as a regular motion picture screenplay (for formatting specifications, see page 236). Some writers prefer to break down their television movie script according to the seven-act breaks, with cliffhangers at the end of each act. Doing so can give you an edge because it shows the production company that you know how a television movie is structured and that you've tailored your script to work within that structure.

On the other hand, you might want to refrain from breaking down your script into seven acts for two reasons. First, all television movie production companies anticipate a spec submission to arrive in the regular motion picture feature format (you won't seem like an amateur if your script isn't divided into seven acts). Second, your television movie script might actually get sold as a feature movie (in which case you'll probably get a lot more money and the seven-act breaks won't matter). After you sell your script as a television movie, you can get together with the production company to put your script into the seven-act formula.

If you still want to break the script into acts, here are the average page lengths for the average television movie, as outlined in David Trotter's *The Screenwriter's Bible* (Silman-James Press). Notice the first act is the longest (to draw the viewer into the story), and that the rest of the acts get progressively shorter (the viewer is already hooked so why not toss in more commercial breaks?):

    Act One: 18–23 pages

    Act Two: 12–15 pages

    Act Three: 12–15 pages

    Act Four: 9–12 pages

    Act Five: 9–12 pages

    Act Six: 9–12 pages

    Act Seven: 9–12 pages

If you have a choice, you need an agent with enthusiasm and clout, but enthusiasm is more important. Enthusiasm—faith in you, greed at the prospect of all the dollars she can make off you, true passion about your talent—is what the people she's talking to on the phone will hear.

—ALEX EPSTEIN

author, *Crafty TV Writing: Thinking Inside the Box*

Start each new act on a new page, drop ten lines, center, and put the act number. Then drop three or four lines and begin the new scene. As mentioned earlier, every act except the last one should end with a cliffhanger or a moment of drama (this is done to hook viewers into sticking around for the next act, after the commercial break). The most dramatic act breaks should occur at the end of acts one and three, because these are considered the most crucial times when viewers might try to change channels. You don't want anybody changing channels when your script is on the air, and neither does the network.

Formatting Specs

Follow the same formatting specs as you would for a motion picture screenplay (see chapter eleven).

ELECTRONIC TELEVISION MOVIE SCRIPT SUBMISSIONS

It is rare for an agent, producer, or story editor to request a television movie script via e-mail, but it might happen. If it does, make sure you get detailed guidelines as to how the script should be submitted and follow them meticulously.

QUERY LETTER TO AN AGENT: TELEVISION MOVIE
Comments provided by Jack Scagnetti of the Jack Scagnetti Talent & Literary Agency

Contact information

Jane Q. Writer
123 Author Lane
Writerville, CA 95355
(323) 555-0000
johnqwriter@email.com

March 16, 2009

Jack Scagnetti Talent & Literary Agency
5330 Lankerskim Blvd.
N. Hollywood, CA 91601

Address specific agent. Spell his or her name correctly.

Dear Mr. Scagnetti:

I found the name of your agency in *Screenwriter's & Playwright's Market* and I thought you might be interested in seeing my screenplay, "Hidden Casualties: Battles on the Homefront." While Sergeant Raye was in Saudi Arabia, her ex-husband illegally manipulated the courts in another state and stole custody of her three children. Seventeen lawyers told her that there was nothing she could do; that she had lost her children and it would take years to get them back. Citing violation of rights as stipulated in the Soldiers and Sailors Civil Relief Act, she refused to give up. It wasn't until she went public with her story that the Army stepped in to right the wrong.

Tells where she found agency and what her script is about. She tells a lot but shows this is a timely and unusual subject. She also quickly reveals conflict and tough battles to overcome problems, and the power of not giving up—things that are appealing in a good story.

1" margin

Single-spaced text, block format

"Hidden Casualties" is a story that will appeal to a wide range of audiences, from those interested in legal matters that bridge military and civilian life to those who served or had loved ones serving in the Persian Gulf, even to those who are serving elsewhere. Medical personnel, single parents, and those concerned with women's issues and children's rights will also be interested.

Mention the various audiences who will be interested in this story.

This story is changing the way the military deals with single parents, and has been discussed in meetings with military lawyers throughout the country. It was profiled on CNN and on all major networks in southern Texas.

Reveal the real life results of the action taken by the main character.

I'm a member of SCBWI (Society of Children's Book Writers & Illustrators) and have written multiple books, an educational video, and an audiocassette in the educational field. My books include four story books, activity books, a "how to" book, reader's theater, and a poetry collection.

I look forward to hearing from you. I've enclosed an SASE for your response.

Sincerely,

Tell enough about yourself to show you're not a novice. That tells tells an agent they should at least read what you've sent.

Signature

Jane Q. Writer

Encl.: SASE

Note all enclosures.

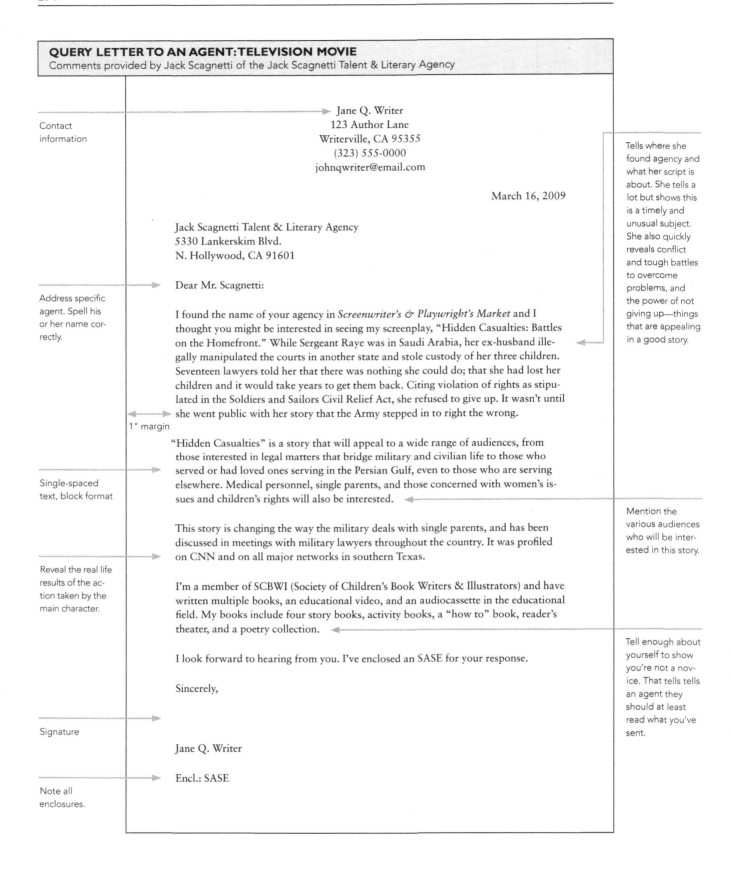

CHAPTER 13:
AUDIO/VIDEO SCRIPTS

Audio/video scripts are used to inform, usually with a goal to instruct (educational videos for corporate clients) or sell (commercials). Video presentations are essential when businesses need to educate those in-house and those outside of the company. They are most often used to train new employees, to convince another company their product is worth investing in, to tell the history and mission of the business, and to explain procedural steps that go into a company's products. On the selling front, audio/video scripts are the backbone of television commercials, and advertising agencies would be lost without them.

FORMAT RATIONALE

Almost all audio/video scripts demand one thing: a clear script that complements the implementation of the ideas on camera. Common elements in audio/video presentations include animation, stock footage, music, illustrations, and narration. The scriptwriter directs the organization and flow of all these elements on the script's page, using an especially effective format—the two-column audio/video (A/V) format. Understanding and using the format is simple: The visual direction and description go on the left side of the page, and the dialogue and audio go on the right. While this certainly is only one way of conveying a message, it is the most effective and popular way to sell a product or communicate a message.

Corporate Programs

If you're producing a short format program to convey a business-to-business message or a business-to-consumer message, the two-column format is most appropriate because it helps clients who don't have a significant background in film or video. They can easily understand the connection between what is heard and what is seen. Also, the two-column format allows for making changes to the first drafts of your script, and ultimately makes it easier to produce.

Commercials

If you're producing a commercial, the two-column format is ideal for the same reasons. Ad agencies and their customers pay thousands upon thousands of dollars for broadcast time, and many believe you have to stuff each spot with tons of information and images. A lot happens in most ten-, twenty-, or thirty-second commercials, and often most of the images are supported by a narration. It seems like some commercials have more scenes than full-length features. For these reasons, the two-column format allows everyone, even the graphic artists and editors, to know what is happening every second, if not every frame. Be sure not to use too much video jargon; you want to make your script easy to understand for your clients.

Formatting Specs

- Create a header at the top of the page. Include your company's information in the top left corner and the client and project information in the top right corner. This information should be double-spaced, and your company's name should be in all caps.

- Separate the header of the script and the body with a line break.

- Video directions always go on the left side of the page, and audio on the right. The audio directions should always begin on the same line as the last line of the video directions.

- Music directions should be in all caps.

- Narration and dialogue should be in upper- and lowercase text and double-spaced.

- Video directions should be in all caps.

- Sound commentary and direction (other than narration) should be in all caps in parentheses.

- "FADE OUT" at the end of a script indicates that the script is finished.

Other Dos and Don'ts

- Do read your script out loud to make sure the dialogue sounds natural.

- Do set up your A/V script in two columns.

- Don't submit your script via e-mail unless specifically requested.

SCRIPT: AUDIO/VIDEO

Include your company's information on the left. The company name is in all caps.

ALL WORLD MEDIA

2222 Ninth St.

New York, NY 10000

(212) 555-1111

CLIENT: Baby Paper Products

PRODUCT: Happy Heinies

TITLE: "Christmas Diapers"

LENGTH: 45 Seconds

Double-space information in header. Include client and project information on right.

Separate the header of the script and the body with two blank lines.

VIDEO:

AUDIO:

OPEN WITH A FROWNING
BABY IN A SANTA HAT
AND CHRISTMAS OUTFIT.

MUSIC: (AWFUL SOUNDING VERSION
OF "SILENT NIGHT")

Music directions are in all caps.

NARRATOR:

Do you want your little loved one to have a
soggy Christmas?

Video directions are in all caps.

SHOW SHOT OF INEXPENSIVE
SOGGY DIAPERS COMING APART
ON BABY'S BOTTOM.

(A BABY STARTS WHINING AND
CRYING UNCONTROLLABLY IN
BACKGROUND)

Narration and dialogue is in upper- and lower-case text, double-spaced.

SHOT OF SNOWFLAKES FALLING
INTO A DIAPER

MUSIC: ("I'M DREAMING OF A WHITE
CHRISTMAS")

NARRATOR: Or a happy white Christmas?

SHOT OF SMILING BABY, FOLLOWED
BY SHOT OF A CLEAN, WHITE, DRY
STURDY DIAPERON BABY'S BOTTOM

(BABY GOO-GOOS HAPPILY.)

Notice the audio directions begin on the same line as the last line of the video directions.

SHOT OF UGLY YELLOW DIAPER
JUXTAPOSED WITH CLEAN WHITE
DIAPER

NARRATOR: It's up to you, Mom and Dad.

SHOT OF HAPPY BABY HOLDING
HAPPY HEINIES PACKAGE

NARRATOR: This holiday season, make the
right choice.

Sound comments and direction (other than narration) go in parentheses and are in all caps. Video always goes on the left side of the page, audio on the right.

FADE OUT.

Indicate this script is finished.

* * *

CHAPTER 14:
PLAY SCRIPTS

In general, there are three types of stage plays:

- The ten-minute play
- The one-act play
- The full-length play

Ten-minute plays are just that—they run ten pages and last ten minutes. They generally feature two or three characters in one setting and address one central conflict. One-act plays run twenty to sixty pages in length. Full-length scripts are 100 to 130 pages in length and usually feature two or three distinct acts, sometimes with an intermission. Using the following formatting specifics, plan on about one minute per page when performed out loud.

Despite the number of acts and pages a play possesses, all plays should follow the basic dramatic structure and have three overarching movements—a beginning, a middle, and an end. Here's a rough sketch of what the overall dramatic structure of your play should look like, as outlined in Jeffrey Hatcher's *The Art & Craft of Playwriting* (Writer's Digest Books):

Part One
Start of play

- Introduction of characters, place, time, setting or exposition
- Introduction of the primary inciting event
- Initial point of attack or primary conflict
- Introduction of the central dramatic question

Part Two

- Characters embark on journey/struggle/search for answers/goals
- Conflicts with other characters, events, circumstances
- Characters reassess situations, respond to obstacles and challenges, plan new tactics, succeed, fail, attack, retreat, surprise and are surprised, encounter major reversals (rising action)
- A crisis is reached

- Characters embark on an action that will resolve the crisis and lead inexorably to the conclusion

Part Three

- The major characters or combatants engage in a final conflict (climax)
- The character's goal is achieved or lost
- The central dramatic question is answered
- The actions suggest the themes or ideas of the play
- Following the climax is the resolution, in which a new order is established
- End of play

WHAT YOU NEED TO SUBMIT

Along with the stage play script, you need introductory pages, including a title page, an information breakdown page, act and scene breakdowns, and a cast of characters page.

> When something is spelled out, or told directly to us, it simply becomes less because our participation is denied. Imagine being told just seconds before the game that your team will lose by one point on a missed shot with one second left in the game.
>
> **—MICHAEL WRIGHT**
>
> author of *Playwriting in Progress*

TITLE PAGE

Submission Tips

The title page includes the name of the play, how many acts it contains, and your name and contact information (or the agent's name and contact information if you have representation). It also indicates if the play is based on a novel.

Formatting Specs

- The title should be in all caps, centered, about one-third of the way down the page.
- Drop four lines and type "A One-Act Play by," or "A Play in Two Acts by" or "A Play in Three Acts by" (depending on what you write).
- Drop four lines again and type your name. (If your play is written with another person, use an ampersand between your names.)
- If your play is based on a novel or other source, drop six lines and type "Based on the novel *Novel's Title*," then drop two more lines and type "by Author's Name."

You have to write with the practicalities of the theater in mind. Plays are not movies. You can't say, "Scene 1: The peer at Lake Michigan; Scene 2: A skyscraper penthouse; Scene 3: Central Park." That is a nonrealistic play. There are a lot of logistical things that a producer will look at in a script. They may say, "This is an interesting play, but it's got too many characters, it's got too many costumes, it's got too many props."

—TED SWINDLEY

playwright, *Always … Patsy Cline*

- In the lower right corner, put your name and contact information, single-spaced, in upper- and lowercase text.
- If you have an agent, type "Representation:" skip a line and put the agent's name and contact information instead of yours.

Other Dos and Don'ts

- Don't number the title page.
- Do include your agent's name and contact information if you have representation.
- Don't submit your play via e-mail unless specifically requested.

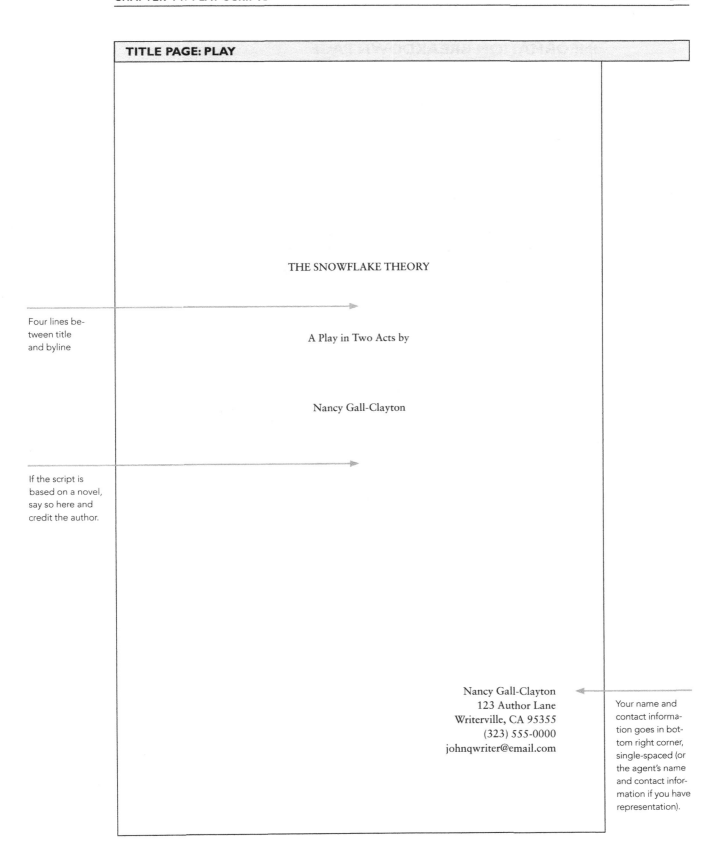

TITLE PAGE: PLAY

THE SNOWFLAKE THEORY

Four lines be-
tween title
and byline

A Play in Two Acts by

Nancy Gall-Clayton

If the script is
based on a novel,
say so here and
credit the author.

Nancy Gall-Clayton
123 Author Lane
Writerville, CA 95355
(323) 555-0000
johnqwriter@email.com

Your name and
contact informa-
tion goes in bot-
tom right corner,
single-spaced (or
the agent's name
and contact infor-
mation if you have
representation).

INFORMATION BREAKDOWN PAGE

Submission Tips

The information breakdown page(s) of a play has several sections and purposes. It lists all the pertinent information about the play, from characters to scene breakdowns and the play's development. This information can last either one or two pages.

Listing Characters

Primary and secondary characters are listed, each with a brief description of the character. The description will be used mostly to help a director or producer in casting the part. Common aspects to include would be the character's age and any overarching characteristics (e.g., "grunge-loving, teen-angst-filled teenage boy"). This section can be broken down into primary characters and secondary characters if need be.

Time and Place

This section illuminates when the story takes place, whether it's present day Boston, or 19th-century London.

Scene Breakdown

Breaking down the acts and scenes helps producers and directors see how many scenes are in the play and the setting of each scene. Include the exact page count for each scene.

Notes

If you anticipate questions from readers, this is your chance to address them upfront.

History of Awards and Development

In this section, elaborate on the play's past development. Has it received a staged reading? A workshop? Multiple workshops? If so, where? Has it placed in any contests? If so, was it a grand-prize winner, finalist or semifinalist? What years? Make sure you include up-to-date information regarding if the work is published anywhere or has had any formal productions. If you're contacting a theater in Colorado, for instance, can you tell them that the work has never been produced in the American West? That way, they understand it's not in consideration for a world premiere, but rather for a regional premiere.

Playwriting is different from all other writing. The story is told exclusively in dialogue and exclusively in the present tense. The challenge is to tell a story in dialogue and the fact that each time it is presented, it's as if the story is unfolding afresh.

—NANCY GALL-CLAYTON
Louisville-based playwright

INFORMATION BREAKDOWN PAGE: PLAY

The Snowflake Theory

The title is at the top, centered, bold, and italicized.

CHARACTERS (in order of appearance)

The "Characters" section is sometimes broken down into two subsections: primary characters and secondary.

Keep character information to a minimum.

Marge Klein	A widowed Jewish woman, 58, primed to reinvent herself
Rebecca Klein	Marge's daughter, 40 (DOB = 1963), never married and doesn't mind, 17 weeks pregnant in Act I
Clark Klein	Marge's son, 33 (DOB = 1970), has been in a fog for years (or so it seemed), but is emerging
Violet Sample	Clark's girlfriend, non-Jewish, 20s, couldn't be less—or more—right for the Kleins, a fan of vintage clothes and fun hair colors
Harris Samuels	A rabbi, 57, he knows humor can heal

Character names flushed left

TIME & PLACE
February–April 2003. A city in the Midwest: Marge's kitchen and Harris's office.

SCENE BREAKDOWN

Act I:	Scene 1, Marge's kitchen, Wednesday, February 26, 2003, pages 1–35
	Scene 2, Rabbi's office, the next day, Thursday, page 35–50
	Scene 3, Marge's kitchen, the next evening, Friday, pages 51–59
	Scene 4, Marge's kitchen, two days later, Sunday, pages 59–70
Act II:	Scene 1, Marge's kitchen, a few minutes later, pages 71–88
	Scene 2, Marge's kitchen, the next evening, Monday, pages 88–94
	Scene 3, Marge's kitchen, eight weeks later, pages 94–106

NOTES
The several lines of Aristophanes' *Lysistrata* quoted in this play come from a version originally published in 1912. It was translated anonymously and is in the public domain. Pronunciations offered for Yiddish and Hebrew are only approximations; explanations of words like chuppah and bris are not all encompassing.

1" margin

HISTORY OF AWARDS AND DEVELOPMENT
The Snowflake Theory was presented as a staged reading at "Beyond the Borscht Belt: The Jewish Theatre Festival" at the Jewish Community Center in Columbus, Ohio, and the Ohio State University Hillel Foundation on October 26 and 27, 2008 and at ScriptFEST at Southern Appalachian Repertory Theatre on October 24, 2008. Previously, it was a Finalist for the Southeastern Theatre Conference Charles M. Getchell Award and a Semifinalist for the Dorothy Silver Playwriting Competition. Earlier versions were selected for readings at the New Voices Series of the Cincinnati Arts Association and the Cincinnati Playwrights Initiative at the Aronoff Center for the Arts and for the Kentucky Voices Play Reading Series at Kentucky Repertory Theatre in Horse Cave, Kentucky. This play has never been produced or published.

Depending on the length of your notes and play history, this information can go more than one page—but try and keep it to two pages maximum.

Explain if the play has any readings, workshops or productions.

SCRIPT PAGES

After the introductory page(s) comes the play script itself. The script pages include the following information, which should be formatted as specified.

Dialogue

Following the scene description, double-space and begin the dialogue. Formatting the dialogue is simple. The speaking character's name appears in all caps, centered. Dialogue starts from the left margin on the line below the character's centered name, and should be in regular upper- and lowercase text and single-spaced.

Parenthetical Comments

Parenthetical comments, also known as parentheticals, include description, expression or direction that helps the actor or director know what you intend. There are two types of parentheticals in playwriting:

A parenthetical that appears within the dialogue lines. When the direction indicates an action or emotion to occur while the character is speaking, the parenthetical is put in lines of dialogue. If the parenthetical is used to signal the character's mood or delivery, it is placed between the character's name and the first word of dialogue. All the text is lowercase.

FLOYD
(exasperated)

Then what are you talking about? Huh?

A parenthetical that falls between or outside spoken lines. When there are more detailed directions (often physical directions), the parenthetical will be set apart from the dialogue by a line break. Put the direction in parentheses and indent four tabs in. The text is both upper- and lowercase, and is single-spaced within the parenthetical.

FLOYD

Then what are you talking about? Huh?

(Floyd gets up and pushes his chair over.)

The Act Ending

To end an act, simply type "Curtain Falls" or "Lights Down" (italicize or underline it), centered, at the bottom of the page.

Formatting Specs

- Use 1" margins on all sides.
- Character cues should be placed centered above the line of dialogue.
- The dialogue should be single-spaced with a double space before a new character starts to speak.

- When a character's name is used in an action parenthetical, it should appear in all caps.

- When a character enters a room, the character's name should appear in all caps.

- The act and scene identifications should be centered, bold, and underlined.

Other Dos and Don'ts

- Do number all your script pages and put a period after the number.

- Don't overuse action. Directors want to interpret the movement onstage and make the play "their own," in a way. Actors, too. The less parenthetical emotions and directions you can include, the better.

- Don't submit your script via e-mail unless specifically requested by the publisher.

In plays, the audience gets the big picture. They can't see things close up. Words that the actors say are the most valuable commodity.

—CLAY STAFFORD

Nashville-based playwright

SCRIPT, PAGE 1: PLAY

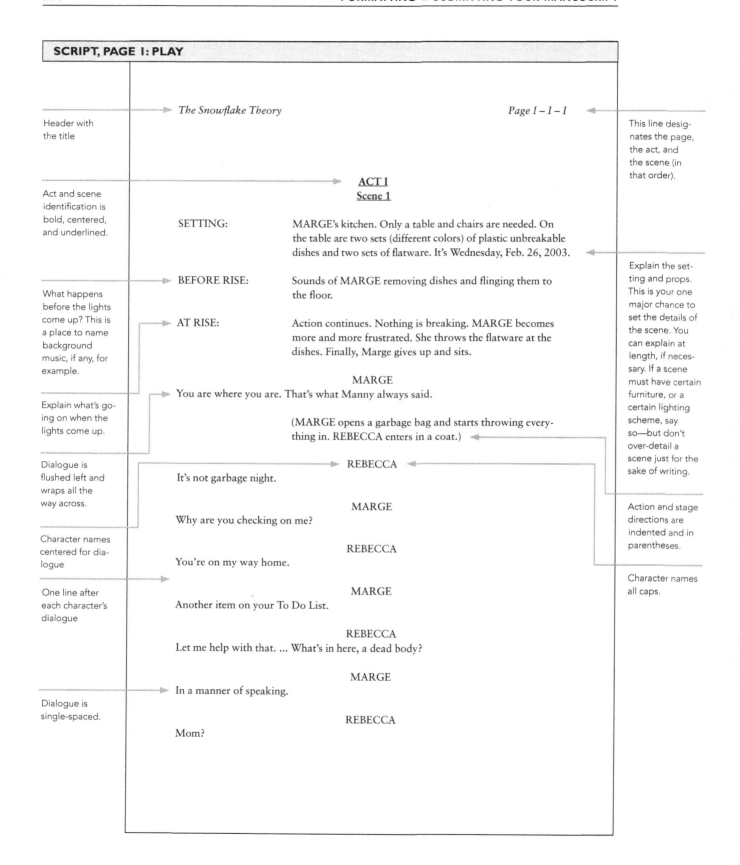

The Snowflake Theory   *Page I – I – I*

<u>ACT I</u>
<u>Scene 1</u>

SETTING: MARGE's kitchen. Only a table and chairs are needed. On
                     the table are two sets (different colors) of plastic unbreakable
                     dishes and two sets of flatware. It's Wednesday, Feb. 26, 2003.

BEFORE RISE: Sounds of MARGE removing dishes and flinging them to
                     the floor.

AT RISE: Action continues. Nothing is breaking. MARGE becomes
                     more and more frustrated. She throws the flatware at the
                     dishes. Finally, Marge gives up and sits.

                              MARGE
You are where you are. That's what Manny always said.

                     (MARGE opens a garbage bag and starts throwing every-
                     thing in. REBECCA enters in a coat.)

                            REBECCA
It's not garbage night.

                              MARGE
Why are you checking on me?

                            REBECCA
You're on my way home.

                              MARGE
Another item on your To Do List.

                            REBECCA
Let me help with that. ... What's in here, a dead body?

                              MARGE
In a manner of speaking.

                            REBECCA
Mom?

Callout labels (margin annotations):

Left side:
- Header with the title
- Act and scene identification is bold, centered, and underlined.
- What happens before the lights come up? This is a place to name background music, if any, for example.
- Explain what's going on when the lights come up.
- Dialogue is flushed left and wraps all the way across.
- Character names centered for dialogue
- One line after each character's dialogue
- Dialogue is single-spaced.

Right side:
- This line designates the page, the act, and the scene (in that order).
- Explain the setting and props. This is your one major chance to set the details of the scene. You can explain at length, if necessary. If a scene must have certain furniture, or a certain lighting scheme, say so—but don't over-detail a scene just for the sake of writing.
- Action and stage directions are indented and in parentheses.
- Character names all caps.

SCRIPT, PAGE 2: PLAY

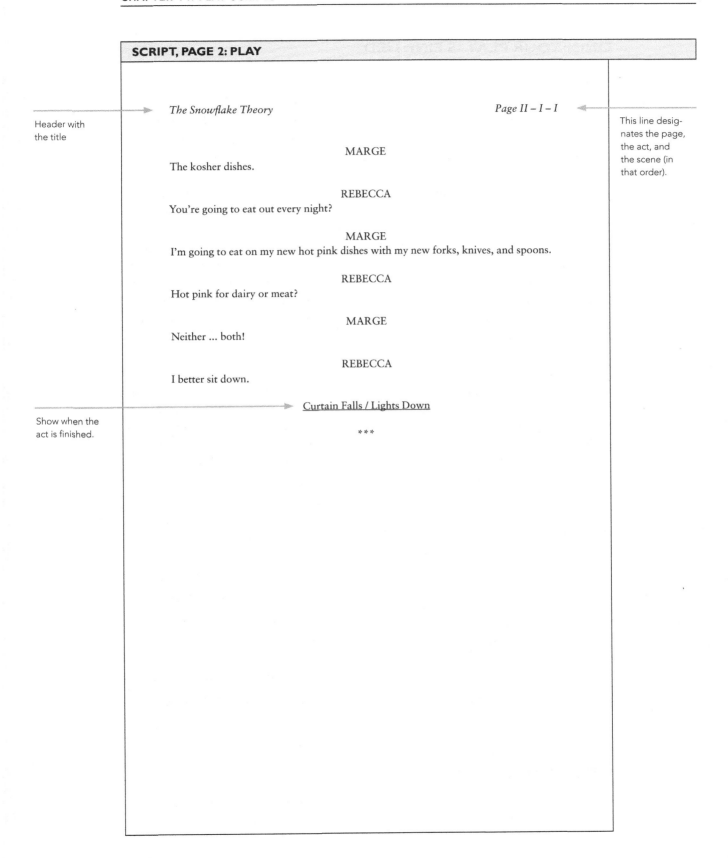

Header with the title

The Snowflake Theory   *Page II – I – I*

This line designates the page, the act, and the scene (in that order).

MARGE

The kosher dishes.

REBECCA

You're going to eat out every night?

MARGE

I'm going to eat on my new hot pink dishes with my new forks, knives, and spoons.

REBECCA

Hot pink for dairy or meat?

MARGE

Neither ... both!

REBECCA

I better sit down.

Curtain Falls / Lights Down

Show when the act is finished.

* * *

ONCE YOUR PLAY IS FINISHED

Network

As is true in many things, whom you know is very important. A glowing recommendation from the right person may be enough to see your play set in the fall schedule two years from now. With that in mind, don't be a shut-in! Get out and network with actors, directors, producers, and everyone else who loves plays or knows someone who has power.

Consider working or volunteering at a local hall. Get to know the staff and how a production functions. Familiarize yourself with all things theater. Sooner or later, there will be a good moment to mention that you, too, write plays. Even try acting in some small productions and see how it feels. The more you know about how actors operate when delving into a character and moving around onstage, the better you can craft a play with their likings in mind. If you get ridiculously lucky, you can bump into an angel or two—a wealthy arts lover who takes on passionate causes and bankrolls projects. Also, you may even be able to build a relationship with a theater that agrees to premiere all of your plays.

Join a Group

If there is a writing group near you solely dedicated to playwrights, you're lucky, so don't pass up the opportunity to join and schmooze. There may not be a specific playwriting group, though, and that's all right, too. Look for a general writers' group in the area. Though not ideal, you will still be surrounded by peers who can offer their ideas on storytelling. Finding other playwrights in the area and seeing how they achieved successes is a good first step. Referrals are born from this.

These days it's tough for a new play to be produced in this country. Tough for experienced playwrights and more than intimidating for the struggling writer—the comer who keeps coming but never seems to arrive, or the novice without a church. But that's a challenge the talented, ambitious writer meets head-on. The tougher climate simply means our plays have to be better. So we'll make them better. We'll write the plays the audience stays for. We'll write the plays that compel.

—JEFFREY HATCHER
author, *The Art & Craft of Playwriting*

A PLAY'S THREE STAGES

A new play typically won't be produced right off the bat. Plays are born in stages—and that happens for a reason. Usually, a work isn't pristine until it's been read aloud by actors and altered appropriately by the writer, who now has heard different perspectives on what works and what doesn't. Here are the three stages that a play takes en route to success.

Staged Reading

The first step for a new play is a staged reading, which allows the writer to hear the work spoken by acting professionals. This involves actors reading parts aloud while sitting down, scripts in hand (usually behind music stands). Stage directions, character descriptions, and act introductions are also simply read aloud, usually by a "narrator" who is sitting with the cast.

A staged reading is an easy way to "work out the kinks" of a new play and see how dialogue plays live. Phrases and sections that once seemed to flow so well on the page may seem awkward when spoken aloud or performed with a thick German accent. As the writer, you sit in the crowd and take notes. The reading will likely have a few rehearsals, so you can also make notes at that time and even tweak dialogue prior to the actual event.

Actors may ask for a little (or a lot) of room to improvise and change dialogue slightly, and it's up to you as to how much slack they have, if any. Staged readings will have a director, but it's not uncommon for a playwright to also act as the director, as duties are minimal.

Readings are commonly performed in front of an audience. This is done for two reasons. First, the audience will chime in with compliments and comments following the performance, giving the playwright more feedback on what worked and what did not. Perhaps more important is the chance for producers and power players to be seated in the crowd.

The process works like this: You call up a theater and explain that you would like to use the venue on an upcoming night for a staged reading and ask to rent the space for a reasonable fee. Once a date is agreed upon, you start to assemble a cast and rehearse. Also in that timeframe, you contact producers and other individuals who choose what plays to produce for their respective theaters and groups. Invite them free of charge to come see the staged reading, giving them a short synopsis of what the play is about. The goal is to get them in the seats and let them see your genius work performed live. So, if any producer is intrigued, he can contact you about producing the work in the future.

Developmental Workshop

The second stage is neither a reading nor a production, but rather something in the middle: a workshop. A developmental workshop involves a loose performance of the play to further see how it will work during a real show. Costumes are worn, some scenes blocked out, some lighting used, etc. Actors may have memorized some dialogue, but they're typically walking around with their scripts.

A workshop may have anywhere from three to a dozen rehearsals, and the goal is to take the play as far as it can go in that limited amount of time. Be prepared to help out in any way necessary. Just like with a staged reading, the writer must work out a location, assemble a crew, and try to get producers in the seats.

Production

The real deal, just like the performances you've seen at theaters. A full production means that everything is in place—costumes, props, memorized scripts, promotion, lighting and everything else. The playwright is likely paid, and hopefully you can get reviewers to see the play. A favorable review can serve as a stepping-stone to getting a larger, more prominent theater to also consider producing the work.

Contests can be a good way to get noticed. Many playwriting contests offer as a prize at least a staged reading and often a full production. Once you've had a reading or workshop production, set your sights on a small production. Use this as a learning experience.

PART 5:
VERSE

CHAPTER 15:

POETRY

The poetry market consists mostly of magazines, literary journals, and online sites. While poems can vary greatly in length and style, all publications are concerned about two things: 1) the quality of the work; and 2) a professional presentation—especially if you're sending multiple submissions at one time.

COVER LETTER

Submission Tips
Until recent years, most editors didn't expect or want cover letters along with a poetry submission; however, now many editors do specify that they want cover letters.

The best approach is to read a publication's listing in *Poet's Market* or to request a copy of its submission guidelines.

Formatting Specs
- The cover letter should be no longer than one page, and not a tightly packed page.
- Use a standard font, 12-point type. Avoid bold or italics except for titles.
  - Use 1" margins on all sides.
- Use block format (no indentations, an extra space between paragraphs).
- Put your name and contact information at the top of your letter, centered, or in your letterhead.
- Introduce the work you are submitting (i.e., Enclosed are three poems ...).
- Provide a brief biography that includes listing some of your published work if you have any and your background, including occupation, hobbies, interests, or other life events that have bearing on your work.
- Note why you think the poetry you're submitting would be appropriate for the publication (giving you a chance to show your familiarity with the publication).
- Mention if the work you are submitting has been previously published or if you are making simultaneous submissions. Check to make sure simultaneous submissions are accepted by the publication before sending them.

Other Dos and Don'ts

- Do address your letter to a specific editor. Call to get the appropriate name and gender.

- Don't request guidelines in the cover letter of your submission. It's too late at this point.

- Don't ask for criticism. It's not the editor's job to coach you.

- Don't submit handwritten poems.

- Do take note if a journal specifically requests poems that either have not been previously published, or poems that were previously published.

ELECTRONIC COVER LETTER

Submission Tips

Before you send a cover letter and poems to a publication via e-mail, make sure they accept electronic submissions by contacting the publication directly or checking out their writers' guidelines. Never send poems via e-mail unless you have permission from the editor or if the publication's submission guidelines state it is acceptable.

Formatting Specs

- Include the same information as you would in a paper cover letter, including your name and contact information. With e-mail letters, put your contact information at the lower left under your signature. It's not necessary to include your e-mail address in the body of the e-mail, since the editor can easily click "Reply" to respond.

- Use a subject line that introduces the theme or concept of your poems, unless the publisher's guidelines indicate what you should type there.

- Follow the same format you would with a paper cover letter, including the date, salutation, and block paragraph format. Find out how many poems a publication wants from their submission guidelines.

Other Dos and Don'ts

- Don't use all caps or exclamation points in the subject line.

- Don't insert clip art graphics or other images in your cover letter. Keep it simple.

- Do use formal communication like you would in a paper cover letter.

> Note, too, the number of poems the editor recommends including in the e-mail submission. If no quantity is given specifically for e-mails, go with the number of poems an editor recommends submitting in general.
>
> *—POET'S MARKET*

COVER LETTER: POETRY

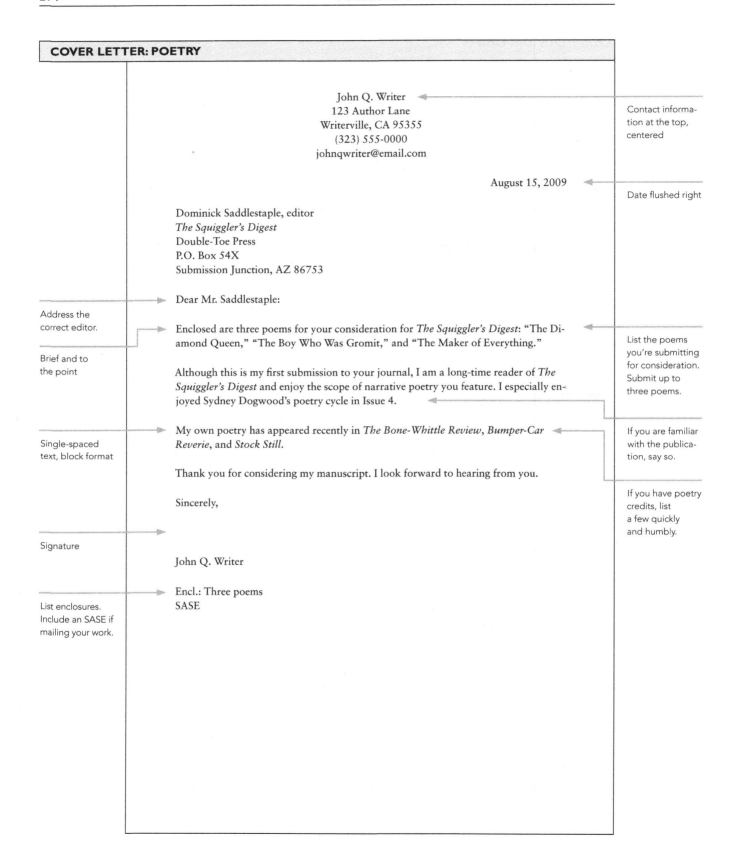

John Q. Writer
123 Author Lane
Writerville, CA 95355
(323) 555-0000
johnqwriter@email.com

August 15, 2009

Dominick Saddlestaple, editor
The Squiggler's Digest
Double-Toe Press
P.O. Box 54X
Submission Junction, AZ 86753

Dear Mr. Saddlestaple:

Enclosed are three poems for your consideration for *The Squiggler's Digest*: "The Diamond Queen," "The Boy Who Was Gromit," and "The Maker of Everything."

Although this is my first submission to your journal, I am a long-time reader of *The Squiggler's Digest* and enjoy the scope of narrative poetry you feature. I especially enjoyed Sydney Dogwood's poetry cycle in Issue 4.

My own poetry has appeared recently in *The Bone-Whittle Review*, *Bumper-Car Reverie*, and *Stock Still*.

Thank you for considering my manuscript. I look forward to hearing from you.

Sincerely,

John Q. Writer

Encl.: Three poems
SASE

Contact information at the top, centered

Date flushed right

Address the correct editor.

Brief and to the point

List the poems you're submitting for consideration. Submit up to three poems.

If you are familiar with the publication, say so.

Single-spaced text, block format

If you have poetry credits, list a few quickly and humbly.

Signature

List enclosures. Include an SASE if mailing your work.

COVER LETTER, MISTAKES TO AVOID: POETRY

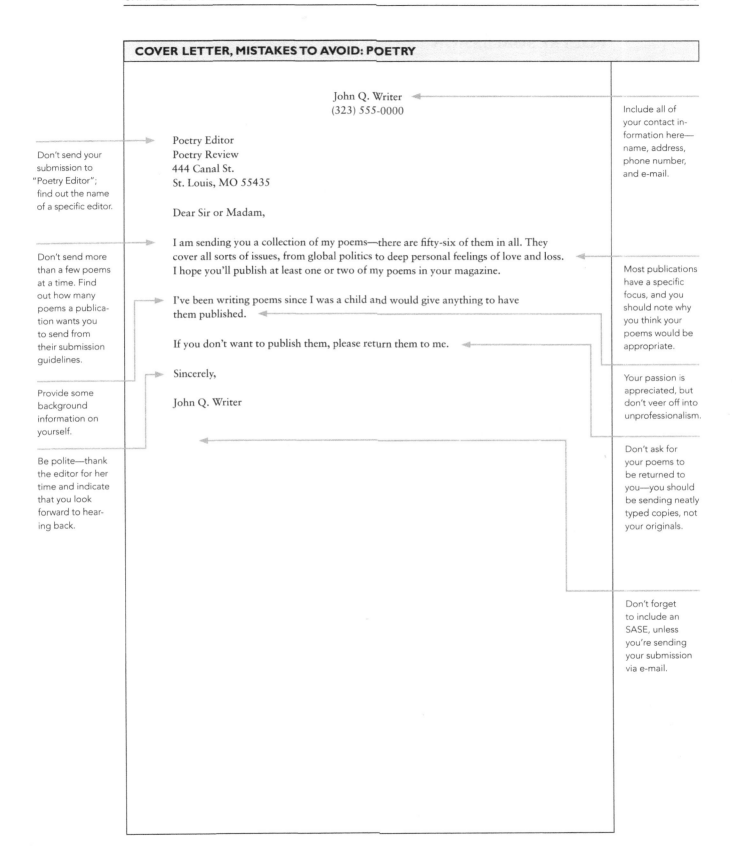

John Q. Writer
(323) 555-0000

Include all of your contact information here—name, address, phone number, and e-mail.

Poetry Editor
Poetry Review
444 Canal St.
St. Louis, MO 55435

Don't send your submission to "Poetry Editor"; find out the name of a specific editor.

Dear Sir or Madam,

I am sending you a collection of my poems—there are fifty-six of them in all. They cover all sorts of issues, from global politics to deep personal feelings of love and loss. I hope you'll publish at least one or two of my poems in your magazine.

Don't send more than a few poems at a time. Find out how many poems a publication wants you to send from their submission guidelines.

Most publications have a specific focus, and you should note why you think your poems would be appropriate.

I've been writing poems since I was a child and would give anything to have them published.

Provide some background information on yourself.

If you don't want to publish them, please return them to me.

Your passion is appreciated, but don't veer off into unprofessionalism.

Sincerely,

John Q. Writer

Be polite—thank the editor for her time and indicate that you look forward to hearing back.

Don't ask for your poems to be returned to you—you should be sending neatly typed copies, not your originals.

Don't forget to include an SASE, unless you're sending your submission via e-mail.

POETRY SUBMISSION

Submission Tips

In poetry, above all other forms, substance supersedes format. Your submissions should be neat and correspond to the rules of the medium. You don't get any points for fancy fonts or colored paper. In fact, your submission is likely to be viewed less favorably if you garnish it in such ways.

Generally, submit three to five poems at a time, though some editors prefer seven or more poems if they feature a poet. Again, the publication's guidelines will help here.

> Arranging poems into a collection is a lot like arranging lines into a poem. I think there should be the same kind of movement, from problem to solution, from buildup to crescendo, from exposition to denouement, whatever it may be.
>
> **—TOM C. HUNLEY**
>
> poet, full-length collection, *Octopus*

Formatting Specs

- Use standard white bond, laser, or ink-jet paper.
- Submit each poem on a separate page, except for haiku.
- Center a title in all caps above the poem. If there is a subtitle, use upper- and lowercase and underline it. Skip one line and center below the title.
- Include your name and contact information.
- If your poem continues over to a second sheet, start the second page with a new stanza whenever possible or applicable.
- Editor preferences vary on whether submissions should be double- or single-spaced. Check the publication's guidelines. Unless otherwise directed, single-space.
- If the line of poetry extends beyond the margin, indent the second line. If you are double-spacing the entire poem, single-space the continuation of a line.
- Put in an extra line space (or two, when double-spacing) before the beginning of a stanza.
- Margins will vary, depending on the poem, but generally run at least 2–2.5" on the sides, with the poem roughly centered top to bottom on the page. These margins do not apply to electronic submissions.
- If you don't use a cover letter, find out if the publication wants biographical information and include such information on a separate sheet under the centered, capitalized heading "BIOGRAPHICAL INFORMATION" or "ABOUT THE POET."

- If your poem runs more than one page, use a header (generally, the title or your last name) in the top left corner and a page number in the top right corner on the second and subsequent pages.

- Fold the poems together into thirds for insertion into the envelope. Fold the cover letter separately and place it on top of the poems. Better yet, use a large envelope and don't fold your cover letter or submission at all.

- Paper clip pages of the same poem together, but submit one-page poems loose leaf, folded.

Other Dos and Don'ts

- Do enclose an SASE, which makes it easier for the editor to respond.

- Don't handwrite your poems.

- Don't use onion skin, colored, or erasable paper.

- Don't put copyright information on your poem. It's copyrighted regardless of this, and you'll likely insult the editor's intelligence or intentions.

- Do address your submission and cover letter by name to the poetry editor or other editor who routinely reviews poetry submission.

- Don't submit previously published work or make simultaneous submissions unless you know the publication accepts them and you note it in a cover letter.

> I try to be as systematic as possible in terms of sending out, by conceptualizing "submission packets" of 4–5 poems each: poems that offset each other well, that advance a certain theme or stylistic gesture. I'll match a packet with whatever I think the editors at that particular magazine will like best. It makes me nervous if I don't have things out at least three journals at any given time. As you can probably guess from that statement, I prefer places that consider simultaneous submissions. As someone who has worked at a number of magazines, I just don't see any reason not to be open to simultaneous.
>
> **—SANDRA BEASLEY,**
>
> poet, winner 2007 New Issues Poetry Prize

ELECTRONIC POETRY SUBMISSIONS

Submission Tips

E-mail submissions are only acceptable when you have permission from the publication or if their submission guidelines indicate it is acceptable. Don't forget to include your cover letter in the body of your e-mail.

Formatting Specs

- Before you send the poems, find out how the editor prefers to receive files. He may want the poems attached as separate files or included in the body of the e-mail. A lot of editors don't like to open attachments, especially from unfamiliar people.

- Follow the same formatting specs as for a paper manuscript submission (see page 296).

- If the editor doesn't specify a particular file format for an attached file, save it as a text file. Most word processing programs can read basic text files.

Other Dos and Don'ts

- Don't use all caps in your subject line.

- Do ask for specific file format guidelines to make sure the editor can open your files.

- Don't justify text or align the right margin.

- Don't put any copyright information on your poem. It's copyrighted when you write it, and the editor is aware of this.

The same poem written with line breaks and without them—can have an entirely different effect. And meaning. I think choosing a form is like choosing a design for a house. If you have a big open space with skylights and a stage, that's one kind of experience. If you build a large house with a bazillion tiny rooms, that's another experience.

—NIN ANDREWS

poet, full-length collection *Sleeping With Houdini*

ELECTRONIC COVER LETTER AND MANUSCRIPT: POETRY

Don't send an
e-mail submission
unless the publi-
cation requests it.

Address the cor-
rect editor to show
that you've done
your research.

Follow standard,
professional cover
letter guidelines.

Contact informa-
tion, on the bot-
tom of the e-mail

Five lines between
your contact in-
formation and the
poem title

Include a
line count.

Copy and paste
your poems into
the e-mail body.
Editors don't
like to open at-
tachments.

It's never a bad
idea to copy
yourself (CC or
BCC) on e-mail
correspondence
to keep a record.

Title is all caps.

Single-spaced
text, not center
aligned

TO: wicktora@bwr.com
CC: johnqwriter@email.com
SUBJECT: Poetry Submission

Ms. Wicktora:

Pasted below is the following poem I'm submitting for your consideration: "Kubla
Khan." I've noticed that *Bone-Whittle Review* has published quite a bit of traditional
poetry, so I thought my work might be of interest to you.

My poetry has appeared in journals in the U.S. and U.K., including *Wordsworth's Pal.*
I've won prizes from Stanzaloosa '02.

Thank you for your time and consideration. I look forward to hearing from you.

John Q. Writer
123 Author Lane
Writerville, CA 95355
(323) 555-0000
johnqwriter@email.com

KUBLA KHAN
(88 lines)

In Xanadu did Kubla Khan
A stately pleasure dome decree:
Where Alph, the sacred river, ran
Through caverns measureless to man
Down to a sunless sea
So Twice five miles of fertile ground
With walls and towers were girdled round
And there were gardens bright with sinuous rills,
Where blossomed many an incense-bearing tree;
And here were forests ancient as the hills,
Enfolding sunny spots of greenery …

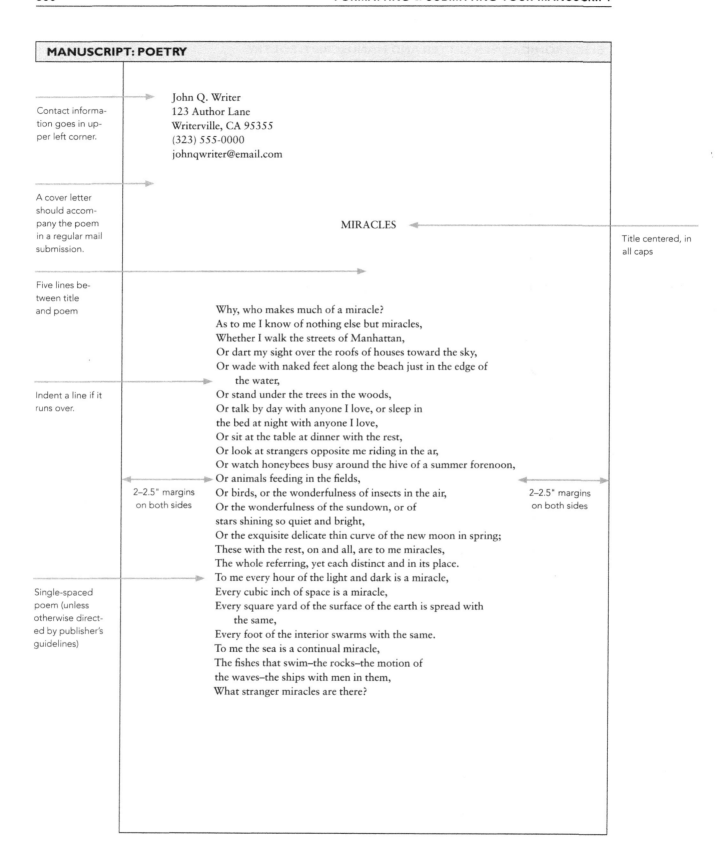

MANUSCRIPT: POETRY

Contact information goes in upper left corner.

John Q. Writer
123 Author Lane
Writerville, CA 95355
(323) 555-0000
johnqwriter@email.com

A cover letter should accompany the poem in a regular mail submission.

MIRACLES

Title centered, in all caps

Five lines between title and poem

Why, who makes much of a miracle?
As to me I know of nothing else but miracles,
Whether I walk the streets of Manhattan,
Or dart my sight over the roofs of houses toward the sky,
Or wade with naked feet along the beach just in the edge of
    the water,
Or stand under the trees in the woods,
Or talk by day with anyone I love, or sleep in
the bed at night with anyone I love,
Or sit at the table at dinner with the rest,
Or look at strangers opposite me riding in the ar,
Or watch honeybees busy around the hive of a summer forenoon,
Or animals feeding in the fields,
Or birds, or the wonderfulness of insects in the air,
Or the wonderfulness of the sundown, or of
stars shining so quiet and bright,
Or the exquisite delicate thin curve of the new moon in spring;
These with the rest, on and all, are to me miracles,
The whole referring, yet each distinct and in its place.
To me every hour of the light and dark is a miracle,
Every cubic inch of space is a miracle,
Every square yard of the surface of the earth is spread with
    the same,
Every foot of the interior swarms with the same.
To me the sea is a continual miracle,
The fishes that swim–the rocks–the motion of
the waves–the ships with men in them,
What stranger miracles are there?

Indent a line if it runs over.

2–2.5" margins on both sides

2–2.5" margins on both sides

Single-spaced poem (unless otherwise directed by publisher's guidelines)

APPENDIX:

RECORD KEEPING AND FORMS

Some freelancers keep detailed forms tracking submissions of queries and manuscripts to publications and other markets, but the time required and paperwork yields questionable value. In the interest of saving time and forests, sensible use of your computer can eliminate need for tedious sets of specialized logs. With computer memory as cheap as it is today, there's no reason not to keep everything you do on your computer hard drive in perpetuity. The trick is simply organizing your hard drive in a way that will permit you to go back and grab the information when you need it. Just remember to back it up regularly.

Following is an outline of the types of records you need and the easiest ways to keep them.

SUBMISSION TRACKING CHECKLIST

Use your calendar or appointment book along with your computer to keep a record of your queries and manuscript submissions.

Keep a special folder on your hard drive for queries, with file names descriptive enough that you'll be able to understand what they represent. When you need to see how long it has been since you made a query, display your queries by date. Your saved queries are a ready supply of templates for creating new ones. A simple Microsoft Excel spreadsheet is an easy way to track your queries and editor responses. Use a similar strategy for manuscript submissions by keeping a file of cover letters.

The spreadsheet can also keep a record of when a query or manuscript was accepted or rejected, and the rights sold or the fee.

CONTACT TRACKING

It's a good idea to track contacts, either in the marketing or preparation of articles and books. Keep files that make sense for you, such as a folder with magazine editors, book editors or editors in a particular specialized market where you work. Likewise, keep files of contacts for each project or a master file of all your contacts. Database programs were designed to keep this kind of information, but you may find it easier to store your contact list as a word processing file and use the Find function to retrieve the names or other information you need.

INCOME AND EXPENSE TRACKING

You can track expenses several different ways. Regardless of whether you're reimbursed by a publisher for expenses, you'll need to track them for tax purposes. The

IRS expects some kind of regular record-keeping system for both income and expenses; this can be through one of the many personal or professional accounting packages out there or a paper ledger system. You'll also need an auto mileage log if you use your car in your work, and you may need to log business and personal time spent on your computer or mobile phone so you can appropriately deduct equipment costs.

Here are a few tips to make expense tracking as pain-free as possible:

- For phone expenses, either arrange with your long-distance carrier for account codes (which is possible for all business and some home lines) or assign each publication or client to a particular carrier (for instance, your main line for your biggest market, 10-10-321 long-distance service for another client, etc.).

- Keep a daily calendar or appointment book that shows what projects you're working on and who you called. You can check this against long-distance bills.

- Keep your appointment book along with your tax records each year to substantiate the business nature of long-distance calls and business use of your home office.

- If you use a personal computer for both business and personal use, keep a daily log of how many personal and business hours you spend on it. Tally these numbers at year-end for deduction purposes.

- If you use a mobile phone, get detailed billing, which will make the job of determining business and personal use much easier.

- Keep a separate checking account for business, and keep detailed records in your check register, recording the payer for checks you deposit and details of the expense for the checks. This can serve as a record-keeping system, or at least allow you to construct a more elaborate one at year-end.

FORMS, FORMS, FORMS

There are still a few paper forms that you will need from time to time. They include permission forms for using copyrighted material, model contracts and agreements, and release forms for photographic subjects. (Note: You don't need the latter for photojournalism-type shots in public places, but you do need these for models or when using a photograph in a home or on private property.) While it always helps to have a contract or a form, many articles are written without them. You can generally write articles safely without a formal contract, and the risk is relatively slight. If you're worried, however, it doesn't hurt to send the editor a letter of agreement spelling out terms you've agreed to verbally or a model contract that you use.

In the absence of a verbal or written agreement on rights, the default is First North American Rights or one-time use. Publishers or clients cannot make a work-for-hire agreement or buy unrestricted use without an explicit written agreement. Publishers have their own model contracts in many cases. Keep in mind that these are negotiable; if you see terms you don't like, you can often change them.

What follows are a permission form, a release form, consent of parent or guardian, and a letter of agreement that can make your life easier.

PERMISSION TO USE COPYRIGHTED MATERIAL

I hereby grant permission to _____

to quote or otherwise reprint the following: _____

_____

_____

From: (Publication's name) _____

By: (Author's name) _____

This material will be published in a _____

by the title _____

to be published by _____

Address: _____

_____

_____

This request shall apply to all future editions and adaptations of

_____

I am the copyright holder or authorized by the copyright holder to grant this permission.

Signed:

Print name: _____

Title: _____

Date: _____

RELEASE FORM

Date: _____

I, _____ hereby consent that my picture, portrait, and/or name and

reproductions thereof may be used by _____

as (s)he may desire in connection with professional activities and may be used, exhibited or published through any or all media, including for advertising or commercial purposes. This release is irrevocable.

I am (am not) over 18 years old.

Name _____

Address _____

City, State, ZIP _____

Signature _____

CONSENT OF PARENT OR GUARDIAN

I, _____ , certify that I am parent/guardian of
_____ and hereby consent that his/her name, picture, portrait, or

representation may be used by _____
_____ in connection with his/her
professional activities and may be exhibited, reproduced, published, or used through
any medium in connection with those professional activities, including for advertising
or commercial purposes. This release is irrevocable.

Name _____

Address _____

City, State, ZIP _____

Signature _____

LETTER OF AGREEMENT (Note: This is similar to a contract.)

John Q. Writer
123 Author Lane
Writerville, CA 95355
(323) 555-0000
johnqwriter@email.com

October 12, 2009

Kim Paul
Greenfield Digest
101 Warsaw Parkway
Rochester, NY 10322

Dear Ms. Paul:

This letter is to confirm the assignment we discussed for the article tentatively titled "Brownfield to Greenfield—The Challenges Ahead" on the following terms:

1) The article will be approximately 1,500 words, including one sidebar.

2) The article is due November 15, 2009.

3) Payment of $750 is due upon acceptance.

4) *Greenfield Digest* will review and either accept or seek revisions of the article within thirty (30) days of receipt.

5) A revised version will be due within ten (10) days of notice, with final decision on acceptance within fourteen (14) days of receipt of revised article.

6) *Greenfield Digest* buys First North American Rights. Electronic and reprint rights are negotiable.

7) Should *Greenfield Digest* cancel the assignment before completion, a kill fee of $325 will immediately become due.

8) *Greenfield Digest* will pay reasonable telephone, database research and incidental fees, due upon receipt of an invoice and documentation of expenses.

Thanks for the assignment and for your time. If you have any questions or concerns, please feel free to call. Enclosed is an SASE in which you can return a signed copy of this letter. You may keep the original for your records.

Sincerely,

John Q. Writer

I understand and agree to the terms stated above.
Kim Paul, Editor, *Greenfield Digest,* Date:

INDEX

ABOUT THE AUTHOR

By day, Chuck Sambuchino is an editor for Writer's Digest Books (an imprint of F+W Media). He is the editor of two annual resource books: *Guide to Literary Agents* and *Screenwriter's & Playwright's Market*. He also assists in editing *Writer's Market* (www.writersmarket.com). Chuck is a former staffer of several newspapers and magazines—most notably *Writer's Digest*. During his tenure as a newspaper staffer, he won awards from both the Kentucky Press Association and the Cincinnati Society of Professional Journalists.

By night, Chuck is a writer and freelance editor. He is a produced playwright, with both original and commissioned works produced. He is also a magazine freelancer, with recent articles appearing in *Watercolor Artist*, *Pennsylvania Magazine*, *The Pastel Journal*, *Cincinnati Magazine*, and *New Mexico Magazine*. During the past decade, more than 500 of his articles have been published in newspapers, magazines and w. Chuck also teaches online instructional courses through Writers Online Workshops (www.writersonlineworkshops.com). He is a frequent speaker at writers' conferences and retreats across the country.

To sign up for free newsletter about agents and publishing, visit www.guidetoliteraryagents.com. Visit his blog at www.guidetoliteraryagents.com/blog.

MORE GREAT RESOURCES FROM WRITER'S DIGEST BOOKS

The Fire in Fiction
Passion, Purpose and Techniques to Make Your Novel Great
by Donald Maass

How do widely published authors keep their stories burning hot? Learn how to supercharge every story with deep conviction and, conversely, turn fiery passion into effective story. *The Fire in Fiction* shows you not only how to write compelling stories filled with interesting settings and vivid characters, but how to do it over and over again. With examples drawn from current novels, this inspiring guide shows you how to infuse your writing with life.

ISBN-13: 978-1-58297-506-1, paperback, 272 pages, #Z1080

You Must Be This Tall to Ride
Contemporary Writers Take You Inside the Story
by B.J. Hollars

To truly understand works of short fiction, you must become aware of the process behind the stories, as well as the challenges the author encountered and how he or she worked through them. *You Must Be This Tall to Ride* is a collection of short fiction with analytical and instructional essays and exercises by a diverse group of contemporary authors. Not only will you become engaged with the content, but you will also become a more critical student of technique, recognizing decisions and strategies that can be employed in your own writing.

ISBN-13: 978-1-58297-574-0, paperback, 304 pages, #Z3053

Take Ten for Writers
Generate Ideas and Stimulate Your Writing in Only 10 Minutes a Day
by Bonnie Neubauer

Writers are constantly looking for ideas and this book of ten-minute writing exercises provides 100 exercises with ten different variables for a whopping 1,000 prompts. Guaranteed to get the words flowing, you'll get a creative boost by playing around with starting phrases, the last sentences of stories, locations and more. It only takes ten minutes to open up your writing to boundless possibilities!

ISBN-13: 978-1-58297-533-7, paperback, 224 pages, #Z2008

And Here's the Kicker
Conversations with 32 Top Humor Writers About Their Craft
by Mike Sacks

In this book for aspiring humor writers and fans of comedy, practitioners of the craft including Jack Handey (Saturday Night Live), Judd Apatow (The 40-Year-Old Virgin) and Roz Chast (The New Yorker) discuss the comedy writing process, their influences, their likes and dislikes, and their experiences in the industry. Funny and informative, *And Here's the Kicker* is a must-have guide for aspiring humor writers and simply a great read for fans.

ISBN-13: 978-1-58297-505-4, paperback, 320 pages, #Z1028